YOUR GARDEN
WEEK BY WEEK

A. G. L. Hellyer, a gardening writer and plantsman of
the very first rank, is particularly well qualified to
advise on the practical side of the gardener's work. His
life-long experience of gardening and his close contact
with amateur gardeners have given him a special
awareness of their problems and interests.

This book tells the reader just what to do in the
garden during each week of the year. Every operation
is described in detail so that the volume as a whole has
become a manual of garden craft as well as a calendar
of seasonal operations. Food crops are considered with
as much care as ornamental plants, and the management
of greenhouses, frames and cloches receives due
attention. Successful planning of the garden is made
easy by unusually comprehensive lists of flowers,
vegetables and fruit in season from January to
December. The arrangement of the matter as a whole
and the comprehensive index make it easy for the
reader to find any information required without delay
or fuss. This is of vital importance in a book that is
intended not merely to be read once but to be referred
to time and again, year after year. There are very
many illustrations to supplement the text.

A. G. L. HELLYER

M.B.E., V.M.H., F.L.S.

YOUR GARDEN
week by week

COLLINGRIDGE BOOKS

LONDON · NEW YORK · SYDNEY · TORONTO

Published for Collingridge Books by
THE HAMLYN PUBLISHING GROUP LIMITED
LONDON . NEW YORK . SYDNEY . TORONTO
Hamlyn House, Feltham, Middlesex, England

First published in 1936
Thirteenth impression 1972
© The Hamlyn Publishing Group Limited, 1936

Printed by C. Tinling & Co. Ltd.
London and Prescot

ISBN 0 600 44296 9

Contents

Illustrations

7

LINE DRAWINGS
by Cynthia Newsome-Taylor

Introductory

I N this book I have set out to provide something more than a mere calendar of operations. Week by week I have tried to show not only *what must be done* but also *the best way in which to do it*. The volume is intended primarily for beginners, and so I have not included stove plants and orchids, nor the more uncommon vegetables usually grown only by connoisseurs.

The plan of the book demands a few words of explanation. It is divided into twelve monthly sections each of which is further split into five sub-sections under the headings General Work, First Week, Second Week, Third Week, and Fourth Week. The first of these sub-sections contains all those tasks which cannot be referred to any particular week but must be spread more or less continuously throughout the month. In the other four sections the remaining work is more precisely allocated. The expert may feel that this is too arbitrary a scheme, contending that most garden tasks can be done over a longer period than I have indicated, but I would remind such that the book is intended for beginners and that these invariably desire precise guidance. As they gain in experience they will learn just what liberties they can take, but at first they will be more likely to get good results by following rather rigidly a definite calendar of operations than by trying to sort out a mass of vague information. The formalized scheme of four weeks per month will, I hope, simplify and not complicate the application of the information to each and every year. The odd days in the month must be tacked on at the end, or the beginning of the next as common-sense suggests.

The calendar is based mainly upon experience around London and may need a little adaptation for certain parts of the country. Differences, however, are likely to be most apparent in late winter and early spring and are of little account at other seasons. From February to April the extreme south-west may be anything from a fortnight to a month ahead, while very cold northern districts may be almost as much behind London and the Midlands, but, of course, these big differences are only applicable to outdoor work.

The lists of flowers, vegetables, and fruits in season are intended for reference when planning the garden in all its branches. They have been made as complete as possible and I make no apology for the strings of

15

botanical names which they contain, for these provide the beginner with the only certain means of turning up further information and of explaining to the nurseryman exactly what he needs.

There are certain tasks which are 'in season' from January to December, and to avoid monotony and save space I have not repeated them month by month. Here is a list of them.

Dutch Hoeing. This can be done whenever the surface of the soil is dry enough not to stick to the blade of the hoe. Its object is twofold: first to destroy weeds, and second to break up the surface soil and so prevent loss of water by evaporation. Always keep the blade of the hoe sharp, and work it backwards and forwards just beneath the surface so that weeds are severed from their roots, not pulled up and left lying on the surface to grow again.

Weed and Moss Killing. Another method of killing weeds is by means of plant poisons, but it must be remembered that few of these are very selective in action, and so it is not safe to apply them to ground in which garden plants are growing. Simazine is one of the best and most recent of these, in that when watered on to the soil it will stay exactly where it has been applied, and will not 'creep' sideways. Weedkilling may be slow but it will clear the ground completely and keep it clean for at least twelve months. Sodium chlorate is a similar type of plant poison, but it is quicker acting and correspondingly not so long-lasting. It can be used in water in solutions varying from $\frac{1}{4}$ to 1 pound per gallon according to the toughness of the weeds that have to be killed. Like simazine it can be used to clear vacant ground of weeds and will remain effective for anything from a fortnight to six months, according to the rainfall and the nature of the ground. Its effect will be lost more quickly in sand than in clay.

Another method of killing weeds is by giving excessive doses of certain plant hormones. These are frequently referred to as selective weed killers because they are extremely potent to some plants and almost harmless to others. The one in most common use, often known as MCPA, can be purchased in proprietary brands either as a liquid to be further diluted according to manufacturer's instructions and then applied from a watering can fitted with a fine rose, or else in powder form already mixed with a carrier for immediate application as purchased. MCPA is particularly valuable for the treatment of lawns because it affects grass very little indeed but is deadly to most lawn weeds.

Several excellent proprietary preparations are made for killing moss on lawns, and these can be used at any season, so long as manufacturer's

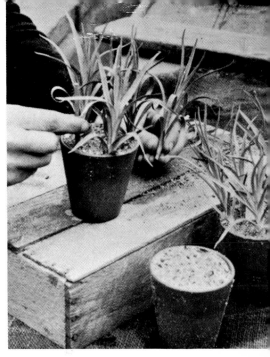

Left: Preparing perpetual-flowering carnation cuttings. *Right:* Three or four cuttings of perpetual-flowering carnations may be inserted round the edge of a small flower pot.

Imported lily bulbs generally require placing in damp fibre to plump up before planting or potting. Dust with sulphur as a precaution against disease.

Left: Removing hyacinths from the plunge bed, ready for forcing in the greenhouse.
Right: Preparing seakale thongs. Note the slanting cut that is made to distinguish the top from the bottom of the thong.

Inserting root cuttings of anchusa in a deep box.

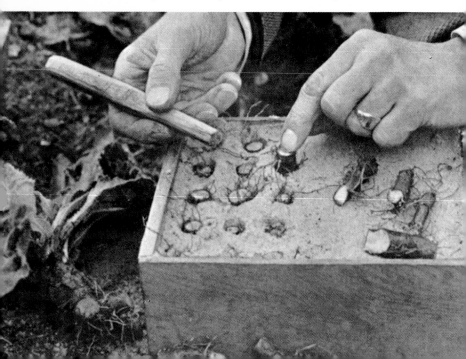

instructions regarding strength are not exceeded. Raking vigorously with a spring-toothed grass rake will remove a lot of the moss, but you must not overlook the possibility that the cause of the growth is poverty of soil or bad drainage—two conditions that must be rectified if you wish to effect a permanent cure.

Greenhouse Fumigation. August is often a convenient time of the year at which to fumigate greenhouses, as during that month it is often possible to empty greenhouses completely and use smokes that would hardly be safe if there were any plants about. But this must not be misinterpreted as implying that all smokes are dangerous to vegetable growth. On the contrary, nicotine can be used safely at any time of the year and, indeed, is really only effective if the houses are stocked, as the pests which it kills are on the plants and would be carried out and in again on them. Azobenzene, for the control of red spider, can also be used safely when plants are in the house, but sulphur fumigation requires more care, and should really only be attempted by the expert. Manufacturer's instructions should always be followed.

Lawn Mowing and Rolling. There is a widespread but mistaken notion that the lawn mower and roller should be put away for the winter. Really good lawns cannot be produced in this way, for though it is true that winter mowing will be infrequent and that the roller must never be used on waterlogged soil, it is equally certain that complete neglect from October to April will result in coarse grasses ousting those of a finer nature. I have referred to this in the notes for April, General Work.

January

GENERAL WORK

Dig All Available Ground. When the ground is frozen so hard that it cannot be dug is the ideal time for wheeling out manure and placing it about in handy heaps for spreading and digging in as soon as conditions improve. It is not wise to dig soil immediately after a thaw nor during or immediately after a heavy fall of snow, for it is then too wet on the surface to break up properly. The clods will lie in the bottom of the trenches and gradually harden into brickbats, especially if the ground is of a clayey nature. But whenever the soil is soft enough to be dug, and yet not so wet that it sticks to the spade badly, digging can proceed—and it is an axiom of gardening that the early digger gets the crops.

Prick over Bulb Beds. During the month tulips, daffodils, and hyacinths will appear through the soil. As soon as the green sprouts can be seen clearly, go over the beds carefully with a small border fork, pricking up the soil between the bulbs, but only to a depth of about an inch. This will improve aeration and kill moss, green, scummy growth, and weeds. At the same time give the soil a dusting of some good and properly blended chemical fertilizer. If you wish to make your own mixture, do so with seven parts of superphosphate of lime, five parts of sulphate of ammonia, two parts of either sulphate or muriate of potash, and one part of steamed bone-flour (all parts by weight). Use this at 4 ounces per square yard. Of course, you must choose a fine day for this work and one when the soil is neither very wet nor frozen.

Prune Roses. Continue to prune bush and standard roses (see November, General Work).

Take Chrysanthemum and Carnation Cuttings. A task which can be carried on as opportunity permits throughout January is that of taking late-flowering chrysanthemum cuttings. It is rather early yet to start on the outdoor flowering chrysanthemums, though even with these I would not hesitate to have a few cuttings of such a variety as old Roi des Blancs if there are any good ones showing, because this is notoriously shy in producing cuttings. Later on, when the proper time arrives, there may be no suitable shoots to be had—and a cutting in the pot is certainly worth two in the bush.

Nevertheless in the main it is the late-flowering kinds that are to be propagated in January and particularly the incurves and exhibition

18

Japanese kinds. Full particulars are given in the notes for **December, Third Week.**

You should also propagate perpetual-flowering carnations as opportunity occurs. This task I have described in detail in the General Work notes for December.

A POT OF CHRYSANTHEMUM CUTTINGS

The leaves are still flagging— an indication that the cuttings are not yet rooted. As soon as growth recommences the cuttings should be potted individually.

Pot Rooted Carnation and Chrysanthemum Cuttings. During the month keep a careful watch on carnation cuttings taken during December, and if these are in pure sand get them potted up singly in 2-inch pots as soon as they are well rooted (which means that roots ½ inch long have been formed). It is quite easy to tell when a cutting is rooted, because it will start to grow at once. Until then it will remain quite at a standstill. There is not the same urgency with carnation cuttings that are in soil and sand, nor with chrysanthemum cuttings, which are almost always rooted in soil and sand, but even with these it is a good plan to get them singly into pots before the roots get tangled together. Use 3-inch pots for the chrysanthemums, for these grow more rapidly. Propagating boxes must be ventilated freely as soon as cuttings commence to grow. Use a compost of three parts of fibrous, rather heavy loam and one part containing equal proportions of wood ashes, old soot, mortar rubble, and sand for potting the carnations. The chrysanthemums will do well in a mixture of four parts of medium loam, coarsely sifted, one part of moss peat or leaf-mould, and two parts of sharp sand with a sprinkling of fine bonemeal and ground chalk. Shade the plants from direct sunlight for a few days and then start to harden them off by placing on a shelf near the glass and ventilating more freely.

General Greenhouse Management. The well-managed greenhouse should be full of plants during January, many of them in flower and all wanting careful watering. Greenhouse calceolarias are particularly susceptible to bad watering and may collapse quite suddenly if given too much; yet dryness is equally bad. Chinese primulas are apt to suffer severely if water is allowed to collect at the base of the leaves and in the heart of the plant. Do not forget the golden rule of all watering—namely, that when water is given it must be supplied in sufficient quantity to moisten the soil in pot or box right through. There is nothing worse than keeping the surface wet and letting the lower soil remain dry.

Ventilation is also bound to be a tricky matter, especially in a small house or one that is not too well heated. The ideal is a constant circulation of air without draughts or sudden variations of temperature. Only the top ventilators will be needed during January, and even these must be closed at night. Open them a little during the day provided it is not freezing or foggy, but, if there is any choice in the matter, be sure to open them on the side away from the wind—and be equally sure to get them closed well before the sun goes down, for a little sun heat trapped late in the afternoon will go a long way towards keeping up the night temperature. Watch carefully for decaying leaves—a sure sign of a stuffy atmosphere (see November, General Work).

The ideal average temperature to be aimed at for the common winter-flowering plants such as primulas, cinerarias, calceolarias, and cyclamen is 55° to 60° by day and 45° to 50° at night. If winter-flowering begonias are grown, it will be all to the good to have 5 or 10 degrees more, but most plants are able to stand quite a wide variation in temperature. A good deal of nonsense is talked upon this subject, and one is sometimes left with the impression that there are many plants which cannot be grown in anything but a thermostatically controlled atmosphere. A thermostat is certainly an immense help, but it is by no means a necessity. The great thing to avoid is any very sudden fluctuations, especially in the early morning or evening.

Bring Bulbs into the Greenhouse. Successive small batches of tulips, narcissi of all types, including trumpet daffodils, hyacinths, and *Iris tingitana*, should be brought into the greenhouse from plunge bed or frame to maintain a continuity of flowers later on (see November, First Week).

Force Seakale and Rhubarb. You should also bring in at least two batches of seakale and rhubarb to force in heat if you wish to maintain an unbroken succession. These, of course, are forced in complete darkness. (See November, Second Week).

Pot and Plant Lilies. There is no doubt that early autumn is the best time to pot and plant most lilies, but it is sometimes impossible to get certain varieties then, especially if they have to be imported from the Far East. Such should be dealt with as soon as they are available, and this often adds quite appreciably to the extent of one's January tasks. Bulbs that have travelled a long distance may have become rather soft

POTTING A LILY BULB

(a) *Crown of bulb and* (b) *the base. The pot should be well crocked* (e), *half filled with compost* (d) *and the bulb set in a finer soil* (c), *allowing space for top-dressing later.*

or shrivelled and it is wise to plump them up before potting or planting them. This is done by placing them in seed trays, partly surrounding them with moist moss peat, and keeping this damp by daily syringeing. As soon as the bulbs get plump and firm, plant or pot without further delay.

Ventilate Violets, etc., in Frames. Violets and other hardy or nearly hardy plants in frames, such as violas, pansies, anemones, penstemons, bedding calceolarias, antirrhinums from late summer seeds and cuttings, sweet peas, cauliflowers, and bulbs, and alpines in pots, etc., must be ventilated just as freely as the weather permits. On all mild, sunny days remove the lights altogether for a few hours. If there is a cold wind blowing, tilt the lights with blocks of wood placed on the leeward side. At night the frames should be closed, and if the weather is very cold it is advisable to throw a few sacks over them into the bargain. An occasional stirring of the soil between the plants with a pointed stick does a lot of good.

VENTILATING FRAMES

The block of wood in three steps is very useful for controlling the ventilation of garden frames.

Take Root Cuttings. Many plants can be raised more readily from root cuttings taken during January than in any other way. Well-known examples are Oriental poppies, perennial statices, anchusas, perennial verbascums, *Romneya Coulteri*, *Phlox decussata*, and gaillardias. The roots are cut up into pieces about 1 to 2 inches in length. In all except the last three these cuttings are pushed vertically, right end up, into a sandy compost in well-drained pots. The tops of the cuttings should be just level with the soil. Romneya, phlox, and gaillardia cuttings are simply strewn thinly over the surface of the soil and covered with a further ¼ inch of compost. Place in a frame or greenhouse (slightly heated or unheated) and water moderately. Shoots will form slowly, and in late spring, after proper hardening off, the small plants can be established outdoors.

Protect Broccoli. The curds of broccoli will require protection as they commence to form. (See November, General Work).

Sow Small Salads under Glass. Various small salads may be sown during the month in a slightly heated greenhouse or a frame placed on a hotbed.

MAKING A HOTBED

A frame is placed on a heap of decaying manure which is best placed in a hollow and allowed to extend beyond the frame on all sides.

This latter is prepared by making a flat-topped mound of fresh horse manure or placing the manure in a wide, flat-bottomed hole. There should be at least 18 inches depth of manure well trodden down. This is covered with 5 or 6 inches of fine soil, and a frame is placed on top. When the first fierce heat of fermentation has died down, but the soil is nicely warm, seeds are sown in it and the lights are placed in position. Mustard and cress can be grown very readily in this manner or in shallow boxes in a warm greenhouse. Sow the mustard every week and the cress about once a fortnight, as it lasts longer. A couple of small sowings of radishes and Tom Thumb lettuces made at fortnightly intervals under similar conditions in a frame or in deeper boxes or beds in the greenhouse will provide useful saladings later on.

Spray Fruit Trees with Tar Oil. When the weather is favourable spray all outdoor fruit trees and bushes with tar oil wash. The object of this is to kill any insect eggs which may be left in the crevices of the bark and to clean the trees of green, scummy growth, scale insects, etc. It is at this season of the year that really powerful insecticides can be used without fear of damaging the trees, and the gardener who neglects his opportunity must not be surprised if his trees in the summer are more freely attacked by pests and diseases than those of his more alert neighbour.

Tar oil washes are sold under many different trade names and can be purchased from any dealer in horticultural sundries. They are prepared by diluting with water, the usual strength being six parts of the neat tar oil to a hundred parts of water—*i.e.*, 6 gallons in 100 gallons, 6 pints in 12½ gallons (100 pints), etc.—but instructions are always given on the tin, and you should consult these in case the purchased brand is not of standard strength.

The important thing in tar oil spraying is to employ a machine that will give a fine but driving spray capable of penetrating well down into the crevices of the bark. A powerful coarse spray is efficient but wasteful. It is also wasteful to attempt to spray trees when the weather is windy, and it is not effective to spray while it is freezing; so choose a calm and comparatively mild day for the work, and not one when it is raining, or the dilution will be upset.

Complete Fruit Tree Pruning. Fruit tree pruning should really be done in November and December, but, if it is delayed then for one reason or another, it can be completed in January—but the sooner the better. Work on the peaches, nectarines, and apricots first, then do the plums, gooseberries, and red and white currants, and leave the pears and apples till the last. Very soon sap will be on the move once more, and the wise gardener will always get his trees pruned while they are quite dormant.

Collect Scions for Grafting. This is a good time to collect suitable shoots for grafting if you intend to do any later on. Ordinary prunings do quite well. Select strong, well-ripened shoots formed the previous summer. Label them carefully and then heel them in in a trench about 4 inches deep prepared in a cool, shady place, preferably under a north wall or fence. The object is to keep them dormant until grafting-time (see March, Fourth Week). Old trees that are to be reworked should also be headed back now—*i.e.*, the main branches should be sawn off about a couple of feet from the trunk. Apples and pears stand this treatment best. Plums, cherries, and other stone fruits resent the hard cutting back.

Open Orchard House and Vinery. The orchard house and vinery should still be ventilated as freely as possible (see November, General Work), except early houses (see later). No heat must be used, and ventilators should be opened widely whenever it is not actually freezing hard. Light frost will do no harm, but rather good, preparing the trees for very rapid growth when the house is closed later on.

FIRST WEEK

Order Seeds and Seed Potatoes. The very first task for January should be to compile a complete list of all seeds that will be required during the

SPROUTING SEED POTATOES

Place the potatoes, eyes (A), uppermost in trays in a frost-proof shed, room or greenhouse to form sprouts. Extra protection may be given in very frosty weather as shown in the illustration.

following two or three months, and to get these ordered without delay. It is true that a good many of the seeds cannot be sown before March or even April, but later on seedsmen become inundated with orders and even with the best of organizations there may be delay in execution. There is no sense in risking that, because the seeds can be kept quite as well at home as in the seedsmen's store, and they will then be at hand the very moment that the most favourable opportunity arrives. Order seed potatoes at the same time, and as soon as they arrive set them up in shallow trays, eyed ends uppermost, and place them in a light but frost-proof room, shed, or greenhouse to form sprouts. This is particularly important with early varieties, but is worth doing with all kinds.

Bring Shrubs and Roses in Pots into Greenhouse. The first week in January is a good time to bring into the greenhouse the first batch of bush roses well established in pots. Give them a light, airy place preferably on the staging, not too far from the glass. Water the soil moderately and syringe with slightly warm water every morning. Maintain a temperature of about 55° to 60°. All the roses must be pruned, previous year's growth being shortened to within an inch or so of the older wood. It is also a good plan to bring in a few deutzias, Indian azaleas, lilacs, viburnums, etc., to provide a succession to earlier batches (see November, First Week). A start may also be made with hydrangeas and astilbes, both of which require rather liberal watering once they have started into growth.

Prune Climbers in the Greenhouse. Several of the permanent climbers commonly grown in greenhouses should be pruned now. These include *Plumbago capensis* and the passion flower. The plumbago is pruned by cutting each of last year's growths back to 9 inches or thereabouts. This applies to fully developed specimens. With young plants which have not yet filled their space, some shoots may be left unpruned. The passion flower is pruned by cutting out weak shoots altogether and reducing the remainder of the previous year's growths to about two buds each.

Sow Onions for Exhibition. If you aspire to great successes on the vegetable show bench later in the year, you must make a sowing of exhibition onions in a heated greenhouse. It is no use to sow onion seed as yet outdoors or in an unheated frame. But if sown thinly in loamy soil with plenty of sand and a little peat moss in well-drained seed trays and placed in a greenhouse with an average temperature of from 55° to 60°, the seed will soon germinate and provide sturdy seedlings for transferring to the open ground in the spring. The best method is to sow the seeds singly 1 inch apart; then the seedlings need not be pricked off.

Sow Shorthorn Carrots on a Hotbed. If a hotbed is available, you can make a first sowing of shorthorn carrots. Sow these directly in the soil in the frame and not in boxes. The rows should be about 6 inches apart. If the seedlings are thinned to a couple of inches apart later on, there will be a nice supply of young roots in the early spring. An alternative method is to sow in a frame heated with hot-water pipes or special electrical soil-heating cables.

Start Early Peaches, Nectarines and Apricots. With the aid of a heated orchard house it is possible to have ripe peaches, nectarines, and apricots at any time during the summer. If you wish to eat ripe fruits in June, this is the time to start the trees into growth. Close doors and ventilators and maintain an average temperature of 45° at night, rising 5° or 10° by day. Syringe the trees every morning with slightly warm water, and damp the floor of the house to maintain the moisture in the atmosphere.

Start Early Vines into Growth. You may also start early vines such as Black Hamburgh, Foster's Seedling, and Buckland's Sweetwater into growth, provided you have a heating apparatus installed in the vinery adequate to maintain a temperature of 55° at night during February and March. Five degrees less than this, rising to 60° by day, will do for the present, however. The higher temperature is only necessary when growth actually starts. Syringe the vines several times daily to keep the atmosphere moist, and give a little top ventilation by day whenever outside conditions permit this without lowering the temperature or causing cold draughts. Soak the border thoroughly with clear water and fill any evaporating trays over the pipes. Spread a 2-inch thick layer of well-rotted stable manure all over the border to feed the roots.

Prune Late Vines. Late-fruiting vines such as Alicante and Gros Colmar should be pruned. Details of this are the same as for the pruning of early vines (see November, Fourth Week).

SECOND WEEK

Sow Exhibition Sweet Peas. This is the time for the exhibition grower to sow sweet peas in pots if this was not done in a frame in September. A warm greenhouse will be needed for germination, but a great amount of heat is not desirable; 50° to 55° will be ample. Sow four or five seeds in each 3-inch pot. A fine compost for this purpose—and, indeed, for most seed sowing—is two parts of medium loam, one part of best moss peat, and one part of sharp silver sand. To each bushel of this mixture should be added ¾ ounce of ground chalk and 1½ ounce of superphosphate of lime. It is all to the good if the loam can be sterilized by steaming in a suitable apparatus. Several reliable soil sterilizers of moderate size are available which will enable you to do the work conveniently and well.

Start Begonia and Gloxinia Tubers. If you own a well-heated greenhouse, you may start tuberous-rooted begonias and gloxinias into growth. The begonias can be managed quite satisfactorily in a temperature of 55°, but a little more is advisable for the gloxinias. If the two have to be

STARTING TUBEROUS-ROOTED BEGONIAS
The tubers are set out in trays nearly filled with damp moss peat.

grown in the same house, the extra warmth will not do the begonias any harm. Prepare some rather deep seed trays with good drainage in the bottom and then a layer of moss peat. Set the tubers almost shoulder to shoulder in this and just cover them with more peat. Be careful to moisten the peat thoroughly some while before it is actually required. This is a tip that always applies when using moss peat. When it is quite dry it is very difficult to make it take up water, which runs off the granules instead of soaking into them, but once they have become moistened they go on soaking up water like a sponge. If the peat is well wetted a few days before the begonia and gloxinia tubers are to be boxed, no further watering will be needed at first, but do not let it dry out. Keep it just nicely moist until growth appears, and then give rather more water.

Sow Tomatoes for an Early Crop. Sow tomatoes now if you want a crop in June, but do not forget that this means plants 3 or 4 feet high by the beginning of May. They will take some accommodation, and the June crop may not be worth it if it means ruining your bedding plants. If you sow now, do so very thinly in well-drained seed boxes, using the compost referred to on page 26. Germinate in a temperature of 55° or rather more. Tomatoes love warmth, and will get hard and blue in the cold, obstinately refusing to grow and becoming more miserable every week. Germination will be more rapid if each box is covered with a sheet of glass and brown paper. Keep the soil well moistened, but not sodden.

THIRD WEEK

Sow Begonias, Gloxinias, etc. Sowings to be made now in the warm greenhouse are begonias, gloxinias, streptocarpus, cannas, verbenas, antirrhinums, and scarlet salvias. With the exception of cannas, all can be managed in an average temperature of 65°. The antirrhinums will even do with rather less, but for preference the gloxinias should have a little more, for they will then germinate more rapidly and grow more sturdily. Cannas need 75°, and even then germinate very irregularly. Do not forget that plants from these early sowings will be quite big by May, the time when many plants accommodated in the greenhouse during the winter can be put out in the open once more. If your greenhouse is already rather full and you plan to sow half-hardy annuals later on (see February, Third Week) and take a lot of cuttings, it may be wise to omit these first sowings and be satisfied with smaller plants. But if space is not pinched there can be no gainsaying the advantage of an early start. It will be reflected in the abundance and quality of the flowers.

Plant Potatoes in Frames and Pots. Potatoes in frames and pots are not difficult to grow, but they do take up a good deal of valuable space. However, it you want them, this is the time to start, with one well-sprouted tuber in each 8-inch pot, or, if in a frame on a hotbed, tubers 9 inches apart in rows 1 foot apart. The layer of soil in the hotbed will need to be a good deal deeper than for seedlings—at least a foot instead of the 4 or 5 inches mentioned earlier (see Small Salads, General Work). A compost of equal parts of turfy loam and sweet beech leaf-mould is ideal, with a sprinkling of any good potato fertilizer, but not more than 4 ounces per bushel.

GROWING POTATOES IN POTS
Place one tuber well down in an 8-inch pot. Later, as the haulm grows more rich soil is added.

Mulch Asparagus Beds. If possible, get some well-rotted manure (farm-yard manure is best, though stable manure will serve), break it up well, and spread it a couple of inches thick over the asparagus beds. This will have a marked effect upon the quality of the shoots later on, and the only condition under which this is inadvisable occurs when the soil is of a heavy, cold nature and is already inclined to be water-logged. In these circumstances a light dressing of hop manure will be more suitable.

Protect Fruit Trees from Birds. From now onwards birds are very liable to attack the buds of fruit trees, particularly pears, plums and goose-berries. The best protection for small bush fruits is obviously a properly constructed fruit cage covering the whole plantation. Pear and plum trees can be protected by passing black thread from twig to twig, but it is a laborious and troublesome proceeding. An easy and reasonably efficacious measure is to spray with a strong quassia wash. This makes the buds so bitter that the birds usually leave them alone. Another good bird protection is Scaraweb, which consists of strands of nylon fibre stretched over bushes or trees. This disintegrates gradually within about six to eight weeks.

FOURTH WEEK

Start Early Hippeastrums. You can start a first batch of hippeastrums by bringing the bulbs in the pots in which they flowered the previous year into a temperature of 60° or thereabouts and giving them a gradu-ally increasing quantity of water. If any of the bulbs that have been resting since October (see October, General Work) show signs of starting, select these in preference to those that are still dormant.

Pot on Greenhouse Calceolarias. It is time to give greenhouse calceolarias their final shift into the pots in which they will flower. These should be 7 or 8 inches in diameter. Use the compost referred to on page 44. Stand the plants in a light, airy place on the staging, water very carefully, and maintain an average temperature of 55°.

Force Rhubarb and Sea-kale Out of Doors. This is a good time to start forcing rhubarb outdoors. There is not much point in starting earlier, as it will be well-nigh impossible to generate sufficient heat to start any growth. The essentials for successful forcing are complete darkness and a mild, even temperature. First of all, the roots must be covered with something: either special earthenware forcing pots, which are not unlike chimney pots with a lid on the top, or with old barrels or large boxes. Whatever you use, make some arrangement for having a removable lid on top so that the sticks of rhubarb can be gathered without having to move the whole contraption. Place the boxes, barrels, or pots in position and heap up dead leaves around them, the more the better so long as they are not completely covered. The leaves will keep the rhubarb crowns at a nice even temperature and encourage steady and early growth. Never attempt to force newly planted or semi-established crowns. Only really strong roots should be covered, preferably those three or four years old.

Sea-kale can also be forced outdoors where it is growing by covering each strong crown with a large flower pot inverted and placing a piece of turf to block up the drainage hole in the bottom of the pot. Complete darkness is essential.

Sow Leeks. This is a good time to make a first sowing of leeks if large stems are required. Sow the seeds singly 1 inch apart in well-drained seed boxes, using an ordinary compost (see p. 26). Germinate in a greenhouse or frame with an average temperature of 55°.

Sow French Beans for Forcing. You can obtain a May crop of french beans by sowing now—five or six in each 8-inch pot filled to within a couple of inches with good loamy soil with which a little sand and leafmould has been mixed. Cover with a further inch of soil, water freely, and place in the greenhouse in a temperature of from 60° to 70°.

FLOWERS, VEGETABLES, AND FRUITS IN SEASON
DURING JANUARY

Hardy Herbaceous Plants. *Adonis amurensis, Helleborus antiquorum, H. colchicus, H. corsicus, H. foetidus, H. niger, H. orientalis* vars., *Iris unguicularis (stylosa), Petasites fragrans, Pulmonaria angustifolia azurea, P. rubra, P. saccharata, Saxifraga ligulata, S. ciliata.*

Hardy Bulbs and Tubers. *Brodiaea Leichtlini, Bulbocodium vernum, Colchicum Decaisnei, C. hydrophyllum, C. libanoticum, Crocus alatavicus, C. Billotti, C. Boryi, C. caspius, C. hyemalis, C. Imperati, C. Korolkowii, C. Tommasinianus, Cyclamen coum, Eranthis hyemalis, Galanthus cilicicus, G. plicatus, Iris Histrio, I. histrioides, I. reticulata* and vars., *Leucojum vernum carpaticum, Sternbergia lutea angustifolia.*

IRIS RETICULATA

This is one of the earliest irises to bloom and it is quite easy to grow either in the open or in pans indoors. Its very sweetly scented violet, purple and yellow flowers are produced in January and February on 6-inch stems.

Rock Plants. *Polygala Chamaebuxus, Primula Juliana* vars., *P. megaseaefolia, P. Winteri, Saxifraga Kellereri.*

Evergreen Shrubs. *Azara integrifolia* (shelter), *Daphne Laureola, D. odora, Erica Carnea* and vars., *E. darleyensis, E. lusitanica, Garrya elliptica, Lonicera fragrantissima, Mahonia japonica, Viburnum Tinus* and vars.

Deciduous Shrubs. *Chimonanthus fragrans, Corylus Avellana* and vars., *Daphne Mezereum grandiflora, Hamamelis japonica, H. mollis, Lonicera Standishii, Osmaronia cerasiformis, Rhododendron mucronulatum, Viburnum fragrans.*

Deciduous Trees. *Crataegus monogyna praecox, Prunus Davidiana, P. subhirtella autumnalis.*

Hardy Climbing Plants. *Clematis calycina, C. cirrhosa, Jasminum nudiflorum.*

Greenhouse Plants. Arum lilies, azaleas (Indian in variety), *Begonia fuchsioides, B. manicata, B. socotrana*, hybrid begonias of the Optima and

Gloire de Lorraine types, *Boronia heterophylla*, *B. megastigma*, bouvardias, *Browallia speciosa major*, camellias, carnations (perpetual-flowering), cinerarias (hybrids), *Coleus thyrsoideus*, cyclamen (Persian), *Daphne indica*, *Erica gracilis*, *E. melanthera*, epacris, *Euphorbia fulgens*, freesias, gardenias, hyacinths (Roman and large-flowered), *Iris tingitana*, *I. reticulata*, *Jasminum primulinum*, lachenalias, narcissi (Paper White, Soleil d'Or, Christmas Cheer, etc.), poinsettias, *Primula kewensis*, *P. malacoides*, *P. obconica*, *P. sinensis* and vars., *Sparmannia africana*, tulips (Duc van Thol).

Plants in Frames. *Anemone coronaria* vars. (St Brigid and du Caen anemones), *Helleborus niger* vars. (Christmas roses), violets (double and single).

Vegetables in Store. Jerusalem artichokes, beetroots, carrots, onions, parsnips, potatoes, turnips, shallots.

CHIMONANTHUS PRAECOX (WINTER SWEET)

The fragrant flowers of the winter sweet, a hardy shrub, are often out before Christmas. They are yellow, with a dark red or purple blotch, and they are produced on the leafless twigs. The shrub is ideal for training against a wall.

Vegetables in Garden. Jerusalem artichokes, broccoli (maincrop), broccoli (sprouting), brussels sprouts, celery, coleworts, endive, kales, leeks, lettuces, parsnips, savoys, spinach (sown August), turnips.

Vegetables under Glass. Endive, lettuce, mushrooms, mustard and cress, radishes, rhubarb, seakale.

Fruits in Store. *Apples:* Adams' Pearmain (D), Annie Elizabeth (C), Baumann's Red Winter Reinette (CD), Barnack Beauty (CD), Beauty of Kent (C), Beauty of Stoke (CD), Belle de Boskoop (CD), Bismarck (C), Blenheim Orange (D), Bramley's Seedling (C), Brownlees' Russet (D), Christmas Pearmain (D), Claygate Pearmain (D), Cornish Gillyflower (D), Court Pendu Plat (D), Cox's Orange Pippin (D), Cutler Grieve (D), Edward

Starting hippeastrums in a warm greenhouse.

Left: Heeling in well-labelled fruit tree prunings ready for grafting later.
Right: Sowing broad beans in deep drills.

Left: Begonia tubers are started into growth by being placed in boxes of compost in a greenhouse. *Right:* Removing a cutting from a chrysanthemum stool.

Shallots are planted by pressing them firmly into the soil.

VII (C), Gascoyne's Scarlet (D), Houblon (D), Imperial (D), John Standish (D), King of Tompkin's County (D), King's Acre Pippin (D), Lane's Prince Albert (C), Laxton's Pearmain (D), Lord Hindlip (D), Madresfield Court (D), Margil (D), May Queen (D), Monarch (C), Newton Wonder (C), Norfolk Royal (D), Orlean's Reinette (D), Reinette du Canada (D), Ribston Pippin (D), Rosemary Russet (D), Roundway Magnum Bonum (D), Royalty (D), Saltcote Pippin (D), St Cecilia (D), Superb (D), Triumph (D), Wellington (C), Wyken Pippin (D). *Grapes:* Alicante, Appley Towers, Canon Hall Muscat, Golden Queen, Gros Colmar, Gros Guillaume, Lady Downe's Seedling, Lady Hutt, Mrs Pearson, Mrs Pince, Muscat of Alexandria, and Prince of Wales. *Pears:* Bellissime d'Hiver (C), Beurré Easter (D), Blickling (D), Catillac (C), Foreile (D), Glou Morceau (D), Joséphine de Malines (D), Le Lectier (D), Uvedale's St Germain (C), Vicar of Winkfield (CD), Winter Nelis (D).

Nuts in Store. Cobnuts, filberts, walnuts.

C

February

GENERAL WORK

Finish Planting Trees and Shrubs. There is still just time to plant fruit trees, and also deciduous ornamental trees and shrubs, including roses, but the earlier this can be done in February the better, provided soil conditions are good. There is considerable controversy about the pruning of fruit trees transplanted as late as this, some experts urging that it is unwise to give the tree two shocks at once, root disturbance and a curtailment of branches. This group argues that it is better to leave the late-planted trees unpruned until the following November and then, if they have not made much new growth, to cut them hard back into the older wood; in other words, to prune them to just about the point where they would have been cut had the work been done at planting time. My own view is that this is a waste of time, and that in any case the idea that proper pruning is a shock is a fallacy. I would not hesitate to prune late-planted fruit trees immediately before planting. Ornamental shrubs and trees should certainly be cut back fairly drastically to encourage vigorous growth later on. February-planted roses are better left unpruned until the end of March.

Complete Digging and Break Down Soil. The good gardener will certainly have completed all his digging and trenching by this time, but sluggards may still have some work to do. The quicker it is finished the better. Ground that was turned over earlier in the winter and left rough should be broken down to a fine surface some time during February. It is essential to choose a day when the surface is fairly dry. You will do more harm than good if you walk about on beds that are soaking wet. Still, the right day often turns up several times during this month, and may be looked for after a period of steady east winds. Lawn sites that are to be sown or turfed later should also be prepared now.

Prune Roses. Continue to prune bush and standard roses (see November, General Work).

Complete Planting of Lilies. There is still time to plant lilies outdoors and also to transplant established lilies from one part of the garden to another. The latter will be in growth and must be handled in the same way as herbaceous plants—that is to say, they must be lifted carefully and with a good body of soil, which should be kept around the roots while replanting.

34

Continue to Pot Rooted Cuttings. Throughout the month you must keep a sharp eye on chrysanthemum and perpetual-flowering carnation cuttings, and pot them singly as soon as they start to grow freely (see January, General Work).

Take Chrysanthemum and Carnation Cuttings. As opportunity occurs during the month continue to take chrysanthemum and perpetual carnation cuttings. It is getting late for exhibition Japanese chrysanthemums in full-size pots, but decorative varieties can still be propagated with advantage, and February is the ideal month to start on the hardy border varieties.

General Greenhouse Management. Plants in flower or coming into flower in the greenhouse are very much the same as those for January,

WATERING BY PARTIAL
IMMERSION
*Each pot or pan is held almost
to its rim in a tub until the
rising water darkens the
surface of the soil.*

and for general management I refer you to notes in that month (see January, General Work). If there are any bright, warm days, seize the opportunity to give more top ventilation, but beware of cold winds. An occasional thorough airing, so long as it does not involve a drop in temperature or cold draughts, does the greenhouse a lot of good. Most plants will require rather more water, but begonias of the Optima type should have less.

Seedlings from January sowings of begonias, tomatoes, leeks, onions, etc., should now be appearing. At any rate, it is essential to examine the seed trays and boxes very carefully every day so that covering materials can be removed before seedlings get thin and drawn. Give water if the soil appears to be dry. The best method is to hold each receptacle almost to its rim in a pail of water for a few moments and let the water soak up

from below, but if there are a number to be done and this method takes
too long, water from an ordinary watering-pot fitted with a very fine
rose. Be sure to go over the surface several times, because the fine spray
of water tends to collect on the top and not soak in immediately.

Ventilate Frames According to the Weather. There is little to add to my
remarks on this subject in the General Work for January. As the days
get a little longer you will be able to ventilate more freely, but run no
unnecessary risks with frost.

Continue to Protect Broccoli. The curds are still liable to be damaged by
frost, and must be protected as they form (see November, General
Work).

Sow Small Salads for Succession. To maintain a supply of mustard and
cress and radishes, make further small sowings as advised in the notes
for January, General Work.

Harden Off Autumn-sown Cauliflowers. Cauliflower seedlings growing
in frames from late summer sowings must be gradually hardened off
during February in readiness for planting out next month. Take the
lights right off during the daytime if the weather is not frosty and the
wind is not very cold. Even at night a little ventilation can be given on
the leeward side if weather conditions are at all reasonable.

Continue to Force Seakale. Continue to pot and force seakale roots for
succession (see November, General Work). There is not much point in
bringing in any further supplies of rhubarb, however, as successional
supplies will be obtained from the roots covered outdoors (see January,
Fourth Week).

Pollinate and Disbud Early Peaches, Nectarines, etc. Peaches, nectarines,
and apricots in the early orchard house will be in flower during the
month, and as there will certainly not be enough insects about to effect
pollination it is necessary to do this by hand. The best method is to
have a camel-hair brush and scatter the dry pollen from bloom to bloom
with this, the most favourable time being towards mid-day when the sun
is shining.   While the fruit trees are in bloom it is necessary to dis-
continue syringeing and to raise the temperature by about 10° night
and day and keep the atmosphere dry by judicious ventilation (see
January, First Week). When the fruit is set syringe the trees freely again
once every morning.

As shoots grow you must, on peaches and nectarines, start the process
known as disbudding. The small side shoots that form on the fruiting

laterals are gradually pinched off, a few at a time, until only two are left
to each lateral, one at its base and the other at its extremity. Then in the
winter the old fruiting lateral is cut right out and the young basal shoot
is trained in its place. The object of leaving the terminal shoot is simply
to encourage the flow of sap through the branch and so help the fruits
to swell. This method of disbudding is only fully practised on established
trees that have filled their space. Small young trees may be allowed to
form new laterals wherever there is room for these to be trained in as
branches. Apricots bear on old as well as new wood, and with these
only shoots that are awkwardly placed are removed. Other side growths

DISBUDDING A PEACH
*Left; a typical fruiting
lateral before disbudding.
Right; the same lateral at
a later stage. Two young
shoots have been retained
near the base, but these
may be reduced to one
later.*

are cut back to four or five well-developed leaves each as soon as they
commence to get hard and woody at the base.

Pollinate and Train Early Vines. Vines started into growth last month
(see January, First Week) will also come into flower during February
and will need hand-pollination just like the peaches. The young laterals
must be pulled down little by little until they lie along the training wires.
If more than one lateral forms at each spur, pinch out the growing point
of the weaker at the earliest opportunity. The points of the flower-
bearing laterals must also be pinched just beyond the second leaf formed
after the truss. If any secondary laterals form, pinch these just beyond
the first leaf. While the vines are in flower, raise the temperature to

65° at night, rising about 10° by day. From this stage onwards you should soak the border occasionally with very weak liquid manure. Give sufficient to wet the soil to a depth of a couple of feet, and repeat the application as soon as the soil looks at all dry an inch or two below the surface.

FIRST WEEK

Prune Flowering Shrubs and Clematises. Flowering shrubs which should be pruned now include *Hydrangea paniculata*; *Spiraea japonica* (and varieties such as Anthony Waterer), *SS. Douglasii, Menziesii, bullata, salicifolia, ariaefolia, Aitchisonii, arborea, Lindleyana,* and *sorbifolia*; *Tamarix pentandra*; *Hypericum Moserianum*; all kinds of willows, unless grown principally for bark effects (see April, First Week); also *Cornus alba* and its varieties. In all these, stems made last year should be cut hard back to within one or two joints of the older wood. With the bigger shrubs you can, if you wish, allow some strong branches to remain at three-quarter length to build up a main framework of growth and so lay the foundation of larger specimens than could be obtained by constant hard pruning.

This is also the time to prune all clematises of the lanuginosa type. Cut out all weakly or imperfectly ripened and consequently soft vines to make room for the sturdier growths, which should be retained at full length.

Pot Annuals for the Greenhouse. If you were able to sow various annuals in September (see September, First Week) for flowering in the greenhouse during the spring, you should get the plants potted singly into 5- or 6-inch pots, according to the growth they have made. Use a rather light compost, about two parts of loam, one part of leaf-mould, and one part of really coarse sand. Stand on the staging or a shelf quite close to the glass to encourage sturdy growth. Schizanthus sown in August (see August, Third Week) must also be potted on in the same way. If you want very bushy plants pinch out the tips of the shoots.

Force Roses, Flowering Shrubs, etc. Bring further batches of bush roses, azaleas, deutzias, lilacs, astilbes, etc., well established in pots, into the greenhouse to provide a succession of flowers after those introduced in January (see January, First Week).

Start Achimenes. Place achimenes tubers thinly in shallow boxes half-filled with a light sandy compost and just cover them with the same mixture. Water very moderately and place on the staging in a temperature of about 60°. Very soon shoots will appear, and when these are a couple of inches in length the plants should be transferred to pots or pans. Five or six roots can be grown in a pot 5 inches in diameter. An alternative method is to grow them in hanging baskets, but in any case the initial starting process is the same. Do not start all the tubers at once. Successional starting will give a longer display.

Sow Broad Beans under Glass. You can make a sowing of broad beans in boxes or pots during this week. Do not scatter the seeds haphazard, but set them out at regular intervals 2 inches apart each way, and cover them with about ¾ inch of soil. Germinate in a slightly heated greenhouse or even a frame, provided the latter is well covered with sacks or mats on frosty nights. This method of sowing early in boxes gives far more reliable results, at any rate on all save the lightest of soils, than the old-fashioned scheme of sowing out of doors in the autumn.

Sow Lettuces, Culinary Peas and Cauliflowers. If you want a really early outdoor supply of lettuces make a small sowing of a cabbage variety in seed boxes and place in a warm greenhouse to germinate. An average temperature of 55° will be sufficient to ensure this. Seedlings from this indoor sowing will be planted out later, after proper hardening.

It is also an excellent plan to make a sowing of an early culinary pea in boxes and germinate in the same way as the lettuces. These seedlings will also be planted outdoors later. If you happen to live in a very mild part of the country or have an unusually sheltered garden you may even make an outside sowing of peas on a border with a southerly aspect, but you must certainly choose a really hardy variety, such as Meteor or Peter Pan.

Cauliflowers require a long and steady season of growth if they are to be a real success and if you have a warm greenhouse you should certainly make a first sowing now. A temperature of 55° to 60° will be quite adequate for germination. It is even possible to germinate them satisfactorily on a good hotbed made up as described for carrots (see January, General Work). Sow the seeds as thinly as possible, either in deep seed trays or, if in a frame on a hotbed, directly in the soil in shallow drills.

Sow Cucumbers for an Early Crop. Sow a few cucumber seeds for an early crop if you have a well-heated greenhouse. Place the seeds singly in 3-inch pots filled with a compost of loam, leaf-mould, and sand in about equal parts and germinate in a temperature of 75° in a close frame, preferably with bottom heat. It is an excellent plan to half-fill the frame with moss peat or coconut fibre and plunge the pots to their rims in this. Cucumbers need more warmth than tomatoes in the early stages, as they must be kept in rapid growth.

Plant Jerusalem Artichokes. Plant Jerusalem artichokes at the earliest opportunity. These are amongst the hardiest of all vegetables, and as they make a lot of tall, sunflower-like growth they may well be used as a windbreak in exposed gardens. They will grow almost anywhere, and good crops are to be had from soil that would be far too poor to produce potatoes. Simply plant the tubers 15 inches apart in rows 3 feet apart. Cover with 3 inches of soil.

Prune Autumn-fruiting Raspberries. Autumn-fruiting raspberries such as Hailsham and November Abundance must now be cut right back to within 6 inches of the ground. These varieties fruit on the young growth produced after pruning. The variety Lloyd George can also be pruned in this way for autumn fruiting, but is really more profitable as a summer fruiting variety, when it is pruned in August (see August, Second Week).

Start Second Early Vines into Growth. If you have more than one vinery and wish to have a succession of ripe grapes, or if you were afraid to start vines in January owing to lack of artificial heat you may do so now. It is still necessary to maintain the same temperatures as before (see January, First Week), but with lengthening days and more sun heat this is not so difficult.

SECOND WEEK

Plant Anemones and Ranunculuses. This is an excellent time to make a good planting of anemones of the St Brigid, du Caen, and fulgens types, and also of turban ranunculuses for a summer display. The anemones should be 2½ to 3 inches deep and the ranunculuses about 1 inch less. The latter are queer-looking things, like dried-up claws, and the claws should be planted downwards. Space both subjects about 6 inches apart each way.

Prune and Start Greenhouse Plants. Several well-known greenhouse plants require pruning now. Bougainvilleas should have last year's growth cut hard back unless you wish to retain some growths for extension. Bouvardias, gardenias, fuchsias, zonal and ivy-leaved pelargoniums, and *Diplacus glutinosus* should be cut sufficiently to give them a solid foundation for the coming season's growth and so prevent the least suspicion of untidiness. You can give all these plants water in gradually increasing quantity from now onwards as growth commences. A slightly higher temperature will also be all to the good, though it is not essential. All need as much light as they can get.

Sow Parsnips. If the weather is at all favourable do not hesitate to sow parsnips out of doors, for the longer and more steadily they can grow the better. However, there is no sense in sowing if the ground is sodden or frozen. Better wait two or three weeks than have all the seeds rot away. Sow in drills 1 inch deep and about 18 inches apart, scattering the seeds as thinly as possible, for later on the seedlings must be thinned to at least 9 inches apart in the rows. Those who grow for exhibition very often make a hole for each parsnip with a large iron crowbar. This is driven in to a depth of about 2 feet, the hole is then almost filled with fine potting soil, two seeds are sown, and a little more fine soil placed on top. The object of this is to encourage the tap root to grow straight down into the soft potting soil, and so obtain specimens of perfect shape. If both seeds germinate the weaker seedling is pulled out.

Lift and Store Parsnips. Parsnips that have been left in the ground all the winter will soon be starting to grow again, and it is best to lift them without delay and store in some cold place. A position beneath a north wall will do very well. It is only necessary to place the roots in a heap and cover them with a little soil; they are quite hardy and will not be injured by frost.

Plant Shallots and Potato Onions. There used to be an old-time idea that shallots should be planted on the shortest day of the year. There are, no doubt, some gardeners who follow this out still, but my own opinion is that, at any rate around London and on heavy soils generally, it is much better to wait until the second week in February. Indeed, even then, I would not plant unless the surface of the bed can be broken down reasonably fine. Better wait than plant in mud. The method of planting is simply to push good bulbs firmly into the soil until only the top third can be seen. Plant 9 inches apart in rows 1 foot apart. Potato onions, which are very much like shallots, are planted in exactly the same way and at the same time. Choose an open position and, for preference, ground that is well drained and has been adequately manured earlier in the winter.

Plant Out Spring Cabbages. Cabbages for a spring supply are sown in July or August and are usually planted out in the early autumn in the beds in which they are to mature. But sometimes one cannot find sufficient room for all the seedlings, and if there are some still left in the seed beds, now is the time to get them planted, always provided the weather is reasonably good. If it is not, seize the first favourable opportunity. These late plants are not likely to make such big hearts as the earlier ones, so it will be sufficient to plant them 10 inches to 1 foot apart in rows 18 inches apart.

THIRD WEEK

Sow Half-hardy Annuals and Greenhouse Plants. I usually make this week a busy one in the greenhouse, reserving it for sowing a great number of half-hardy annuals, greenhouse plants, etc. The half-hardy annuals are principally required for summer bedding, but some of them

VENTILATION FOR SEED PANS

Most seeds germinate more quickly if the seed pans are covered with glass and paper, but the latter must be removed as soon as the seedlings appear and the glass should be tilted a little. After a few days it can be removed.

may also come in useful for potting later on and growing as greenhouse plants during the summer (see my notes on hardy annuals in the greenhouse, March, First Week).

The principal half-hardy annuals to be sown now are ageratum, amaranthus, anagallis, antirrhinums, *Begonia semperflorens*, brachycome, cobaea, cosmeas, *Dianthus Heddewigii*, eccremocarpus, kochia, limonium (statice), lobelias, marigolds of both French and African types, marguerite carnations, nicotianas, nemesias, *Phlox Drummondii*, petunias, scarlet salvias, salpiglossis, schizanthus, ten-week stocks, and verbenas. The greenhouse plants include balsams, begonias, celosias (including cockscombs), celsias, *Clerodendrum fallax*, gloxinias, *Impatiens Sultani*, and *I. Holstii*, mimulus, *Rehmannia angulata*, streptocarpus, and trachelium. You may have sown some of these already (see January, Third Week), but even so plants from this later sowing will prove very useful for succession. Dahlias also come very well from a sowing made at this time, and make good strong plants for putting out

early in June. They will all germinate in a temperature of from 55°
to 60°.

For all these use the compost of two parts of rather light but fibrous
loam (preferably steam sterilized), one part of moss peat, and one part
of coarse silver sand that I have already recommended, and do not forget to add 1½ ounce of superphosphate and ¾ ounce of ground chalk to
each bushel of the mixture. Seed boxes will do for all seeds, though
perhaps it is a little better to have the really choice greenhouse seeds,
such as celosias, begonias, and streptocarpus, in earthenware seed pans.
Whichever you use be sure to make them thoroughly clean by scrubbing
them out with a stiff brush, and then provide plenty of drainage material,
first of all with a layer of broken pots and then with a thin scattering of
either rough leaf-mould or sphagnum moss. Prepare the boxes a day
before you actually intend to sow the seeds and give the soil a thorough
watering. Then stand the boxes on the staging to drain. Never fill a seed
receptacle right to the rim; leave at least ½ inch for watering. The day
after watering sow the seeds very thinly and evenly, cover lightly with
soil (a good general rule is to cover a seed with twice its own depth of
soil), and then place a sheet of glass over each pan or box and a large
piece of brown paper over the lot. Any more water that may be needed
must be given either from a can fitted with a very fine rose or else by
holding the pan or box almost to its rim in a tub of water.

Start Dahlia Tubers for Cuttings. If you wish to increase your stock of
dahlias considerably, get the old dahlia tubers out of store and place
them in boxes in the greenhouse to start into growth. Old apple boxes

STARTING DAHLIA
TUBERS

*The old roots are
arranged in boxes and
surrounded with light
soil, then placed in a
warm greenhouse and
watered moderately.*

serve very well for this purpose, or orange cases can be used—indeed,
anything that is deep enough to take a dahlia tuber. Any old potting
compost can be utilized. Place a little in the bottom of the box, then
stand the tubers on it, as many in a box as can be accommodated
comfortably, and place more soil around them until the fleshy tubers
themselves are just covered, but the stumps of last year's stems are

exposed. Give a moderate watering and place in any light or semi-light place. They can go under the greenhouse staging for the time being, but as soon as growth starts they must be brought out into full light or the shoots will be blanched and useless. Give more water as necessary, sparingly at first but much more freely when growth appears. Any temperature over 55° will be sufficient to start growth.

Pot Early Begonias and Gloxinia Tubers. If you were able to start begonia and gloxinia tubers into growth during January they will almost certainly need potting up by this time. It is not wise to leave them until their roots become matted together in the trays. Get them out when they have two or three leaves each and place them separately in the smallest sized pots that will accommodate them comfortably. A good compost for this purpose is seven parts of medium loam, three parts of moss peat, two parts of coarse sand, with 1½ ounce of hoof and horn meal, 1½ ounce of superphosphate, ¾ ounce of sulphate of potash, and ¾ ounce of ground chalk added to each bushel. This, incidentally, will be found a very good standard compost for most potting. The tubers should only just be covered with soil. Make them moderately firm, give them a thorough watering, and stand them at the warmest end of the house. A temperature of from 60° to 65° will not be too much for a few days. Syringe every morning with slightly warm water to prevent flagging, and shade for a few days from strong direct sunshine.

Start Begonias, Gloxinias, and Hippeastrums. A further batch of begonias, gloxinias, and hippeastrums may be started into growth to provide a succession after those started in January (see January, Second and Fourth Weeks). Even if you were unable to start any then you may be safe in doing so now, for it will be easier to maintain the requisite temperatures.

Start Clivias and Vallotas. These plants may also be arranged to make growth now, but as they are never dried off to the extent of hippeastrums this simply means increasing the water supply a little and standing in a warmer part of the house. A temperature of from 55° to 60° will be ample unless very early flowers are required.

Sow Early Celery. This is the time to make the earliest sowing of celery to give fully blanched stems by the end of August. I do not advise you to attempt this first sowing unless you have plenty of frame space available and are fairly accustomed to handling plants under glass. It is much easier to grow celery from a March sowing, and from this you should have good sticks by Michaelmas. However, if you intend to enter in some August shows a few sticks of celery may make all the difference. A temperature of from 60° to 65° will be necessary for germination. The seeds should be sown as thinly as possible in the usual seed compost (see p. 26). It is an advantage to cover each box with a sheet of glass and another of brown paper. Of course, an early variety should be chosen for this purpose.

Sow Maincrop Tomatoes. A second sowing of tomatoes (see January, Second Week) will provide you with good sturdy plants for planting in the greenhouse in May as soon as you have cleared it of bedding plants, early-flowering plants, etc. Details of sowing are as before.

Pot Tomato Seedlings. Tomato seedlings from the January sowing should be potted separately in 3-inch pots as soon as they have made two or three rough leaves each beyond the first pair of plain seed leaves. Transfer them carefully to these pots, using the same kind of compost as that advised for the seed boxes (see January, Second Week). Water freely and keep shaded from direct sunshine for a day or so until they get over the shift. Later sowings may be pricked off into deeper boxes before potting, but I find that for the earliest crop it is better to pot separately as soon as possible.

Sow Turnips. Make a first sowing of turnips outdoors in a warm, sheltered place. Sow the seeds thinly in drills ½ inch deep and 10 inches apart. You should only sow a few seeds now and subsequently make small successional sowings every fortnight or so until the end of July, as by this method you will have a constant supply of young roots instead of a lot of old, tough, and strongly flavoured ones.

Start the Unheated Orchard House. Give considerably less ventilation to the unheated orchard house containing peaches, nectarines, etc. By day the top ventilators may be opened a little if the weather is fine, but early in the afternoon the house should be closed completely. This will encourage the trees to start into growth.

FOURTH WEEK

Prick off Early Seedlings. It should now be possible to prick off some of the early seedlings such as begonias, gloxinias, streptocarpus, etc., sown in January (see January, Third Week). They will be very small and it may be necessary to use a small forked stick to lift them, but early pricking out before roots become matted together is amply repaid. Fill rather deep seed trays or big earthenware pans with the same kind of compost as that used for seed raising, and dibble the seedlings in about 2 inches apart each way. Water freely and keep rather warm and shaded for a few days until they recover from the shift, after which they may be placed on the ordinary greenhouse staging in a temperature of about 60°.

RAISING BEGONIAS
FROM SEED

The seed pans are covered with glass until the seeds germinate but then air must be admitted in increasing quantity until, after a few days, the glass can be removed altogether. Prick out the seedlings, when they have made two or three leaves, into pans or boxes. A forked stick, as shown, is useful for pricking out the tiny seedlings that are difficult to handle.

Plant Chives. Chives are not a very important vegetable crop, but a small bed comes in very useful for flavourings. This is the time of year to plant it or to divide old clumps that have got overcrowded. Simply lift the plants and pull them apart, replanting small tufts about 9 or 10 inches apart in rows 1 foot apart. Any ordinary soil and reasonably open position will do.

Plant Potatoes in a Sheltered Border. If you have a very sheltered border, preferably one with a south aspect, and you are not afraid to take a small risk, you can now make a first planting of early potatoes. They will need watching later on and you will probably have to protect the young shoots with dry straw or bracken, but if you are successful there is no reason why you should not be digging new potatoes early in June. Of course, for this first planting it is essential to choose a quick-growing variety such as Arran Pilot or Sharpe's Express. Also you should use only well-sprouted sets. Reduce the number of sprouts to two or three sturdy ones on each tuber. Plant in trenches about 5 inches deep and 2 feet apart, setting the tubers 9 inches apart with the eyes pointing upwards. Surround each tuber with a couple of handfuls of leaf-mould or moss peat and sprinkle a little potato fertilizer in the bottom of each trench (about 2 ounces per yard run). Then refill the trenches but do not firm the soil much. Plenty of good potato fertilizers can be bought ready to use, but if you prefer you can make your own with eight parts of superphosphate of lime, five parts of sulphate of ammonia, and three parts of sulphate of potash. This mixture will keep for quite a long time in a dry place. If it sets hard after a few days, break it up thoroughly with the back of a spade.

Plant Out Autumn-sown Onions. Directly the soil is in good condition— that is to say, as soon as you can walk on it without it sticking to your boots—plant out seedling onions from the August sowing. The method is to plant with a small dibber, just dropping the seedlings into holes about 2 inches deep. Plant 9 inches apart in rows 15 inches apart. Incidentally, the position chosen should be fully open and the soil must have been well cultivated earlier in the winter—plenty of manure in the bottom spit and any quantity of wood ashes mixed with the surface soil. Onions growing in rough, hard soil are almost certain to be misshapen.

Prick off Lettuce and Cauliflower Seedlings. These seedlings from the sowings made three weeks ago should now be ready for pricking off into deeper seed boxes filled with the same kind of compost as that used in the seed trays. Lift the seedlings very carefully with a sharpened wood tally and dibble them in 2 inches apart each way. Water freely and keep shaded for a day or so until they start to grow again.

Sow Parsley in a Sheltered Place. Make a small sowing of parsley in a warm, sheltered place. It is much too early yet for the main sowing, but plants raised now will be useful in early summer before the main crop is ready. Parsley seed is quite cheap, so there is no great loss even if the sowing does not prove a success.

Sow French Beans for Succession. Sow some more french beans in 8-inch pots if you wish to keep up a successional supply under glass during the spring (see January, Fourth Week).

Sow Melons in a Heated Greenhouse. This is a good time to sow melon seeds. Sow them singly, $\frac{1}{2}$ inch deep, in small pots (those $2\frac{1}{2}$ inches in diameter will be admirable), and start them into growth in a temperature of from 60° to 70°. It is a good plan to plunge the pots to their rims in moss peat or coconut fibre in a propagating box placed over the heating apparatus (see p. 40).

Prune Cobnuts and Filberts. Cobnuts and filberts must be pruned as soon as the small red female flowers can be seen. These, by the way, are rather insignificant and you must look closely to find them. It is the male catkins that make the show. The leading shoots of established bushes which fill their space are shortened to a couple of buds each. If there is still room for the bushes to extend there is no need to prune these leaders at all, or at the most only to remove their tips. Side shoots are cut back to the first catkin, reckoning from the tip, or, if there are no catkins, to the first female flower. Some shoots may have catkins only. These should be left unpruned until the catkins fade and then be cut right back to two buds. There is no point in keeping them, as they will not produce any nuts. Badly placed branches which crowd up the centre of the bush

TYPICAL SHOOTS OF COBNUT IN FLOWER

The upper shoot is bearing catkins only, while the lower forked stem has been cut back to the female flowers nearest the extremities. Later, when the catkins have faded, the upper shoot must be shortened to two buds or leaves.

should be removed altogether, even if this means using a saw. The ideal nut bush is roughly in the form of a goblet, with a short main trunk and branches radiating from it at regular intervals.

Spray Peaches and Nectarines Outdoors. If your outdoor peaches or nectarines were attacked by red spider the previous summer, spray them now with lime-sulphur wash at the usual winter strength advised by the manufacturers. This treatment will also check the leaf-curl disease.

Above: Peach blossom pollinated
with a rabbit's tail. *Above, right:*
Pot-grown roses, hard pruned
and placed in a greenhouse ready
for forcing.
Right: A shrubby spiraea that
has been winter pruned.

A knife is used to sever dahlia cuttings from the tubers.

Tying down the laterals of a vine.

FLOWERS, VEGETABLES, AND FRUITS IN SEASON
DURING FEBRUARY

Hardy Herbaceous Plants. *Adonis amurensis, Arisarum proboscideum, Euphorbia biglandulosa, Helleborus abchasicus, H. antiquorum, H. caucasicus, H. colchicus, H. corsicus, H. foetidus, H. guttatus, H. odorus, H. olympicus, H. orientalis* vars., *H. viridis, Iris unguicularis* and vars., *Petasites fragrans, Pulmonaria angustifolia, P. rubra, P. saccharata, Ranunculus Ficaria* vars., *Saxifraga ciliata, S. ligulata, S. Stracheyi.*

Hardy Bulbs and Tubers. *Chionodoxa Luciliae, Colchicum crociflorum, C. hydrophilum, C. libanoticum, C. montanum, Crocus aerius, C. alatavicus, C. ancyrensis, C. aureus* and vars., *C. Balansae, C. banaticus, C. biflorus* and vars., *C. candidus, C. carpetanus, C. chrysanthus* and vars., *C. corsicus, C. dalmaticus, C. etruscus, C. Fleischeri, C. gargaricus, C. Imperati, C. Korolkowii,*

CROCUS IMPERATI

Among the early-flowering crocuses C. Imperati *is very popular. Its lilac flowers are produced from January to March.*

C. Olivieri, C. sativus and vars., *C. Sieberi, C. stellaris, C. Tommasinianus, Cyclamen coum, C. ibericum, Erythronium Dens-canis, Eranthis hyemalis, Galanthus byzantinus, G. Elwesii, G. latifolius, G. nivalis* in var., *G. plicatus, Hyacinthus azureus, Iris Bakeriana, I. Danfordiae, I. histrioides, I. persica, I. reticulata, I. sindjarensis, I. Rosenbachiana, Leucojum vernum carpaticum, Merendera caucasica, Narcissus Bulbocodium* and vars., *N. minor* and vars., *N. Pseudo-Narcissus pallidus praecox, Scilla amoena, S. bifolia* and vars., *S. sibirica, Tulipa biflora, T. saxatilis.*

Hardy Rock Plants. *Anemone angulosa, A. blanda, Cardamine diphylla, C. polyphylla, Corydalis angustifolia, C. bracteata, C. tuberosa, Doronicum caucasicum, Draba pyrenaica, Lithospermum rosmarinifolium* (shelter), *Omphalodes verna, Polygala Chamaebuxus, Primula Allionii, P. megaseaefolia, P. Juliana* vars., *P. Winteri, Saxifraga apiculata, S. Borisii, S. Burseriana* and vars., *S. Elizabethae, S. Haagii, S. Irvingii, S. Jenkinsii, S. juniperifolia, S. Kellereri, S. kewensis, S. megasaeflora, S. oppositifolia* and vars., *S. Paulinae, S. scardica* and vars., *Sisyrinchium grandiflorum, Synthyris reniformis, Viola florariensis.*

D

Evergreen Shrubs. *Azara integrifolia, A. microphylla, Camellia reticulata* (shelter), *Daphne Laureola, D. odora, Erica arborea* and vars., *E. carnea* and vars., *E. darleyensis, E. lusitanica, E. mediterranea, Garrya elliptica, Lonicera fragrantissima, Mahonia aquifolium, M. japonica* and vars., *Pieris japonica, Ribes laurifolium, Sarcococca humilis, Ulex europaeus* vars., *Viburnum Tinus* and vars.

Deciduous Shrubs. *Chimonanthus fragrans, Cornus Mas, Corylopsis Griffithii* (shelter), *Corylus Avellana* and vars., *C. maxima* and vars., *Cydonia japonica* and vars., *Daphne Mezereum, Edgeworthia papyrifera, Hamamelis mollis, H. japonica* and vars., *H. vernalis, Lonicera Standishii, Osmaronia cerasiformis, Stachyurus praecox, Viburnum foetens, V. fragrans, V. grandiflorum.*

HAMAMELIS MOLLIS (WITCH HAZEL)

The yellow flowers of the witch hazel appear early in the year on the bare stems and add a welcome touch of colour to the winter scene.

Deciduous Trees. *Alnus incana* vars., *A. japonica, A. oregana, Corylus Colurna, Prunus cantabrigiensis, P. Davidiana, P. pseudocerasus, P. subhirtella autumnalis, P. Conradinae.*

Hardy Climbing Plants. *Clematis calycina,* C. *cirrhosa, Jasminum nudiflorum.*

Greenhouse Plants. Arum lilies, *Acacia armata, A. Baileyana, A. dealbata,* azaleas (Indian and Mollis), camellias, begonias (as Jan., except Optima type), *Boronia heterophylla, B. megastigma, Browallia speciosa major,* camellias, carnations (perpetual), cinerarias (hybrids), *Coleus thyrsoideus, Coronilla glauca,* correas, cyclamen (Persian), *Daphne indica, Eupatorium vernale,* freesias, gardenias, hyacinths, bulbous irises (*tingitana,* Spanish, etc.), *Jasminum primulinum,* lachenalias, narcissi (including Golden Spur, *praecox,* etc.), primulas (as Jan.), *Sparmannia africana,* tulips (early-flowering vars.), also forced shrubs such as deutzias, cherries, almonds, peaches, viburnums, etc.

Plants in Frames. *Anemone coronaria* vars. (St Brigid and du Caen anemones), *Helleborus niger* vars. (Christmas roses), violets (double and single).

Vegetables in Store. Jerusalem artichokes, beetroots, carrots, onions, parsnips, potatoes, turnips, shallots.

Vegetables in Garden. Jerusalem artichokes, broccoli, sprouting broccoli, brussels sprouts, coleworts, celery, endive, kales, lettuces, leeks, spring onions, parsnips, savoys, spinach, turnip tops.

Vegetables under Glass. Endive, lettuces, mustard and cress, mushrooms, radishes, rhubarb, seakale.

Fruits in Store. *Apples:* Adams' Pearmain (D), Annie Elizabeth (C), Barnack Beauty (CD), Beauty of Kent (C), Beauty of Stoke (CD), Belle de Boskoop (CD), Brownlees' Russet (D), Cornish Gillyflower (D), Court Pendu Plat (D), Cox's Orange Pippin (D), Duke of Devonshire (D), Edward VII (C), John Standish (D), King's Acre Pippin (D), Lane's Prince Albert (C), Laxton's Pearmain (D), Lord Burghley (D), Lord Hindlip (D), May Queen (D), Monarch (C), Newton Wonder (C), Norfolk Royal (D), Reinette du Canada (D), Rosemary Russet (D), Roundway Magnum Bonum (D), Superb (D), Wellington (C), Wyken Pippin (D). *Grapes:* Alicante, Gros Guillaume, Lady Downe's Seedling, Mrs Pearson, Mrs Pince, Muscat of Alexandria, and Prince of Wales. *Pears:* Bellissime d'Hiver (C), Bergamotte d'Esperen (D), Beurré Easter (D), Catillac (C), Joséphine de Malines (D), Olivier de Serres (D), Uvedale's St Germain (C), Verulam (C), Winter Orange (C).

Nuts in Store. Cobnuts, filberts, walnuts.

March

GENERAL WORK

Transplant and Divide Herbaceous Perennials. March is usually the best month of the whole twelve during which to transplant the majority of herbaceous plants. There are a few exceptions, but they are not very important. German irises are usually planted by experts at the end of June because they will then give a full display of flowers the following year, but they can be transplanted with equal safety in March, the only drawback being that there will be few flowers the following summer. Similar

DIVIDING HERBACEOUS PLANTS

(*a*) *Cut solid crowns with a knife, taking care not to damage the roots.*

remarks apply to pyrethrums, which are also moved by experts immediately after flowering. Peonies and eremuruses are often quoted as examples of plants that benefit greatly by autumn transplanting. My own opinion is that this is well enough on properly drained soil, but that even with these plants it is better to wait until March if one has to contend with heavy clay. The actual moment during the month chosen for planting may be decided to some extent by opportunity and pressure of other work, but do not fail to seize any really good days early in the month or you may find that later on persistent rain holds you up.

When transplanting old clumps always break them up into smaller pieces, and if you have plenty of stock throw away the hard central portions of the clumps and keep only the young outside pieces. This is particularly important with vigorous spreading things such as Michaelmas daisies, heleniums, rudbeckias, and solidagos. Split up by hand where possible, and for very tough clumps use a couple of small border forks thrust back to back through the middle of the mass and then levered apart. Only use a knife with plants that make a solid crown— *e.g.*, peonies, delphiniums, and Caucasian scabious—and even then be careful only to cut the crowns and not the roots; pull these apart.

Always replant with a spade or trowel and not a dibber. Prepare good wide holes, spread roots out well, work some fine dry soil around them

DIVIDING HERBACEOUS
PLANTS

(b) Where possible divide herbaceous plants by pulling them apart ensuring that each division has its fair share of roots.

(it is an excellent plan to prepare a barrow-load of this in advance), and make thoroughly firm.

Prune Roses. Continue to prune bush and standard roses (see November, General Work).

Lay Turves. This is a good month for turf-laying, and also for repairing bare places in lawns. So, if you have any of this work to do, choose any day during March when the surface is dry enough to be walked on without sticking to your boots and it can be broken down reasonably well with the fork or rake. Beat the turves down on to the soil with a special wooden turf beater or roll them with a light roller, first in one direction and then transversely.

General Greenhouse Management. The greenhouse will now be filling with many more seedlings and young rooted cuttings than before. These must have plenty of light and air if they are to be kept short-jointed and sturdy and are not to be attacked by the deadly damping-off fungus. In consequence it is not usually possible to do with much less fire heat in the general utility greenhouse than in January or February because, though the days may be a little warmer, more ventilation must be given, and yet the temperature inside the greenhouse must still be at an average of 55° to 60° for the majority of popular greenhouse plants. If you have a separate house or a section of a house that can be devoted to seed germination, starting bulbs and tubers, rooting soft cuttings, etc., this can be ventilated less and the necessary temperature of 60° to 70° maintained with considerably less artificial heat than formerly.

In the main greenhouse, in which you have flowering and foliage plants, seedlings, and cuttings that have been removed from the propagating box and are being hardened off, etc., avoid sudden large rises of temperature caused by direct sun heat. On a bright, still day the thermo-

THE USE OF A GREENHOUSE FRAME

The seeds when germinated in the frame may be pricked off into beds made up on the staging.

meter may easily rise 15° or 20° in an hour or so if you are not on the watch. Give increased top ventilation to counteract this, so avoiding rises of more than 10° and preventing serious scorching of both foliage and flowers.

Roses started in the greenhouse during January or February will benefit from an occasional syringeing with a nicotine or malathion insecticide just in case there should be any greenfly about. On warm, bright days many plants not in bloom will benefit from syringeing with tepid water. It should be done in the morning, but not too early. Plants must not be syringed while they are in bloom.

Harden Autumn Seedlings and Cuttings. Various seedlings and cuttings that have been in frames during the autumn and winter must now be hardened off. This simply means that more ventilation should be given, the lights being removed altogether during the day when the weather is mild and being tilted a little at night unless it is actually freezing or blowing very cold. The hardiest of these plants, and therefore the most able to stand exposure, will be pansies, violas, and violets. Antirrhinums (either from autumn seed or cuttings), penstemons, and calceolarias need a little more protection as yet.

Take Cuttings of Bedding and Greenhouse Plants. In a moderately heated greenhouse such popular bedding plants as heliotropes, marguerites, fuchsias, pelargoniums (geraniums), scarlet salvias, lobelia, and agera-

INSERTING CUTTINGS OF GERANIUMS
Prepared cuttings are inserted in 4-inch pots containing a sandy compost.

tum (it is only worth while keeping very choice varieties of the last two, as ordinary kinds can be raised so readily from seed) will be making suitable growth to provide cuttings. Secure these directly they are sufficiently long. The actual length of the cutting will depend on the type of plant—for example, with geraniums, which have comparatively big stems, cuttings 3 inches in length are ideal, but 2-inch cuttings will do for the thinner fuchsias and heliotropes, while it will only be possible to get 1-inch long shoots of lobelias and ageratums. Prepare all by severing them cleanly immediately below a joint and then insert them in well-drained boxes or 4-inch pots filled with a sandy compost, dropping them in just sufficiently deep to keep them erect. They can be rooted on the greenhouse staging if they are shaded during the day, but better results with all except geraniums are obtained by placing them in a propagating box, especially if this is over the hot-water pipes or other heating apparatus.

You can propagate quite a number of popular greenhouse plants in precisely the same way. It is worth trying a few shoots of any perennial that is just making new growth. A few examples are abutilons, bouvardia, coleus, datura (brugmansia), eupatoriums, gardenia, justicia, lantana, libonia, berried solanums, the double-flowered tropaeolums and petunias. All these should be kept as close as possible in a frame warmed from below until they are rooted. Winter-flowering begonias of the Gloire de Lorraine type make basal growths at this time of the year, and these can be secured as cuttings when 2 inches in length.

If desired the base of each cutting can be treated with a root-forming hormone before insertion. This can be done either by dipping it in powder containing the hormone or by leaving the cuttings to stand for a few hours in a very weak solution of the hormone. Suitable preparations can be purchased from any dealer in horticultural sundries.

Stop Early Carnations. Complete the propagation of perpetual-flowering carnations from cuttings as soon as possible. Cuttings that were rooted in December and January will be ready for stopping some time during the month. This simply means that the top of each cutting is broken off with a sideways movement. The effect of this is to make the plants produce side shoots. The right stage of growth for stopping is when the plant has made about seven joints. One complete joint is broken out.

Pot Chrysanthemum and Carnation Cuttings. You must continue to pot chrysanthemum and perpetual-flowering carnation cuttings as soon as they are well rooted (see January, General Work).

Perpetual-flowering carnations that were potted into 2-inch pots in January and early February will also need a move on into 3- or 3½-inch pots some time during the month. Use the same compost as before, but rather coarser in texture. Do not place the plants in a frame in the same way as the chrysanthemums, but stand them on staging or a shelf in the greenhouse with an average temperature of 55°, and as much ventilation as possible without cold draughts.

Chrysanthemum cuttings that were rooted during December and January should be ready for the second potting into 5-inch pots quite early in the month. Use a rather coarser compost than before and pot a little more firmly. A good mixture is eight parts of good loam, one part of sweet leaf-mould or moss peat, one part of well-rotted cow or horse manure, one part of coarse sand, and one part of old mortar rubble. Add a 5-inch potful of bonemeal to each bushel of this mixture. After potting place the plants in a frame but keep the lights on at first and have plenty of thick sacks or mats at hand to cover them on cold nights.

This is also a good time to purchase rooted cuttings of all kinds of chrysanthemums. Pot the cuttings up singly directly they arrive, and place them in the greenhouse, keeping them shaded from direct sunshine for a few days and syringeing with slightly warm water every morning.

FROST DANGER WITH FRAMES

When protecting frames with mats or sacking on frosty nights make certain that the covering is well fastened down.

Take Chrysanthemum Cuttings and Split Border Kinds. The best way to grow outdoor chrysanthemums is from cuttings, and you can continue to take these throughout March. Instructions are as for indoor kinds (see December, Third Week). However, if you have no facilities for handling cuttings you can still get quite good results by treating the border chrysanthemums like ordinary herbaceous perennials, lifting the roots now and splitting them up into small pieces. Throw away the hard, woody stumps of last year's growth and keep only the young outer shoots. Plant these 18 inches apart in the border or, if in rows, 1 foot apart in lines 2 to 3 feet apart. Propagation of the main stock of late-flowering chrysanthemums should now be almost completed, but towards the end of the month you may take a few more cuttings to be flowered in 6-inch pots.

Make Successional Sowings. Several vegetables that you have already sown will need to be resown during the month to provide a succession. You will need two or three more sowings of radishes as described in the notes for February, General Work. For the first three weeks of the month these should be made in a frame unless you are in an exceptionally favourable district, for radishes must grow rapidly to be of any use. At the end of the month you can make a sowing outdoors in a warm sheltered border. One or two small sowings of turnips (see February, Third Week) will ensure a constant supply in early summer. Mustard and cress may be sown quite frequently in a warm frame or greenhouse (see January, General Work). Make another sowing of lettuces in the greenhouse early in the month (see February, First Week). At the end of the month it will be safe to sow outdoors (see Fourth Week).

Prick off Seedlings. During the month many seedlings raised in the warm greenhouse or frame last month will be ready for pricking out. Usually the ideal time is when the seedlings have made two true leaves each in

A USEFUL TYPE OF
PRICKING-OFF TRAY
One side is held by two screws only and so is quickly removable. When planting time comes it is a simple matter to shovel the plants out with a trowel.

addition to the first seed leaves (these are quite different in character from the true leaves and can be distinguished quite easily). Monocotyledons, such as onions and leeks, make only one seed leaf and are pricked off as soon as they can be handled conveniently. However, if you followed my advice (see January, First and Fourth Weeks) and spaced the seeds singly, no pricking off will be necessary as the tiny plants will have plenty of room.

For general pricking off use the same compost as that advised for the seed trays (see p. 26). Lift the seedlings with as little root injury as possible and dibble them in 2 inches apart each way, making the soil firm around their roots. Water freely and shade for a few days while the tiny plants are recovering from the check of the move. You can either prick off into other boxes like those used for the seeds but preferably a little deeper, or else, if in frames, directly into a bed of fine soil. Among the seedlings needing this attention will be cauliflowers and lettuces sown under glass for planting out, tomatoes (unless you can pot them singly straight away to save time as I described in my notes for February, Third Week), and many half-hardy annuals and greenhouse plants.

Treat Peaches, etc., according to Growth. Peaches, nectarines and apricots in the unheated orchard house will come into bloom early in the month and will require hand-fertilization exactly as described in the notes for February, General Work. Later they must be disbudded little by little, as described in the same place.

Peaches and nectarines which were started in January should now have fruit well set, and you can commence to thin these; but do not complete the work as yet, because there is often a heavy natural fall during the stoning period (see April, General Work). Simply content yourself so far with reducing the number of fruits per cluster so that they have room to swell.

THINNING A BUNCH OF GRAPES
This work must be done at an early stage and with the utmost care. Use a pair of pointed scissors and do not touch the bunch with the fingers.

Start to Thin the Earliest Grapes. Some time during the month bunches of grapes in the earliest vinery will be ready for their first thinning. The ideal time to start is about a fortnight after the grapes first set.

Use a special pair of grape scissors with pointed blades and start thinning at the bottom of the bunch. Leave the extreme point of the bunch, but remove all the berries that are within ¾ inch above it. Berries at the top of the bunch can be left almost twice as thick as this, those between being given an intermediate amount of room. Do not touch the berries by hand, but use a small forked stick to turn them if necessary.

Vines started into growth in February will be in need of pollination, training, and stopping exactly as I described for the earliest vines (see February, General Work).

FIRST WEEK

Sow Sweet Peas Outdoors. If you were unable to sow sweet peas in the autumn or in January under glass you should certainly make an outdoor sowing at the earliest possible moment now. Some growers are successful with sowings made in the open as early as the second week in February, but my opinion is that little is gained in this way, and that the soil is much more likely to be in the right condition during March. Sow the seeds 2 inches deep and 4 inches apart in rows 10 inches apart, with an alleyway at least 5 feet wide between each pair of rows.

This is also the time to pinch out the tips of sweet peas sown in January, a task which must be done even if the peas are to be grown on the single stem (cordon) system. Side growths produce better flowers than the main stems.

Bed out Wallflowers, Forget-me-nots, etc. If it was not possible to complete the planting of wallflowers, forget-me-nots, Canterbury bells, polyanthuses, and double daisies in October, now is the time to get the plants into their flowering quarters. Do not delay this operation if weather and soil conditions are right. (See October, General Work, for particulars).

Sow Annuals for the Greenhouse. A great many of the familiar hardy annuals that are grown for flowering in summer beds also make good greenhouse pot plants. Included under this heading are annual anchusa, calendula, annual chrysanthemum, clarkia, eschscholtzia, godetia, gypsophila, heliophila, ipomoea, larkspur, *Mesembryanthemum criniflorum*, mignonette, nasturtium, nemophila, phacelia, salpiglossis, sweet scabious, annual statice, ursinia, and viscaria. Sow seed now in well-drained seed trays and germinate in the greenhouse in a temperature of 55° to 60°. You will then have good strong plants starting to flower at the end of May, just when your greenhouse has been cleared of most of the winter and spring plants. Prick off the seedlings 2 inches apart each way into similar soil and boxes as soon as they have made two true leaves each.

Repot Foliage Plants, Ferns, etc. Early March is a great time for potting, at any rate so far as summer and autumn-flowering plants are concerned, and also all plants that are grown principally for their foliage. Winter-flowering plants are a different matter, and are generally best repotted as soon as they have finished blooming. Now is the time to deal with palms, aspidistras, ferns of all kinds, including the so-called asparagus fern and *Asparagus Sprengeri*, smilax, coleus, crotons, cacti and succulents generally, dracaenas, marguerites, fuchsias, pelargoniums (this genus includes the familiar bedding geranium), and heliotropes. It is usually advisable to give plants that are to be repotted a shift into a pot one size larger than that which they occupied before. If for any reason it is essential that the

PREPARING POTS
FOR POTTING
The correct method is shown on the left. The large piece of broken pot used to keep the finer rubble from passing down through the drainage hole has been placed the right way up. On the right it is the wrong way, blocking up the hole and doing more harm than good.

plants should be kept in the same size pot you must first reduce the size of the ball of soil around the roots. The way to do this is to tap the plant out of its old pot by rapping the rim of this upside down on the edge of the potting bench and holding one hand close up to the ball of soil to support it as it comes away. If there is any difficulty push a stick through the drainage hole in the bottom of the pot. Then get a pointed stick and carefully loosen the soil around the edge of the ball without injuring the roots. If the compost is neither too wet nor too dry this can be done fairly readily. Do not remove all soil, but just sufficient to get a reasonable quantity of new compost into the new pot. Even when potting for a size larger receptacle it is advisable to loosen roots a little in this way. After potting always give the plants a thorough soaking with water at the same temperature as that of the house and then transfer them to a slightly warmer temperature than that in which they were growing previously. In a small house this can usually be done by moving them to the boiler end. Syringe every morning with tepid water, and shade from direct sunshine. These special precautions need only be maintained for a week or ten days, after which normal conditions should be resumed. The idea is to prevent the leaves from flagging during such time as new roots are being formed, and to encourage rooting as much as possible.

A good general compost for most of this potting consists of seven parts of good quality loam, preferably steam-sterilized (see p. 264), three parts of moss peat, and two parts of coarse sand, with 1½ ounce of hoof and horn meal, 1½ ounce of superphosphate of lime, ¾ ounce of sulphate of potash, and ¾ ounce of ground chalk added to each bushel of the compost. Add one part of leaf-mould for all ferns.

Pot Rooted Cuttings. Another kind of potting which you should do at the earliest opportunity is that of late summer and early autumn rooted cuttings of tender bedding plants, including marguerites, geraniums, heliotropes, and fuchsias. These will be just starting into growth, and if you transfer them singly to 3-inch or 3½-inch pots in the compost just mentioned they will soon grow into sturdy specimens. After potting, shade the plants for a few days, but stand them on the greenhouse staging in a light place as soon as growth recommences.

Start Achimenes for Succession. You should now start another batch of achimenes to provide a succession of flowers to those started in February (see February, First Week).

Sow Cauliflower, Broccoli, etc., in a Frame. If you were not able to sow cauliflowers in the greenhouse (see February, First Week) you should

A HANDY FRAME FOR SEEDLINGS

Drills have been prepared in readiness for the seeds by pressing a length of broom-handle into the soil.

now sow seeds in a frame. It is even worth making this sowing as an addition to the greenhouse one if you choose a rather later variety than that sown before, because you will then prevent any chance of a break in the supply of curds in the autumn. Sow thinly, as advised for cabbages above. Also sow a few seeds of an early broccoli, such as Veitch's Self-protecting or Sandringham Winter White, for these are hardier than the cauliflowers and may stand you in good stead if hard frost comes early in the autumn.

Brussels sprouts must have a long and steady season of growth if they are to be really successful. Sow now in boxes and germinate in a frame (preferably on a mild hotbed) or in a slightly heated greenhouse. If you also want a supply of cabbages in midsummer, sow an early variety now under exactly the same conditions as the brussels sprouts.

Sow Onions. A most important sowing for this first week in March, if the weather is reasonably kind, is that of maincrop onions. Sow in drills $\frac{1}{2}$ inch deep. The drills themselves should be 9 inches to 1 foot apart, the latter if you are after big bulbs for exhibition. As I have already remarked, it is almost impossible to make the surface of the onion bed too fine and light, but there should be plenty of richness in the way of animal manure below. With the top 4 inches, mix only wood ashes and similar lightening things so that the bulbs can swell without restriction.

Sow Spinach in a Sheltered Place. A first sowing of summer spinach can be made in a sheltered border—preferably one with a southern aspect. Sow thinly in drills nearly 1 inch deep and 1 foot apart. Other successional sowings will be made later, so this first sowing need only be a small one.

Sow Broad Beans and Celery. Make another sowing of broad beans in boxes for planting out (see February, First Week). If you were unable to make the first sowing through lack of heat you may yet manage this one, for it is possible to germinate the seeds now in a practically unheated house or in a frame on a mild hotbed.

This is the time to make the main sowing of celery for a supply from October on through the winter. Treat the seeds exactly as described for the earlier sowing (see February, Third Week).

Plant Pickling Cabbage. Red pickling cabbage, sown in August and pricked off in September (see September, Third Week), must now be planted where it is to mature. Choose an open position and rather good ground, and plant the cabbages 2 feet apart each way.

Plant Rhubarb, Horseradish, and Sea-kale. You can make a new rhubarb plantation if you wish now, or transplant old roots from one part of the garden to another. Be certain to dig out a hole big enough to take all the roots and allow the crowns to be just level with the surface of the ground. It is a spade job and not one that can be done with a trowel. The ground should have been well manured first and the position may be open or slightly shaded, but preferably the former.

A small plantation of horseradish is always useful, but you should be certain to make it in an out-of-the-way part of the garden and one where it can be more or less permanent, because once established it is extremely difficult to get rid of. The roots are planted with a dibber 1 foot apart each way, and are dropped right into the soil so that the crowns are 4 inches beneath the surface. The only further cultivation that is necessary is an occasional hoeing to keep down weeds.

The sea-kale thongs that were removed earlier from the planting crowns and tied up in bundles (see November, Second Week) can also be planted outdoors to form new beds. Cut the roots into pieces about 6 inches long and make a nick or sloping cut at the bottom end of each so that you may be certain to plant them the right way up. Plant with a dibber, making holes 6 inches deep so that the cuttings are just level with the soil. Plant them 1 foot apart in rows 18 inches apart.

New stocks can be obtained by sowing seeds outdoors now. Sow in drills 1 foot apart and ½ inch deep.

PLANTING CUCUMBERS IN A GREENHOUSE
Each plant should be planted on the top of a mound to ensure good drainage.

Plant Early Cucumbers. Cucumbers raised last month (see February, First Week) will now be ready for planting. Prepare the bed in a green-

Left: Dividing an aster (Michaelmas daisy) by means of two hand forks placed back to back. *Right:* Sand being placed under each gladiolus corm as it is planted to assist drainage.

Left: Planting well-sprouted potatoes in a drill. *Right:* Seakale thongs being planted with a dibber, 1 foot apart, in rows 18 inches apart.

Well-rooted chrysanthemum cuttings being lifted and potted singly.

Left: Pinching or 'stopping' a chrysanthemum for the first time.　*Right:* Note the method of holding tomato seedlings by the leaves when pricking out.

house or forcing pit in which you can maintain a temperature of 60°
minimum. The bed can be on the ground or on staging, but should not
be more than a couple of feet from the glass. Slates or sheets of corru-
gated iron make a good base. On this spread some old clinkers or straw
for drainage and then spread a 6-inch layer of rough turfy loam mixed
with about one-third its own bulk of well-rotted stable manure and a
good sprinkling of bonemeal and wood ashes. At intervals of 3 feet
make low mounds, each consisting of about 1 bushel of the same compost, and plant a cucumber on the summit of each. Place a stake to each
plant and make it secure to this. Train the main stem, as it grows, towards the apex of the house and tie laterals to horizontal wires stretched
15 inches apart 9 inches below the glass. Water the plants freely and
syringe them twice daily with tepid water to keep the atmosphere moist.
Little air will be needed at first, but open the top ventilators when the
temperature reaches 75°.

Sow Cucumbers. Cucumbers may be sown at almost any time of the year
for successional cropping, but the average amateur gardener will
find that a sowing made now will prove most useful for his general
needs.

Plant Strawberries. The best time for planting strawberries is at the end
of August or early September, but if for some reason it is not possible to
complete planting then, the work may be finished in March. Do not
allow these plants to bear any fruit the first year.

Spray Apple Trees. If apple blossom weevil has been troublesome (this is
the pest which produces small white maggots which feed inside the
opening flower buds, causing them to turn brown and become capped)
spray with DDT insecticide. If for any reason it was not possible to carry
out tar-oil spraying in winter, DNC winter wash can be used now. DDT
can be mixed with the DNC if both applications are deemed necessary.
DNC will kill aphides, capsid bugs, and many other pests, but not the
apple blossom weevil. It is not as effective as tar-oil in cleaning green
scum, lichen and moss from the bark of old trees.

SECOND WEEK

Sow Herbaceous Perennials and Alpines. A great many herbaceous perennials and rock plants can be raised easily from seeds sown at this time
of the year in either a frame or an unheated greenhouse. These include
delphiniums, lupins, perennial gypsophilas, perennial statices, thalic-

E

trums, coloured primroses and polyanthuses, violas and pansies, campanulas, hypericums, meconopses, aquilegias, dianthuses, etc. I make no attempt to give a full list because it is really worth while trying anything of which you can obtain seed. The method is to sow thinly in well-drained boxes or pans (the latter are better in some ways, especially if the seeds happen to be slow in germinating) filled with the compost mentioned on page 26. Cover the seeds to twice their own depth with very fine soil and then place them in the frame or greenhouse and shade from direct sunlight. Remove the shading as soon as the seedlings can be seen.

Auriculas may also be sown now, but are best in well-drained seed pans, as the seeds are slow and irregular in germination. Place the pans in a frame or greenhouse and water as necessary by partial immersion rather than from a watering-pot. Sow very thinly so that seedlings can be pricked off as they appear.

Sow Roses, Trees, and Shrubs. This is also a good time to sow seed of roses and any other shrubs and trees that may be available. It is not worth sowing rose seed saved haphazard, but if you or any of your friends have made some special crosses, it is quite possible that they may yield good results. Do not expect too much, however. One really worthwhile rose out of a hundred seedlings is quite good going. All these seeds should be sown outdoors in a sheltered border of finely prepared soil without any manure, or at most a sprinkling of bonemeal. If the seed has been stratified (see November, General Work) rub the mass of sand, pulp, and seed through the hands to separate the seeds roughly. Then everything can be scattered in the seed drills as evenly as possible. Sow in drills about $\frac{1}{2}$ inch deep and press the soil down fairly firmly on top of the seeds, but not so hard as to make it puddle. Many of the seeds may not germinate the first year, so be certain to sow in a place where you can leave them undisturbed if necessary.

Sow Cacti, Fuchsias, and Geraniums. This is a good time to sow seeds of cacti and succulents, and also fuchsias and geraniums. Sow the seeds very thinly in well-drained pots, using a light, sandy compost. Germinate in a greenhouse in a temperature of about 60°. The pots containing the fuchsia and geranium seeds can be covered with glass or brown paper, but the cactus and succulent seeds should only be covered with glass; they germinate better in the light.

Stop Chrysanthemums. Well-known Exhibition chrysanthemums which should be stopped now are Monica Winterton, James Bryant, Pink Cloud, Shirley Primrose and Yellow Marvel. Stopping simply means pinching the growing tip out of each plant with the object of making it produce side shoots. If your desire is to have very large blooms for exhibition each plant must be kept to one stem and this must not be allowed to carry more than one flower. In this case you must only keep

STOPPING A CHRYSANTHEMUM
Left; The young plant shortly after the first stopping. Right; The same plant later; the side shoots, just visible in the left hand plant, have grown into sturdy stems, each terminated by a flower bud, technically known as a 'first crown bud.'

the uppermost of the side shoots that form after stopping. Rub the others out at the earliest opportunity. If your object is to have several smaller flowers per plant, you may retain about three of the best side shoots after this first stopping.

Sow Herbs. Sundry herbs, including thyme, sage, and marjoram, can be raised from seed sown in a frame or practically unheated greenhouse and treated in exactly the same way as the seed of rock plants or herbaceous perennials.

Sow Culinary Peas Outdoors. Make a first sowing of an early culinary pea outdoors where the plants are to grow. I find the best method is to scoop out a trench with a spade. It should be just the width of the spade (about 9 inches) and not more than 3 inches deep. Place the peas singly in this trench in two lines, one at each side, the peas themselves being about 3 inches apart in the lines, and staggered on opposite sides of the trench. Then cover with an inch of soil. The depression left will provide the tiny seedlings with some protection and will make watering a simple matter. Do not sow all your early peas at once, or they will all mature at once. Practise successional sowing every fortnight or so.

Plant out Cauliflowers sown in September. Cauliflowers raised from a September sowing in a frame may now be planted outdoors if properly hardened off (see February, General Work). Lift the plants with as much soil and root as possible, and plant with a trowel on really good, well-dug soil. Allow 2½ feet between the rows and at least 18 inches between the plants in the rows.

Plant Mint. If you want to make a new plantation of mint now is the time to set about it. Lift some old plants or purchase the necessary roots; divide them up and spread them out thinly over the selected site, which should be in a reasonably open place, and cover with about 1½ inch of finely broken soil.

Pot Early Tomatoes and make Further Sowings. Tomatoes from the January sowing (see January, Second Week) should now be ready for their second potting into 4½-inch or 5-inch pots. Use the compost already recommended for general potting on page 62. Pot the plants rather firmly this time and shade for a day or so as before (see February, Third Week).

A sowing of tomatoes made now will provide good sturdy plants for planting outdoors in June. Sow the seeds exactly as before (see January, Second Week) and germinate them in the greenhouse in a temperature of about 60°.

THIRD WEEK

Plant Autumn-sown Sweet Peas. Seize the first favourable opportunity to plant out sweet pea seedlings raised in pots in the autumn. Contrary to general practice when planting from pots, no attempt should be made to keep intact the ball of soil around the roots. Instead, very carefully shake the roots clear of soil and then plant equally carefully in deep holes prepared with a trowel. Spread the roots out and work fine soil around them, firming it thoroughly with the knuckles. For exhibition purposes the plants should be at least 9 inches apart in the rows. Common practice is to grow double rows a foot apart with 5-foot alleyways between.

Sow Hardy Annuals. This is a good time to make first sowings of all really hardy annuals, provided the soil is in reasonably good condition. Sow thinly broadcast and cover the seeds with fine soil to about twice their own depth. The seeds should be sown where the plants are to flower. If the seedlings are too thick some of them may be transplanted later on, but the best flowers will be obtained from the untransplanted plants.

Among the best annuals for sowing now are sweet alyssum, bartonia, calendula, annual candytuft, annual chrysanthemum, clarkia, collinsia,

Convolvulus minor, annual coreopsis, cornflower, eschscholtzia, godetia, annual gypsophila, larkspur, *Lavatera rosea*, limnanthes, linum (scarlet flax), annual lupins, malope, mignonette, nemophila, nigella, phacelia, cardinal and Shirley poppies, annual rudbeckia, annual saponaria, annual sunflower, Virginian stock, and annual viscaria.

Sow Half-hardy Annuals in a Frame. If you have not a heated greenhouse and were therefore unable to sow half-hardy annuals, etc., as advised in my notes for February, Third Week, you can do so now in a frame. This should be in a sheltered place and it is all the better if it is on a hotbed (see p. 22). The seeds may either be sown directly in the frame or in

PREPARING A BOX FOR SMALL SEEDS

If tiny seeds are to be sown it is essential that the surface should be perfectly smooth and level. For this purpose a firming block should be used. Firm the compost round the edges of the box with the fingers.

boxes or pans as with greenhouse-germinated seeds. The latter method does make for easier handling later on. Dahlias usually germinate very well in a frame at this period and make good flowering plants by August.

This, I find, is a good time to make a first sowing of asters. Seed will germinate easily enough earlier in the year, but the plants tend to get too big by planting time, and are much more liable to damp off.

Plant Gladioli and Montbretias. Make a first planting of gladioli, but do not plant all the corms at once. It is much better to make successional plantings over a period of about a month or six weeks, because this will lengthen the flowering period. Cover the corms with about 3 inches of soil. The small 'primulinus' and miniature varieties may be 3 inches

apart in rows 8 inches apart, but the large-flowered gladioli should be at
least 6 inches apart in rows 1 foot apart—that is to say, if you want the
flowers for cutting. If they are merely to be used for bedding or in groups
in the herbaceous border, let them be at least 6 inches apart each way.

Montbretias are also planted now, and all can go out at once. If you
are purchasing dried corms, I advise you to start them into growth first
in trays filled with a very light compost mainly consisting of moss peat
and sand. Just bury them in this, water moderately, and place in a frame.
Then, as soon as growth starts, transfer them to the beds in which they
are to flower, planting carefully with a trowel and covering the corms
with about 2 inches of soil. A better method of culture is to obtain growing tufts (plants that have never been quite dried off) and plant these as
advised for the started corms. Montbretias should be at least 4 inches
apart each way.

Start Cannas and Dahlias. Cannas and dahlias can now be started into
growth in slightly heated greenhouses, in frames on a mild hotbed, or
even in well-constructed frames standing in a really sheltered place. But
beware of unheated frames as yet if the sides are thin or have gaps between the wood through which draughts can penetrate. The method of
starting dahlias is exactly as in greenhouses (see February, Third Week),
except that there is really no need to use boxes. The roots can simply be
placed in the frames side by side and nearly covered with dry soil. Old
canna roots may be in pots already. There is not any need to repot them
for the moment, as this is better done after growth has restarted. If,
however, you are purchasing new roots or are dealing with old bedding
roots that have been wintered in boxes, pot them singly in 6-inch pots,
using a compost of about two parts of good loam, one part of well-rotted
cow manure, or failing this good leaf-mould, and one part of moss peat,
enough sand to speckle the whole freely.

Take Dahlia Cuttings. Dahlias introduced to the greenhouse last month
will now be making growth, and you can obtain a first batch of cuttings.
Sever the firm young shoots when they are about 2 inches in length.
Some recommend taking each cutting with a small piece of tuber, but I
regard this as wasteful. If the cuttings are severed just above the tuber,
leaving a tiny stump still attached to it, this stump will soon send out
two or three more shoots which can in turn be taken as cuttings. If the
shoot is severed with some of the tuber, no more cuttings will be obtained
from there. The cuttings are prepared by trimming the base cleanly just
below a joint, removing the lower leaves (if any), and inserting ¾ inch
deep in sandy soil. I find the simplest and quickest method in the long

run is to put the soil into 2½-inch pots and place one cutting in each. Then there need be no further root disturbance. The cuttings should be rooted in a propagating box with a temperature of from 60° to 70°. Any sufficiently deep box with a piece of glass on the top will serve. Water rather freely. If desired dahlia cuttings can be treated with a root-forming hormone prior to insertion as described on page 56.

Start Begonia and Gloxinia Tubers. If you have only a small greenhouse or one that is not too well heated and you were therefore not able to follow my advice regarding starting tuberous-rooted begonias and gloxinias into growth in January or February, this is the time to make a start. I have already given full particulars regarding this (see January, Second Week) and there is nothing further to be said, except that you will find it a good deal easier to maintain the required temperature of 55° to 60° in March than in January. Make use of sun heat during the day by closing the ventilators early in the afternoon. An excellent plan with houses that are not too well heated is to have heavy canvas blinds which can be rolled down right over the glass as soon as the sun sets.

Pot Begonia and Gloxinia Tubers. Tubers that were started in January and potted for the first time in February (see February, Third Week) will almost certainly need a shift into their flowering pots, 4 to 6 inches in diameter, according to the size of the plants. Use the same compost and treat as before. Tubers set in fibre in February to start growth will probably be ready for first potting.

Start Hippeastrums. Start another batch of hippeastrums (see January, Fourth Week, and February, Third Week), giving preference to any bulbs that are forming shoots.

Sow Browallia. If you sow seed of browallia now in a slightly heated greenhouse or frame you will have good plants in flower from September to November. Simply scatter the seed thinly in the usual seed compost (see p. 26), cover very lightly with soil, and place a pane of glass and a sheet of brown paper over the pan or box.

Pot Greenhouse Annuals. If you were able to pot some annuals for the greenhouse in February (see February, First Week), the finest should now be ready for a further shift into 7- or 8-inch pots. Use a rather coarser compost than before. That described on page 62 will do well.

Remove Vegetable Seedlings to Frame. Onions and leeks sown in the greenhouse in January (see January, First and Fourth Weeks), also cauliflowers, peas, lettuces and broad beans sown in February (see February, First Week) will now be better in a frame, where they can be hardened off for planting outdoors in April. Ventilate cautiously at first and be ready with sacks for cold nights, but gradually accustom the plants to full exposure.

Sow Carrots and Leeks Outdoors. If the soil is in good working condition, make a small sowing of stump-rooted carrot outdoors, but choose a sheltered place. Sow very thinly, either broadcast or in rows 9 inches apart, and cover with ¼ inch of soil. The main sowings will be made in April (see April, Second Week).

As already explained, the best leeks are raised under glass (see January, Fourth Week), but if you have not got a greenhouse, or even a frame that you can place on a hotbed, you can still have quite good leeks of your own raising by sowing outdoors now. Sow thinly in rows 1 foot apart and cover with ¼ inch of fine soil.

Plant Early Potatoes. Even if you are not favoured with a particularly sheltered border you may now make a first planting of early potatoes. I have already given full particulars of the method to be followed in the notes for February, Fourth Week.

THE WRONG WAY TO PLANT POTATOES

A dibber has been used, and, though this has been worked round and round to enlarge the hole, a space has been left beneath the tuber.

Prick off Early Celery. Celery from the February sowing will be in need of pricking off into deeper seed boxes. Use a compost with plenty of leaf-mould and just a little rotted manure if available, and dibble the seedlings 3 inches apart each way. Water freely and return to the greenhouse in an average temperature of about 55° for the time being, but gradually harden off so that you can remove the boxes to a frame later (see April, Second Week).

Protect Early Fruit Blossom. Outdoor peaches and nectarines should now be coming into flower, and it is an excellent plan to protect these by hanging fish netting in front of the trees. It might seem that this would afford no protection at all, but actually it makes quite a difference, causing eddies and preventing the slow, unbroken flow of air which always accompanies the worst frosts.

FOURTH WEEK

Clip Ivy on Walls. It is an excellent plan to clip ivy growing on walls at this time of the year. The work can be done very quickly with a pair of shears. Simply clip off the leaves, leaving the stems practically bare, and then brush them down with a stiff broom, getting out all dead leaves, dirt, etc. The plants will look very bare at first, but will soon get new leaves and will be much better for a clean up.

Plant Tigridias. Tigridias are not everybody's flower, but they are very lovely and even though the individual blooms only last a day, they are followed by a succession of others. The corms are barely hardy and must be given a sheltered and sunny position. Plant now, placing the corms 4 inches deep and about 6 inches apart each way.

Plant Carnation Layers. Early autumn is usually considered the best time for planting rooted border carnation layers, but in very exposed places I prefer to pot the layers in the autumn and keep them in a cold frame during the winter. Then they are planted outdoors at this time of the year, when conditions are getting steadily more favourable.

Sow Spinach Beet. This is a very useful form of beetroot grown for its leaves, which are used like those of spinach. Sow now in drills 1 inch deep and 18 inches apart and thin out the seedlings to 1 foot apart. This plant is sometimes known as perpetual spinach, because it keeps on cropping all the summer and autumn and most of the winter as well.

Sow Lettuces Outdoors. Unless the weather is exceptionally bad or your garden is very cold, it should now be safe to make a first sowing of lettuces outdoors. You can choose a cabbage or a cos variety according to taste. Sow the seeds very thinly in drills $\frac{1}{2}$ inch deep and about 1 foot apart for the large varieties, or 9 inches apart for the Tom Thumb type.

Sow Broad Beans and Peas Outdoors. This is usually a good time to make the first sowing of broad beans outdoors. The place chosen must be open, and really well cultivated. Sow the seeds 6 inches apart in drills rather over 1 inch deep and about 2 feet apart. The dwarf varieties can be grown as close as 15 inches in the rows, but it is a mistake to crowd the bigger kinds.

Make a second sowing of an early culinary pea exactly as advised in my notes for the Second Week in this month.

Sow Celery and Celeriac in a Frame. Celery may be sown in a frame in a very sheltered position and for preference on a mild hotbed. Sow thinly either directly in soil in a frame or in well-drained boxes. Plants from this sowing will provide a succession for planting out after those raised earlier in the greenhouse (see February, Third Week).

Celeriac, which is a moderately good substitute for celery and has the advantage that it will grow on soil that would be much too poor for that crop, is also sown now. The seeds are treated in exactly the same way as those of the celery.

Sow French Beans for Succession. You may now make a third sowing of beans in 8-inch pots for cropping under glass (see January, Fourth Week, and February, Fourth Week). At this season it will be possible to maintain the necessary temperature in a well-made frame placed in a sheltered but sunny position and covered with sacks at night.

Sow Cucumbers on a Hotbed. Good cucumbers can be grown in frames on a hotbed as well as in heated greenhouses. If sown now they will commence to bear in June, just when the earliest hothouse cucumbers are getting past their first vigour. Make a good hotbed as described on page 22. Spread compost prepared as for glasshouse cucumbers (see First Week), with a low mound in the centre of the space covered by each 6 feet by 4 feet light. Place the frames and lights in position, and, as soon as the soil temperature falls to 85°, sow two seeds on the centre of each mound. If both germinate, pull out the weaker seedling.

Plant Melons. Melons raised in a warm greenhouse in February (see February, Fourth Week) will be ready for planting. The method followed is exactly the same as for cucumbers (see First Week), and similar watering, syringeing, etc., must be carried out.

Graft Apples and Pears. Apple and pear stocks that are well established, and also old trees that were cut back for reworking (see January, General Work) may be grafted now. If the stock and the piece of growth, known as the scion, that is to be joined to it are not far off the same size, use a whip graft, but if there is a big difference between the size of stock and scion, as there is sure to be with old trees that are being reworked, employ the method known as rind grafting (see illustrations). Cover the whole of the cut surface and the part immediately above and below it as well with grafting wax, making everything quite airtight.

HOW TO MAKE A WHIP GRAFT

This method is used when stock and scion are about the same thickness. The cut surfaces must fit together exactly. After fitting them together bind the joint with raffia and wax it over.

RIND GRAFTING AN OLD TREE

The scion is prepared as for whip grafting except that no tongue is made. Then a vertical slit is made in the bark of the stock and the graft is slipped beneath it with its cut surface lying snugly against the bared tissue. It is bound in position and the wounded area is covered with wax.

Start Vines in Unheated Vineries. It is now safe to encourage vines to start into growth even in quite unheated vineries. This is done by closing ventilators altogether at night and opening those at the top only a little by day. Syringe every morning with water that is just slightly warm.

FLOWERS, VEGETABLES, AND FRUITS IN SEASON DURING MARCH

Hardy Herbaceous Plants. *Adonis amurensis, Corydalis tuberosa, Doronicum austriacum, Helleborus abchasicus, H. atrorubens, H. guttatus, H. odorus, H. orientalis* and vars., *H. viridis, Iris unguicularis, Pulmonaria angustifolia, Primula elatior* (polyanthus), *P. rubra, P. vulgaris* (primrose), *Saxifraga ciliata, S. cordifolia, S. crassifolia, S. ligulata, S. purpurascens, S. Stracheyi.*

Hardy Bulbs and Tubers. *Anemone coronaria* and vars., *A. fulgens, Brodiaea uniflora, Chionodoxa Luciliae, Colchicum montanum, Crocus Bolansae, C. biflorus, C. candidus, C. chrysanthus, C. corsicus, C. etruscus, C. minimus, C. stellaris, C. susianus, C. veluchensis, C. vernus, Cyclamen coum, C. ibericum, C. libanoticum,* crocuses (large-flowering), *Eranthis cilica, E. hyemalis, Erythronium Dens-canis, E. Hartwegii, Fritillaria pudica, Galanthus byzantinus, G. Elwesii, G. Fosteri, G. latifolius, Hyacinthus azureus,* hyacinths (large-flowered), *Iris Bakeriana, I. persica, I. sindjarensis, I. Rosenbachiana, Leucojum vernum, Narcissus Bulbocodium, N. minor,* narcissus hybrids in var. (including trumpet daffodils), *Romulea rosea, Scilla amoena, S. bifolia, S. sibirica, Tulipa biflora, T. Kaufmanniana.*

CYCLAMEN COUM

This hardy cyclamen produces its red flowers in February and March on 6-inch stems. It thrives best in a shady part of the rock garden or under trees, in a leafy soil.

Rock Plants. *Anemone angulosa, A. apennina, A. blanda, A. nemorosa* vars., *A. ranunculoides, A. vernalis, Cortusa Matthiolii, Daphne Blagayana, Doronicum caucasicum, Gentiana acaulis, G. alpina, G. kochiana, G. verna, Iris pumila* vars., *I. verna, Lithospermum rosmarinifolium, Morisia hypogaea, Omphalodes cappadocica, O. verna, Primula cortusoides, P. denticulata* and vars., *P. Forrestii, P. glaucescens, P. Juliana* vars., *P. marginata, P. viscosa, Pulsatilla vulgaris, Sanguinaria canadensis, Saxifraga apiculata, S. Arco-Valleyi, S. aretioides, S. Borisii, S. Boydii, S. Burseriana* and vars., *S. diapensioides, S.* Faldonside, *S. Elizabethae, S. Griesbachii, S. Haagii, S. Irvingii, S. Jenkinsii, S. juniperifolia, S. kewensis, S. lilacina, S. marginata, S. oppositifolia* and vars., *S. Paulinae, S. Petraschii, S. porophylla, S. racemiflora, S. sancta, S. scardica, S. Sibthorpii, S. Suendermannii, S. Vandellii, Schizocodon soldanelloides, Sisyrinchium grandiflorum, Soldanella alpina, S. minima, S. montana, Synthyris reniformis, Viola calcarata, V. canadensis, V. florariensis.*

Hardy Aquatics and Bog Plants. *Caltha palustris, Primula Giraldiana, P. rosea, P. sino-purpurea.*

Hardy Evergreen Shrubs. *Arctostaphylos Manzanita, Azara integrifolia, A. microphylla, Berberis buxifolia, B. replicata, Camellia japonica* vars., *Daphne collina, D. Dauphinii, D. Laureola, D. tangutica, Epigaea repens, Erica arborea* and vars., *E. carnea, E. darleyensis, E. lusitanica, E. mediterranea,*

Lonicera fragrantissima, Mahonia aquifolium, M. japonica and vars., *M. napaulensis, Pieris floribunda, P. japonica, P. taiwanensis, Raphiolepis Delacourii, Rhododendron arboreum* (shelter), *R. calophytum, R. neriiflorum, R. praecox, R. strigulosum, R. sutchuenense, R. Thomsonii, Ulex europaeus* vars., *Viburnum Tinus.*

Hardy Deciduous Shrubs. *Cassandra calyculata, Colletia infausta, Cornus Mas, Corylopsis Griffithii, C. pauciflora, C. platypetala, C. spicata, Cydonia japonica, Daphne Mezereum, Forsythia intermedia* vars., *F. ovata, F. suspensa, Lonicera Standishii, L. syringantha, Magnolia stellata, Osmaronia cerasiformis, Prinsepia sinensis, Prunus nana, P. spinosa* (sloe, blackthorn), *P. tomentosa, Salix gracilistyla, S. Caprea* (palm, goat willow), *Spiraea Thunbergii, Stachyurus praecox, Viburnum grandiflorum.*

Hardy Evergreen Trees. *Arbutus Andrachne.*

Hardy Deciduous Trees. *Acer Opalus, A. rubrum, Alnus cordata, A. firma, A. japonica, A. oregona, Magnolia Campbellii* (shelter), *Parrotia persica, Prunus Amygdalus* (almond), *P. Blireana, P. Conradinae, P. dasycarpa, P. Davidiana, P. incisa, P. Mume, P. pendula, P. Persica* and vars. (peach), *P. Pissardii* (purple plum), *P. subhirtella* and vars., *P. triloba, P. yedoensis, Salix Smithiana.*

NARCISSUS BULBOCODIUM

The little hoop-petticoat daffodil grows 6 inches tall and in its many varieties is ideal for the rock garden, for naturalizing in grass, or for growing in pans.

Hardy Climbing Plants. *Clematis calycina, Ercilla volubilis.*

Greenhouse Plants. Abutilons, acacias, arum lilies, astilbes, azaleas (Indian and mollis), *Boronia megastigma*, carnation (perpetual-flowering), cinerarias (hybrids), *Coleus thyrsoideus*, correas, *Epacris hyacinthiflora*, forget-me-nots, freesias, hippeastrums, hyacinths (large-flowered), lachenalias, *Leucocoryne ixioides*, lilies of the valley, *Lilium Harrisii*, narcissi (including trumpet daffodils), *Primula obconica, P. sinensis* and *stellata, P. malacoides*, primroses, polyanthuses, rhododendrons (Javanese), roses, tulips (earlies and May-flowering), wallflowers, also shrubs in pots such as cherries, deutzias, genistas, lilacs, peaches, etc.

Vegetables in Store. Same as January, and parsnips.

Vegetables in Garden. Broccoli (maincrop), sprouting broccoli, cabbage (sown July, August), kale, leeks, spring onions, rhubarb, seakale, spinach (sown August), spinach beet, turnip tops.

Vegetables under Glass. Carrots, lettuces, mushrooms, mustard and cress, radishes.

Fruits in Store. *Apples:* Adams' Pearmain (D), Annie Elizabeth (C), Barnack Beauty (CD), Beauty of Kent (C), Beauty of Stoke (CD), Belle de Boskoop (CD), Bramley's Seedling (C), Brownlees' Russet (D), Cornish Gillyflower (D), Court Pendu Plat (D), Crawley Beauty (C), D'Arcy Spice (D), Duke of Devonshire (D), Easter Orange (D), Edward VII (C), Encore (C), John Standish (D), King of Tompkin's County (D), King George V (D), Lane's Prince Albert (C), Laxton's Pearmain (D), Lord Burghley (D), Lord Hindlip (D), May Queen (D), Monarch (C), Newton Wonder (C), Norfolk Royal (D), Ontario (CD), Roundway Magnum Bonum (D), Royalty (D), St Cecilia (D), Sanspareil (CD), Sturmer Pippin (D), Superb (D), Wellington (C), Wyken Pippin (D). *Grapes:* Gros Guillaume, Lady Downe's Seedling, Mrs Pearson, Mrs Pince, Muscat of Alexandria, Prince of Wales. *Pears:* Bellissime d'Hiver (C), Bergamotte d'Esperen (D), Beurré Easter (D), Catillac (C), Joséphine de Malines (D), Olivier de Serres (D), Uvedale's St Germain (C), Winter Nelis (D), Winter Orange (C).

April

GENERAL WORK

Mow Lawns More Frequently. From April onwards lawns will require mowing considerably more frequently. There is a widespread belief that the mowing machine should be put away during the winter, but this is entirely erroneous. It is folly to mow when the surface is frozen, and side-wheel mowers should not be used when it is soft after heavy rain, but well-oiled, easy-running roller machines can be used without damage even when the ground is fairly wet. Occasional winter mowing keeps the lawn neat and prevents the deterioration of the sward. In unmown lawns coarse grasses tend to take the place of fine ones. During the winter one mowing per month will probably be ample, but from now onwards grass will be growing rapidly and the mower must be used to keep it reasonably close. Give a dressing of a good proprietary lawn fertilizer or of a mixture of two parts of sulphate of potash, one part of sulphate of ammonia, two parts of dried blood, and twenty parts of silver sand, well blended and applied at the rate of 6 ounces per square yard.

This is the time of year at which the various patent worm-killers may be used most effectively. Choose a day when the soil is likely to be moist to a considerable depth and be sure to soak the worm-killer well into it.

Complete Planting of Herbaceous Perennials. There is still time to plant hardy herbaceous perennials, but the sooner the work is completed the better, for the plants will now be making quite a lot of growth. (For details see March, General Work.)

Plant Gladioli for Succession. Throughout the month you should continue to plant gladioli in small batches for succession, as already explained in my notes for March, Third Week.

Plant Alpines. Alpine plants are almost invariably grown by nurserymen in small pots and can be transplanted to the rock garden from these at any time of the year, provided sufficient care is taken. But April is the ideal month, and the one in which there is least risk. Even plants grown in the open ground can be shifted now, unless they happen to be in flower—*e.g.*, aubrietas, arabis, early saxifrages, etc.—when they should

79

be transplanted as soon as they have finished flowering. When planting from pots, simply tap the plants out, remove the crocks from the bottom of the pot ball, and loosen the mass a little with the fingers, but not so much as to damage any of the roots. Plant with a trowel and make firm. Only when planting in the moraine is it advisable to shake all the soil from the roots and then spread these out carefully in the new compost.

Plant Evergreen Shrubs. This is the best time for planting evergreen shrubs but if continued spells of cold east wind should follow planting, it may be necessary to erect some kind of protection around the shrubs, either by making screens of sacking or placing wattle hurdles or evergreen boughs in position, paying particular attention to the east and north sides. Later on, as the weather becomes warm, a nightly syringeing with tepid water will do good, and mulching will help to keep the soil moist.

Propagate Shrubs, etc., by Layering. Layering is a very simple method of propagating quite a number of shrubs, fruit trees, etc. It is worth trying practically any variety, with the exception of the big fruits such as apples, pears, cherries, plums, etc., and also very hard-wooded shrubs such as hawthorns, beech, etc. Many evergreens grow freely from layers; rhododendrons, for example, and also laurels and aucubas. Rambler roses

HOW TO LAYER A
ROSE

A stray shoot from the parent plant is bent down, covered with good soil and tied to a stake. After a few months roots will be formed and the layer can be severed and planted on its own.

Left: Onion drills being covered over and made very firm. *Right:* Pruning a bush rose hard back, to two or three buds from the ground.

Cucumbers require adequate wires to support their vigorous growth, as shown in this illustration.

Whip and tongue grafting. *Above, left:* Cutting a tongue in the scion. *Above, centre:* Scion and stock placed in position. *Above, right:* Grafting wax is applied after the graft has been tied with raffia.
Left: An apple tree cut back and rind-grafted. Note the tapes securing the scions in position.

form roots without difficulty, and so do many of the more vigorous climbing varieties.

The method is similar with all these. Choose a good, supple branch or stem, preferably one formed last year, make an upward incision through one of its joints, not too near the tip but at a point that can easily be bent down to soil level, press the cut portion of stem into the soil and hold it in position with a wooden peg or a heavy stone. If the soil is very heavy or poor, make up a good mixture of loam, peat moss, and sand in about equal parts, and peg the layer into this. Keep well watered during the summer and by the autumn the branch will have formed roots round the cut surface and can be detached from the parent plant and established on its own.

Greenhouse General Management. There will now be much less difficulty in maintaining sufficient temperature in the greenhouse. It may even be necessary to have some temporary shading for a good many plants dur-

MAKING THE MOST OF SPACE

Dahlias are being started into growth beneath the staging, stock geraniums and other plants are growing above them, while the shelves are occupied by rooted cuttings and seedlings that are hardening off.

ing the hottest part of the day, especially in small houses which heat up very quickly, but permanent shading will not be needed as yet. It is not wise to have the temperature running much above 70° in the general utility greenhouse in April, which means ample top ventilation on all sunny and fairly still days. Do not use the side ventilators yet, nor leave the door open, for fear of admitting damaging draughts.

Bedding plants and half-hardy annuals generally must be gradually

F

hardened off. Later in the month (see Third Week) you should remove them to frames, if possible, but you must prepare them gradually for this in the early part of the month by giving increased ventilation whenever the weather is favourable, and keeping them as close to the glass as possible. In a mixed greenhouse it is sometimes difficult to reconcile the needs of all the plants at this stage, but much can be done by erecting shelves, a little below the top ventilators, where the plants that need cool conditions can be placed. Those varieties that require warmth can be kept on the staging and as near to the heating apparatus as possible.

From now onwards you will have to keep a sharp look-out for pests such as greenfly, thrips, and red spider. Should any of these appear, fumigate at once with an appropriate fumigant—nicotine or BHC for greenfly; azobenzene for red spider; BHC or DDT for whitefly or thrips. To obtain good results with fumigation, make sure that the greenhouse is as air-tight as possible. Close down all ventilators and doors, and leave the house closed for several hours. Plants which are to be fumigated should never be dry at the roots, and the higher the temperature the more effective will the fumigant be, though treatment should not be carried out in bright sunlight.

The main batch of calceolarias and autumn-sown schizanthuses will be approaching their flowering period and will benefit by fairly constant feeding, provided you use the manure water or fertilizer really weak. The former should only just colour the water, while where proprietary fertilizers are concerned you should consult manufacturers' instructions and certainly not exceed them; I find that it is usually better to halve the strengths they recommend. Similar remarks apply to hippeastrums which are forming their flower stems.

Harden off Plants in Frames. Onion, leek, cauliflower, pea, broad bean, and lettuce seedlings in frames (see March, Third Week) will require full ventilation whenever the thermometer is above freezing point and the wind is not very cold, for they must be hardened fully for planting out later in the month (see Third Week). Similar remarks apply to violets, violas, pansies, penstemons, autumn-sown antirrhinums, and other nearly hardy plants, but more tender kinds must still be ventilated with some caution.

Prick off Seedlings. Throughout the month you will be kept busy pricking off many seedlings from sowings made earlier (see March, General Work, for details).

General Potting. In addition to pricking off there will be a considerable amount of potting to do. Seedlings pricked off earlier may be getting overcrowded. Pot them singly into 2½- or 3-inch pots directly their leaves touch. The later chrysanthemum and carnation cuttings will be needing a shift (see January, General Work, and March, General Work), while dahlia cuttings can be potted into 3-inch receptacles directly they are rooted, unless you inserted them singly in pots, in which case no further

UNPOTTING A PLANT
Place the fingers around the stem of the plant, turn the pot upside down, and tap the rim of the pot on a bench.

move will be needed as yet. This also applies to miscellaneous green-house plant cuttings such as abutilons, petunias, daturas, etc. (see March, General Work). Begonias and gloxinias started as tubers in January and February and already potted once will be in various stages of growth, and the same applies to many other young greenhouse plants and tomatoes. The safe plan is to tap a typical plant out of its pot occasionally and examine the roots. If the soil is just nicely moist right through, you can do this quite easily without disturbing the plant at all. Simply turn the pot upside down, place one hand over the soil, and give the rim of the pot a sharp rap on the edge of the potting bench. As soon as you see white rootlets forming freely all round the side of the pot ball, transfer the plants to larger receptacles. The usual practice is to shift from 3-inch pots into 4- or 5-inch pots, and from these into 6- or 7-inch pots, or, in the case of tomatoes, directly into the 10-inch pots or large boxes in which they will fruit. But too big a shift at one time is not generally desirable. The compost I have already mentioned several times—namely, seven parts of good fibrous loam, three parts of best moss peat, and two parts of coarse sand, with 1½ ounce of hoof and horn meal, 1½ ounce of superphosphate of lime, ¾ ounce of sulphate of potash, and ¾ ounce of ground chalk added to each bushel of the mixture—can still be used for

PREPARING FOR REPOTTING OR PLANTING

When plants have been removed from pots the old crocks in the bottom of the pot ball must be removed and the roots loosened a little. This is most important when planting out pot-grown plants.

the majority of plants. Most plants should be returned to the greenhouse immediately after potting, but chrysanthemums are better in an un-heated frame, where they may be hardened off gradually.

Repot Indian Azaleas and Camellias. Both Indian azaleas and camellias may be repotted if necessary as soon as they have finished flowering. Use a compost of loam and moss peat in about equal parts with half a part of sand and a good sprinkling of bonemeal. At the most only use a pot one size larger than that occupied formerly—it is all the better if they can go back into the same size pots after teasing out some of the old soil with the point of a stick. After potting the plants must be returned to the greenhouse for a few weeks and should be syringed every morning with tepid water.

Prune Azaleas, Genistas, and Deutzias. As soon as they have finished flowering remove the faded flower heads from Indian azaleas and cut back the flowering branches of deutzias and genistas quite close to the base.

Take Cuttings of Winter-flowering Begonias. It should be possible to take further cuttings of winter-flowering begonias during the month (see March, General Work). Semi-tuberous rooted begonias of the Optima

A WINTER-FLOWERING
BEGONIA CUTTING
*Note the method of trimming
the cutting immediately below
a joint and removing the
lower leaves.*

type will now be starting into growth again, and you may encourage them to do so by giving them rather more water. As soon as the basal growths are a couple of inches in length you can remove some of them as cuttings, treating them exactly as the other winter-flowering types.

Rest Freesias, Lachenalias, etc. Freesias and lachenalias that have been flowering during the winter must now be allowed to go to rest gradually. To effect this, place them on a shelf quite near the glass and gradually reduce the water supply. Rather similar remarks apply to arum lilies that have been used for winter flowering. These cannot be stood near the glass, but they must be kept in a cooler atmosphere. Old cyclamen that have finished flowering may be treated just like freesias, but the young seedlings must be kept growing.

Take Cuttings of Bedding Plants, etc. It is still possible to take cuttings of bedding and greenhouse plants in exactly the same manner as I described in the notes for General Work during March. It is true that the bedding plants will be comparatively late in flower, but they may be none the less useful for that. Some late-struck fuchsias, geraniums, and salvias make admirable pot plants for the greenhouse in autumn. Continue to take cuttings of dahlias as they become available (see March, Third Week).

Stop Early-Flowering Chrysanthemums. From time to time during the month you should pinch out the growing tips of the rooted cuttings of early-flowering chrysanthemums required for spray flowering. The ideal moment to do this is when the cuttings are well rooted, growing freely, and are about 6 inches in height. Most February and March rooted cuttings will reach this stage before the end of April. Note particularly that this stopping applies only to plants that are to be grown for garden decoration or to produce a lot of flowers. The object is to produce a number of branches on each plant, and with this end in view the plants will be stopped again in June. With plants that are grown for large individual flowers, either for exhibition or for cutting, a different method is followed (see May, Third Week), and they must not be stopped now.

Prepare Celery Trenches. Some time during the month you should prepare the trenches for celery. They will not actually be wanted until June, but it is an advantage to prepare them well in advance so that manure and soil may become blended together. The trenches should be 15 inches wide for single rows and 18 inches wide for double rows, and they must be at least 3 feet apart. You can use the ground between the trenches for various salad crops. Remove the soil to a depth of 18 inches and then break up the bottom as deeply as possible with a long fork, mixing well-rotted manure or decayed vegetable refuse with it. Place a layer of manure and good top-spit soil in about equal parts 9 inches deep on top of the forked subsoil and a further layer of 6 inches of good top-spit soil on top of this. This, you will see, leaves you with a depression about 3 inches deep in which the celery will be planted later on. This shallow trench gives some protection to the young plants and makes it very easy to flood them with water.

Make Successional Sowings. You will need to make sundry successional sowings during the month if you wish to maintain an unbroken supply of vegetables later on. In the main these are the same as for last month (see March, General Work). Radishes and mustard and cress may now be sown outdoors, but choose a warm, sheltered place for preference. You should make two further sowings of lettuce at fortnightly intervals (see March, Fourth Week). Similar instructions apply to spinach (see March, First Week). A further sowing of broad beans outdoors (see March, Fourth Week) made towards the end of the month will ensure a crop in the early autumn. Further sowings of carrots will be necessary, but these I have dealt with separately (see Second Week). Most important of all are at least two sowings of peas (see March, Second Week). These are treated as before, but you should now choose a maincrop variety, such as Quite Content or Duke of Albany, in place of the early kinds recommended before.

Train and Top-dress Early Cucumbers. Side shoots formed on the main stems of cucumbers planted in March (see March, First Week) must be stopped from extending too far or there will soon be such a mass of

HOW A GREENHOUSE CUCUMBER IS TRAINED

The fruit-bearing laterals have been stopped some time previously by pinching out their tips, as indicated by the black lines. Further laterals are allowed to form all up the main stem, which is stopped when it reaches the ridge.

foliage in the house that the plants will get unhealthy. Pinch out the soft tip of each side shoot as soon as it carries two tiny fruits, or when it is 2 feet in length if it reaches that before it has two fruits. If secondary side shoots appear, pinch them when they have made a couple of leaves. The tip of the main stem must be pinched out as soon as it reaches the apex of the house.

Keep a sharp watch and as soon as white rootlets appear on the surface of the bed give a top-dressing, a couple of inches thick, of a mixture of equal parts of good fibrous loam and well-rotted manure. Repeat this later if necessary. The plants will want a lot of water now that they are growing freely. You should also syringe them twice daily with tepid water and damp down the paths as well to maintain plenty of moisture in the atmosphere. Open the top ventilators a little when the thermometer reaches 75°. A light permanent shading on the glass will be advisable from now onwards. You can use ordinary limewash with a little white of egg mixed in to make it stick. Syringe the glass quite lightly with this. Heavy shading is not desirable as yet.

Cucumbers growing on hotbeds (see March, Fourth Week) are trained in a slightly different manner from those growing in greenhouses. The tip of each plant is pinched out when it has made four leaves. Then the laterals which form are trained evenly over the bed, being held in position with wooden or wire pegs, and are stopped again as soon as they reach the edge of the frame or interfere with neighbouring plants. Sub-laterals, bearing flowers and subsequently fruits, are pinched from time to time one or two leaves beyond the flowers to prevent gross overcrowding with foliage. Later on some old growths that have finished bearing may be cut out to make room for new growths (see June, General Work).

Water the frame plants freely and ventilate very sparingly on mild days only. Spray overhead when closing for the day in sunny, warm weather.

Train and Pollinate Melons. The training of melons (see March, Fourth Week) is not unlike that of cucumbers. It is, however, necessary to restrict each plant to about four fruits. These should be placed as evenly

FERTILIZING MELON FLOWERS

Male flowers are shown at (A), while one has been partially stripped for pollinating at (C). Female flowers, distinguished by the embryo fruits to which they are attached, are shown at (B). The work of pollination is being carried out at (D).

as possible over the plant. There are two kinds of flowers, male and female, and only the latter will produce fruits. You can recognise the females because each will have a tiny fruit on its stalk just beneath the petals. These flowers must be pollinated by hand, and all on any one plant at the same time. You can arrange to get four suitable blooms open at once by judicious pinching. Backward blooms can be hastened by stopping the shoots on which they are growing one leaf beyond the flower, while forward blooms can be retarded by allowing the shoot to grow unstopped. Scatter pollen from the male blooms on the females when the sun is shining.

Management of the Vinery. The vinery, whether heated or unheated, will require fairly constant attention throughout the month. In unheated houses growth can be encouraged now by giving less ventilation and rolling down heavy canvas blinds (see notes on starting begonias and gloxinias, March, Third Week) an hour before sunset, so as to trap sun heat for the night. In a heated vinery growth will be in full swing, and will be in various stages according to the time at which the house was closed. Some vines will be in flower, and will need a slightly higher temperature and a drier atmosphere; more ventilation should be given and syringeing discontinued for the time being (see February, General Work).

FERTILIZATION IN GRAPES

Left: the flower of a free setting variety. Right: the reflexed stamens are typical of those often found in shy setting varieties and a contributory cause of bad fertilization. Shy setting varieties often require hand pollination.

These will also require training and stopping, as I explained in the same place. Other vines a little more advanced will be in need of fruit thinning, as described in the notes for March, General Work. The earliest vines, started in January, will be forming their pips (this is technically known as stoning), and you must make every effort to avoid severe fluctuations of temperature. A minimum night temperature of 60°, rising to 80° by day with direct sun heat is ideal.

Thin Peaches, Nectarines, etc. In the early orchard house peaches and nectarines will have completed stoning by this period, and it will be all the better if you can increase the temperature by 5° or 10° by day and night. Thinning can be completed as soon as the stones are formed. You can easily ascertain how far things have gone by removing a typical fruit and cutting into it. If the stone is hard and almost full size, with a well-developed kernel, the stoning period is over. Leave an average of one fruit per square foot of tree area. Peaches in unheated houses should be nicely set and you can start thinning as advised in the General Notes for March.

FIRST WEEK

Sow Grass Seed. This is usually the most favourable time for sowing grass seed, but wait a little if the ground is sticky. Rake the surface of the ground quite level and scatter the seed as evenly as possible at the rate of 1-2 ounces per square yard. Cover with a light sprinkling of fairly dry soil or by raking lightly to mix the seed with the soil. If grass seed is obtained pre-treated with a good bird repellant no further protection against birds will be necessary, but otherwise bird scarers or black thread stranded between small sticks should be used.

A GOOD METHOD OF SOWING A NEW LAWN

The plot is divided into yard-wide strips with the aid of two lines and one strip is sown at a time. Measure the length of the strip in yards, multiply by two, and you will have the correct weight in ounces of grass seed for the marked area.

Complete Rose Pruning. You should now prune the more delicate tea roses that I advised you to leave alone until April (see November, General Work). Treatment is the same as for the hybrid teas except that cutting back should be a little more severe, as most of these varieties tend to make weakly growth if pruned insufficiently.

Apply Tonk's Fertilizer to Roses. Give all your roses a dressing of Tonk's fertilizer. It will provide them with most of the food they require throughout the summer. You can purchase this fertilizer ready for use, or, if you prefer, you can make it yourself. The ingredients are twelve parts of superphosphate of lime, ten parts of nitrate of potash, two parts of sulphate of magnesia, one part of sulphate of iron, eight parts of gypsum. Mix thoroughly, crush up fine, and use at 4 ounces per square yard.

Prune Flowering Shrubs. Shrubs to prune now include the hardy fuchsias such as *F. macrostemma, F. gracilis,* and *F. Riccartonii; Buddleia variabilis,* and its varieties, *Leycesteria formosa, Perowskia atriplicifolia, Romneya Coulteri,* and *R. trichocalyx,* also all varieties of cornus and salix (willow) grown for bark effects. With all these pruning should be hard, last year's growth being cut back quite close to the older wood, but with the buddleias you can allow a few branches to remain at three-quarter length to build up a main framework of growth if a large bush is required (for method see February, First Week).

PRUNING A BUDDLEIA
VARIABILIS
Buddleia variabilis *may be cut back really hard each February* (A) *or it may be lightly pruned* (B) *and allowed to form a large bush.*

Stop Exhibition Chrysanthemums. There are some well-known exhibition chrysanthemums which should be stopped in early April, in the south of England, to give flowers by mid-November—namely Audrey Shoesmith, Edith Woolman, John Rowe, Keith Luxford, Oporto, and Souvenir. Exhibition incurved varieties which should also be stopped at this time are Ondine, Progress (and its sports), and Monument.

Pot Cyclamen Seedlings. If you were able to raise any cyclamen from seeds last summer (see August, Second Week), the seedlings will now be ready for transferring singly to 3-inch pots. Use a compost rather rich in humus; two parts of loam and one part of either leaf-mould or moss peat, with a liberal sprinkling of sand and powdered mortar rubble and a dusting of bonemeal and old soot will do well. The corms should be kept on the surface of the soil, not buried. Pot moderately firm, water freely, and then stand the plants on a shelf or staging in a light, airy part of the greenhouse. The temperature should not fall below 50°. An average of just over 60° is ideal at this stage.

Sow Zinnias in a Frame. If you make a sowing of zinnias in a warm, sheltered frame and keep the seedlings growing strongly without check, the plants will flower by July. The secret of success with zinnias is to maintain steady growth. Any kind of check is fatal, and sometimes it is almost impossible to avoid a check with seedlings from an earlier sowing. Sow thinly in boxes or directly in the frame and cover with ¼ inch of fine soil.

Lift Celery and Leeks. If there are still celery and leeks left in the ground from last year, lift these and lay them in behind a north wall or in any other cool place. This simply means digging a shallow trench, laying the leeks and celery in this with their tops exposed, and covering them with a little soil.

Feed Spring Cabbages. Give spring cabbages—*i.e.*, cabbages which are now nearing maturity—a top-dressing of nitrate of soda, at the rate of ½ ounce per square yard, and hoe it in. A further dressing can be given in about three weeks' time.

Plant Second Early and Late Potatoes. If the weather is good and the soil works well, there is no point in delaying the planting of second early and late potatoes. These crop more heavily than the earlies and therefore require more room. Allow at least 3 feet between the rows and 15 inches between the tubers in the rows. I find that it is simplest and most satisfactory to plant with a spade, making the holes just deep enough to allow the tops of the tubers to be covered with 3 inches of soil. If the soil is inclined to be harsh and stony, surround each planting set with a few handfuls of moss peat or leaf-mould. Late potatoes take longer to mature than second earlies, and will give a good succession in spite of the fact that they are planted at the same time.

Protect Early Potatoes. Keep a close watch on the earliest potato bed now, for shoots may soon appear and, if they do, they will certainly need protection. The simplest method is to pull some soil over them with a draw hoe; or, if you prefer, you can scatter some dry straw or bracken over them.

Sow and Plant Globe Artichokes. The globe artichoke can be raised from seed, though a better method is to propagate selected varieties by suckers, as the best forms do not come true from seed. However, if you would like to try seed, now is the time to sow it, either in a frame or a sheltered border. Sow in drills 8 inches apart and cover very lightly.

The best globe artichokes are propagated by suckers or offsets, and this is the time to plant them. Choose a really good piece of ground, well worked and thoroughly manured, and plant the suckers firmly 3 feet apart in rows 4 feet apart. This will seem a lot of space to novices, but it is really necessary because the globe artichoke grows into a very large plant and will not give good results if crowded.

Sow Kohl Rabi. Kohl rabi is useful as a substitute for turnips in seasons or places where the soil is too dry for the latter crop. This is the time to sow the seeds, in shallow drills 2 feet apart.

Sow and Plant Asparagus. Asparagus can be raised from seed sown now in a sheltered border outdoors, but it is a slow process, for three or four years must elapse before the roots are large enough for cutting to commence.

The best method of making new asparagus plantations is by planting sturdy roots. There are many different ways of growing asparagus but one of the best is that in which the crowns are planted in single rows about 4 feet apart, with 15 inches between each plant. The crowns are put into a shallow trench, spreading the roots out as widely as possible, and then covering them with fine soil until they are 4 inches beneath the surface. Two-year-old crowns can be used, although commercial growers often prefer to use one-year-old plants.

This method of growing in flat beds is suitable where drainage is good, but on heavy or poorly drained soils a raised bed is better, making it about 6 inches above the level of the surrounding ground.

Plant Cucumbers. Cucumbers from a March sowing (see March, First Week) will now be ready for planting in a heated greenhouse or pit.

Spray Gooseberries and Black Currants. If your gooseberries have suffered in the past from attacks of mildew, spray them, a few days before the flowers expand, with lime sulphur wash or dinocap at the usual strength recommended by the manufacturers.

Black currants sometimes get very badly attacked by a minute pest which breeds within the buds and causes them to swell up to a great size. This condition is appropriately known as big bud and, if any of your black currants are suffering from it, you should spray them at once with lime sulphur wash at twice the normal winter strength recommended by the manufacturers. The effect of this will be to scorch the tiny leaves that are just appearing, but the bushes will recover later on and the mites will be killed.

BIG BUD

These swollen blackcurrant buds are full of tiny mites. The bushes should be sprayed at this time of year with lime sulphur wash at twice the normal winter strength recommended by the manufacturers.

Finish Grafting Fruit Trees. Early April is a good time for grafting fruit trees in the open—but the earlier the better. I have already given instructions for this operation in March, Fourth Week, and illustrations will be found on page 75.

SECOND WEEK

Plant Violets. It is time to make a new violet plantation out of doors to provide clumps for forcing next winter. If cuttings were rooted the previous autumn, as described in the notes for September, General Work (and there is no better way of growing good, clean violets), the old clumps that have been flowering during the past winter can be discarded altogether. However, if you have no cuttings you will have to be satisfied with young rooted pieces pulled from the outside of the old clumps to make the new plantation. The central portion of each clump should be thrown away, however, for it is very unlikely to give good results another season. Whether you use rooted pieces pulled off the clumps or rooted cuttings the method of making a plantation is the same. Choose a partially shaded border and rather heavy, rich soil if there is any choice in the matter. Plant the big single varieties 1 foot apart in rows 18 inches apart and the doubles 6 inches apart in rows 1 foot apart.

A GOOD VIOLET DIVISION

Young rooted pieces such as this, pulled from the outside of old clumps, are almost as good as cuttings.

Sow Hardy Annuals. Seed of the various hardy annuals will usually germinate more readily and certainly in mid-April than in March, particularly if the soil tends to be heavy and cold. I gave particulars for an early sowing in the notes for March, Third Week, and these apply with equal force now, except that to the list of varieties there given a number of other kinds can now be added, notably nasturtiums of all types, calandrinia, sweet sultan, layia, leptosiphon, canary creeper, *Tagetes signata pumila*, *Mesembryanthemum criniflorum*, ursinia, venidium, dimorphotheca, salpiglossis, and jacobaea. In sheltered gardens it is even possible to sow a number of half-hardy annuals outdoors with success, but if your garden is at all exposed I advise you to leave this until the first week in May. In any case it is bound to be a bit of a gamble at the moment. Given cloche protection, however, immediate sowing is advisable.

Stop Exhibition Chrysanthemums. A number of popular exhibition chrysanthemums should be stopped in the midlands and south if fully developed blooms are required by mid-November. The varieties in question now are Champagne, Cossack, and Margaret Shoesmith in the large exhibition class, and Annie Curry and its sports in the incurved section. It is also a good time to stop all decoratives and single chrysanthemums that are well rooted and growing freely.

Start Achimenes and Hippeastrums for Succession. A third batch of achimenes (see February, First Week) started now will ensure a succession of flowers in late summer and early autumn.

Start the remaining hippeastrum bulbs into growth now to provide late flowers (see January, Fourth Week).

Pot Seedling Begonias, etc. Begonias, gloxinias, and streptocarpuses raised from seed in January and pricked off in February or early March (see February, Fourth Week) will probably be in need of first potting into 3-inch pots. Use the usual compost (see p. 44) and stand in a light, well-ventilated place in a temperature between 55° and 60°.

Sow French Beans under Glass. If you want a supply of french beans in July make a sowing now in seed boxes or pots; the latter method has the advantage that it avoids any root disturbance later on. Place one seed in each 2½-inch pot, or in boxes plant the seeds 2 inches apart each way. Cover with ¾ inch of soil and germinate in the greenhouse or in a frame on a hotbed. A temperature of about 55° is necessary for germination, but no harm will be done if it happens to fall a little below this occasionally. Frost, however, will kill the bean. The seedlings will be hardened off later on for planting out in late May (see May, Fourth Week).

Sow Maincrop Carrots. Now is the time to make the maincrop sowing of carrots. For this you will need an intermediate or long variety instead of the shorthorn type. Sow thinly in drills about ½ inch deep and 1 foot apart. It is quite a good plan to make a small successional sowing of a stump-rooted variety as well and repeat a fortnight or three weeks later, as from these sowings you will have tender young roots after midsummer, but before the main crop is ready. These small varieties need only be sown in drills 9 inches apart.

Sow Salsify. Salsify is by no means everybody's vegetable, but food experts think a lot of it. Sow the seed now in shallow drills 15 inches apart. You must choose an open part of the garden and ground that has been well dug and manured, though preferably a year previously. The roots may be forked and useless if grown on freshly manured ground, and for this reason many gardeners plant salsify on the ground occupied by celery trenches the previous year, with no further manuring except a dusting of bonemeal in the autumn and an occasional sprinkling of a compound fertilizer while the plants are in growth.

Sow Winter Greens. All kinds of winter greens should now be sown. Brussels sprouts, cauliflower, broccoli, and cabbages, either to follow the early sowing made under glass (see March, First Week) or as a first sowing, if that was not possible, and borecole, kale, savoy, and sprouting broccoli for the first time. The simplest and most economical method is

eft: Rock garden plants grown in pots may be planted out at any time of the year.
Right: Treading the soil very firmly after planting a rhododendron.

Spreading the roots out is important when planting asparagus.

Plants require potting on when the roots are showing on the outside of the ball of soil.

A correctly potted plant. Space has been left at the top for watering and feeding.

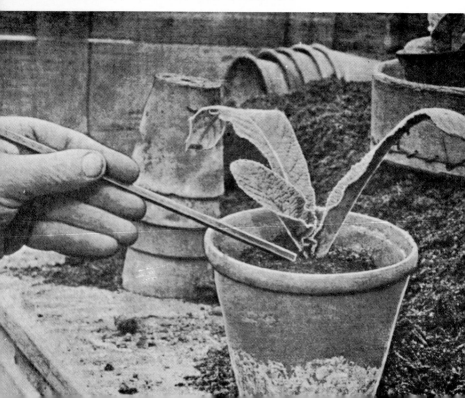

to sow broadcast as thinly as possible on a finely prepared seed bed and cover with fine soil, which can be sifted over the seeds, to a depth of about ¼ inch. Of course, you must take care to keep each patch quite separate and to label it clearly, because seedlings of winter greens are very much alike and you may find difficulty in identifying them later on if you get the seeds mixed. You should note particularly that, altogether apart from sprouting broccolis, there are three groups of broccoli with close white curds—namely, earlies such as Veitch's Self-protecting and Walcheren, ready for cutting from September to Christmas; mid-season varieties such as Adam's Early White, and Snow's Winter White, ready from Christmas to April; and lates such as St George and Late Queen, ready from April to June. Sow some of each kind now and you will be assured of a succession later on. As regards cabbage, choose a quick-maturing variety such as Winnigstadt, Greyhound, or Primo.

Sow Celery in Frame. To supplement earlier sowings of celery made in a warm greenhouse, or as an alternative to these if they could not be made, celery may now be grown in an unheated frame. The method is just the same as before (see February, Third Week), the seed being sown thinly in well-drained seed trays filled with a light, sandy compost.

Remove Early Celery to Frame. Early celery pricked off last month (see March, Third Week) will now be better in a frame, where it can be still further hardened off for planting out.

Prick off Cabbages, Cauliflowers, etc. Cabbages, cauliflowers, broccolis, and brussels sprouts raised in frame or greenhouse in March (see March, First Week) will be in need of pricking off, 3 inches apart each way, in a frame or, provided the weather is mild and they have been properly hardened off, in a sheltered border outdoors.

Plant out Vegetable Seedlings. Culinary peas, onions, leeks, cauliflowers, broad beans, and lettuces raised in the greenhouse and transferred to a frame last month for hardening off (see March, Third Week) may now be planted out in the beds in which they are to mature, provided the weather is fairly mild. If it is frosty or winds are cold, wait a further week. All the ground should have been well dug and manured. The position chosen for the cauliflowers should be sheltered from north and east if possible. Exhibition leeks are usually grown in trenches prepared exactly as for celery (see April, General Work), but quite good leeks can also be grown in ordinary beds if the plants are dropped into holes about 9 inches deep made with a dibber. With this exception, all other planting

G

of seedlings mentioned above is best done with a trowel. Plant the celery 1 foot apart (if there are two rows in an 18-inch-trench, set the rows 1 foot apart). Leeks should be 9 inches apart in rows 18 inches apart for ordinary purposes and 1 foot apart in the trenches for exhibition. Onions are set 9 inches apart in rows 1 foot apart; lettuces from 6 to 9 inches apart, according to the size of the variety, the rows being 1 foot apart to allow easy use of the hoe; cauliflowers 2 feet apart in rows 2½ feet apart; broad beans 6 inches apart in rows from 15 to 30 inches apart, according

ONION PLANTING

A hole has been prepared sufficiently large to take all the roots without any unnatural cramping.

to the size of the variety; and peas 4 inches apart in double rows 10 inches apart, with from 3 to 6 feet between each pair of rows, according to the height of the variety.

Place Early Tomatoes in Final Pots. Tomatoes from a January sowing should now be ready for their final pots. You can, if you prefer, grow them in boxes or plant them out directly into a border of compost prepared on the staging, or on the floor if the house is a light one with low walls or glass right to ground level. Nevertheless, I think 9- or 10-inch pots are best for the first crop, as plants seem to come to maturity more rapidly in them than when grown in any other way. The compost should consist of about four parts of good loam, one part of old, well-rotted manure and sweet leaf-mould, well mixed, and a 5-inch potful of bone-meal added to each bushel of this mixture.

Spray Apples and Pears. If apples were attacked last year by scab disease, spray now with lime sulphur wash, dispersible sulphur or captan as recommended by the manufacturers. Pears similarly attacked should be treated with Bordeaux mixture rather than lime sulphur, as the latter is

DAMAGE CAUSED BY PEAR SCAB

Dry cracks in the fruit are an almost certain sign that this disease has been at work. The fungus also attacks apples.

inclined to cause scorching. The Bordeaux should be used as recommended by the manufacturers; it is not safe to use it later than this, and captan should replace it where necessary.

If caterpillars are active or capsid bug has been troublesome in previous years, add D D T insecticide to the sprays recommended.

THIRD WEEK

Thin Hardy Annuals. Hardy annuals sown in March outdoors where they are to bloom (see March, Third Week) will be in need of a first thinning out. Simply pull out the feeblest seedlings until the remainder are left a clear 2 or 3 inches apart each way and have room to develop. A further thinning will be necessary in May. You can transplant some of the seedlings elsewhere if you wish, but as a rule those with long, unbranched roots (the gardener calls them tap roots) do not recover well from the shift. These include annual lupins, eschscholtzias, poppies, clarkias, godetias, gypsophilas, Virginian stocks, and mignonette. Be sure to firm the soil around the seedlings you leave.

Plant out and Stake Sweet Peas. Sweet peas that you raised in the greenhouse during January will be ready for planting out, provided you have

SWEET PEA SEEDLING

Contrary to practice with most other seedlings, the soil should be shaken from the roots of sweet peas when they are planted out.

hardened them off properly. The method to follow is exactly the same as that for planting out September-sown sweet peas (see March, Third Week).

Sweet peas planted in March should be well established, and it will be time to provide each plant with a bamboo cane at least 7 feet long. This must be pushed really firmly into the soil, and it is a good plan to link all the canes together at the top with string or wire, securing this at each end to a stronger post. You should reduce the number of shoots to one per plant, choosing the sturdiest, and lead this towards its cane with a raffia tie.

If the March-sown peas (see March, First Week) have made 2 or 3 inches of growth, as they should by this time, pinch out the tip of each plant. These late-sown peas are usually grown naturally on bushy pea sticks and are not trained to a single stem on bamboos, so there will not be any need to reduce the number of shoots that form as a result of the stopping.

Plant Violas and Pansies. Plant out violas and pansies, both seedlings and rooted cuttings, if they have been properly hardened off. A rather cool, semi-shaded position is best, though both plants will grow in full sun. The drawback is that they tend to finish flowering sooner. Well worked, rather liberally manured ground will ensure fine blooms. Plant with a trowel and water in freely.

Start Dahlias in Frames. If you were unable to start dahlias early, as recommended in the February and March notes (see February, Third Week, and March, Third Week), you can do so now in an unheated frame. Simply arrange the roots close together in a frame and cover the tubers with light soil. Water moderately, but give increasing supplies as growth commences. Cover the frame with plenty of sacks every night, and remove these in the morning, unless it is very frosty.

Prune Forsythias. This is the time to prune forsythias if you want to keep them as moderately small specimens, or to train them against a wall. The method is to cut back as many as possible of the flowering branches to younger stems that have not yet flowered or to new shoots just starting. Where wall specimens are concerned any small laterals that have not flowered and cannot conveniently be tied in can be cut back severely.

Prune Evergreens grown for Foliage. Hardy evergreen shrubs that are grown principally for their foliage, either in hedges or as topiary specimens, etc., can also be pruned with safety. If there is any really hard cutting back to be done, this is certainly the time to do it. Light trimming can be practised during the summer, but severe pruning is out of place then. Old, worn-out laurel hedges can often be renovated by cutting them back to within a foot of the ground at this time of the year. Of course, the stumps look terrible for a while, but given a little luck and some warm, showery weather, they will soon be a forest of healthy new shoots, with fine, vigorous leaves.

Stop Exhibition Chrysanthemums. Exhibition chrysanthemums to stop now for flowers in mid-November are Lady Docker, Orpheus, and Shirley Champion.

PRUNING A FORSYTHIA

Pruning is carried out immediately after flowering and consists of cutting a few old branches right out (A) and shortening all flowering shoots (B).

Transfer Bedding Plants to Frames. You may now transfer most of the bedding plants and half-hardy annuals which till now have been in the greenhouse to frames for the next stage in hardening off. For the first

HARDENING OFF IN FRAMES

As spring advances bedding plants in frames must be given more and more ventilation. On mild days the lights can be slid right off for most of the day.

few days after this move you should keep the frames closed, and cover them well with sacks at night. Then admit a little air by day if it is fine, steadily increasing the amount until by the end of the month the lights are removed altogether for several hours on all mild days. Be particularly wary of days when the sky clears and the wind drops towards evening. At this time of year these signs often presage frost, and lights should be temporarily closed. Your object should be thoroughly to accustom the plants to full exposure, day and night, by the end of May.

Sow Vegetable Marrows, Ridge Cucumbers, and Melons. Later on you are sure to want vegetable marrows, and you may be glad of a few ridge cucumbers as well. Sow some seeds now, singly, in 2½- or 3-inch pots, and germinate them in the greenhouse or in a frame on a hotbed in a temperature of 60° or thereabouts. They will germinate more quickly if you cover the pots with a piece of brown paper, but this must be removed as soon as the seed leaves appear. Melons that are to be grown in a frame should also be sown now and germinated in exactly the same way.

Sow Parsley Outdoors. Make a small sowing of parsley outdoors to provide a successional crop after that sown in February (see February, Fourth Week). Details of sowing are exactly as before, except that there is no need now to choose a specially sheltered or warm position for the sowing.

FOURTH WEEK

Plant Antirrhinums and Penstemons. Antirrhinums raised in the autumn from seeds or cuttings and also penstemons from autumn cuttings may be planted in their flowering quarters if they have been thoroughly accustomed to full exposure.

Take Chrysanthemum Cuttings for Dwarf Plants. This is the time to start taking cuttings of chrysanthemums that are to make dwarf specimens in pots. You can root them in boxes or beds of soil exactly as the earlier chrysanthemum cuttings, though I think a better method is to insert them singly in 2½-inch pots, or three round the edge of a 3-inch pot. Allow them to root either in a cool greenhouse or a frame. By no means all varieties are suitable for this method of culture. Some of the best are Blanche du Poitou, Blanche Poitevene, Rose Poite vene, Salmon Poitevene, and Pink Poitevene, while others that you might try are Cochineal, Marie Morin, Pearl Angavene, Rigoletto and Spanish Lady.

Sow Greenhouse Primulas. Make a first sowing of the various primulas that flower in the greenhouse during winter, *i.e.*, *Primula sinensis* and its variety *stellata*, *P. obconica*, and *P. kewensis*. Do not sow all your seeds of the first three now, however, but keep some for a second batch in June (see June, Third Week). Sow the seeds thinly in the usual seed compost (see p. 26). I think they are better sown in well-drained pots or pans rather than boxes. Cover the seeds very lightly with fine soil and germinate in the greenhouse in a temperature of about 60°. Cover each seed vessel with a pane of glass until germination takes place. If water is needed, give this by holding the pots nearly to their rims in a tub and not by watering overhead.

Sow Annuals for the Greenhouse. You can now make a second sowing of hardy and half-hardy annuals, for flowering in pots in the greenhouse (see February, Third Week, and March, First Week). Plants from this late sowing will provide a succession of flowers after the first batch is over.

Sow Runner Beans. Make a small sowing of runner beans in exactly the same way as the early sowing of french beans (see Second Week). If you germinate them in the greenhouse you will have some nice forward plants for putting out the first week in June, and these will give you a crop of beans several weeks earlier than would be possible from the earliest outdoor sowing.

Sow Globe Beetroot. You can now make a sowing of globe beetroot in a fairly sheltered border out of doors. This earliest sowing need not be a very large one, as it will be followed by another in May, and also by a much bigger sowing of long beet in the same month. Sow the seeds 2 inches deep in rows 15 inches apart. I find the most economical method is to place three seeds every six or eight inches along the rows and then reduce the seedlings to one at each point later on.

Sow Endive. Make a small sowing of endive; it makes a welcome change from lettuce in summer salads. Sow the seeds thinly in drills ½ inch deep and 1 foot apart.

Spray Gooseberries. If you considered it necessary to spray your gooseberries with lime sulphur before flowering (see April, First Week), you should certainly repeat the treatment as soon as the petals have fallen and you can just see the tiny, fertilized fruits. But for this second spraying you must use the lime sulphur at summer strength or dinocap. Consult manufacturer's instructions regarding these.

AMERICAN GOOSEBERRY MILDEW

This disease causes a mould-like outgrowth on leaves and fruits. Bushes that have been attacked in former years must be sprayed with lime sulphur or dinocap as a preventive.

Remove Greasebands from Trees. You should now remove and burn greasebands that have been round the main trunks or branches of apples, pears, etc., since September.

Thin Outdoor Peaches and Nectarines. The young fruits on outdoor peaches and nectarines should now be about the size of marbles and you must start to thin them out. The work is done in exactly the same way as with indoor peaches (see March, General Work), and so I need not go into it again in detail here. Do not forget that there may be a natural fall during the stoning period with outdoor peaches and nectarines just as with glasshouse-grown varieties, and that it is not wise to complete thinning until this is over. Disbudding (*i.e.*, removal of unwanted young shoots) is carried out with the outdoor trees as with those in the orchard house.

Apricot trees may be allowed to carry more fruits (three or four per square foot), and disbudding is nothing like so drastic, well-placed laterals being merely stopped and not rubbed right out.

FLOWERS, VEGETABLES, AND FRUITS IN SEASON DURING APRIL

Hardy Herbaceous Plants. *Achillea rupestris, Adonis vernalis, Anchusa officinalis, Bellis perennis monstrosa* (double daisy), *Brunnera macrophylla, Cheiranthus Allioni* (Siberian wallflower), *C. Cheiri* (wallflower), *Doronicum plantagineum, Dracunculus vulgaris, Helleborus orientalis* and vars. (Lenten rose), *Heuchera tiarelloides,* Myosotis hybrids (forget-me-nots), *Polygonatum multiflorum* (Solomon's Seal), *P. verticillatum, Primula elatior polyanthus* (polyanthus), *P. vulgaris* vars. (primrose), *Pulmonaria angustifolia, Ranunculus bullatus plenus, Saxifraga ciliata, S. cordifolia* and vars., *S. crassifolia, S. purpurascens, S. Stracheyi.*

Hardy Bulbs and Tubers. *Anemone coronaria* and vars., *A. fulgens* and vars., *Chionodoxa Luciliae, Convallaria majalis* (lily of the valley), crocuses (large-

TRILLIUM GRANDIFLORUM

The American wood lily or wake robin is a plant for a shady, moist border or rock garden. The large white flowers are produced on stems 1 foot tall. The plants prefer a rich, leafy soil.

flowering), *Cyclamen repandum, Erythronium californicum, E. Dens-canis, E. grandiflorum, E. Hartwegii, E. Hendersonii, E. revolutum, E. tuolumnense. Fritillaria citrina, F. imperialis, F. Meleagris, F. oranensis, F. pluriflora, F.*

Purdyi, F. pyrenaica, F. recurva, F. verticillata, hyacinths (large-flowered), *Iris bucharica, I. melanostricta, I. orchioides, I. tingitana, I. warleyensis, Leucojum vernum, Milla uniflora, Muscari botryoides, M.* Heavenly Blue, *M. latifolium, M. moschatum, M. paradoxum, Narcissus Bulbocodium, N. minor,* narcissus hybrids in var. (including trumpet daffodils), *Puschkinia scilloides, Romulea rosea, Scilla amoena, S. bifolia, S. nonscripta* (bluebell), *S. sibirica, S. pratensis, Tecophilaea cyanocrocus* (shelter), *Trillium erectum, T. grandiflorum, T. ovatum, T. recurvatum, T. sessile, T. stylosum, Tulipa australis, T. chrysantha, T. Clusiana, T. dasystemon, T. Didieri, T. Eichleri, T. Fosteriana, T. Greigii, T. Hageri, T. ingens, T. Kuschkensis, T. linifolia, T. orphanidea, T. praestans, T. primulina, T. pulchella, T. saxatilis, T. sylvestris, T. Wilsoniana,* tulips in var. (early singles and doubles, Mendels and Triumphs).

Rock Plants. *Aethionema coridifolium, Ae. iberideum, Ae. grandiflorum, Ae. pulchellum, Ae.* Warley Rose, *Alyssum saxatile* and vars., *A. serpyllifolium, A. spinosum, Androsace carnea, A. lactea, A. pyrenaica, A. sarmentosa* and

OMPHALODES CAPPADOCICA

This rock garden plant blooms in the spring and again in the autumn. A trailing plant, it has masses of forget-me-not blue flowers on 6-inch stems.

vars., *Anemone angulosa, A. apennina, A. ranunculoides, A. sylvestris* and vars., *A. vernalis, Arabis albida* and vars., *A. alpina, A. aubrietioides, Arctostaphylos Uva-ursi, Armeria caespitosa, Arnica montana, Aubrieta deltoidea* and vars., *Bellis perennis* vars., *Bellium bellidioides, Calceolaria biflora, Cheiranthus alpinus, Cornus canadensis, Corydalis tuberosa, C. Wilsonii, Cortusa Matthiolii, Cotyledon simplicifolius, Daphne arbuscula, D. Blagayana, D. Cneorum, D. tangutica, Dicentra eximia, Doronicum caucasicum, Draba Aizoon, D. Dedeana, D. imbricata, D. olympica, Epigaea repens, Epimedium alpinum, E. concinnum, E. macranthum, E. pinnatum, E. rubrum, Gentiana acaulis, G. verna, Geum Borisii, G. montanum, Houstonia serpyllifolia, Iberis saxatilis, I. sempervirens, Iris cristata, I. ensata, I. pumila* and vars., *Isopyrum thalictroides, Lathyrus vernus, Lithospermum rosmarinifolium* (shelter), *Macrotomia echioides, Mazus Pumilio, M. reptans, Morisia hypogaea, Myosotis rupicola, Omphalodes cappadocica, O. verna, Orobus vernus, Papaver alpinum, Primula Allionii, P. Auricula* and vars., *P. cortusoides, P. darialica, P. denticulata* and vars., *P. frondosa, P. glaucescens, P. Juliae, P. Juliana* hybrids, *P. marginata, P. minima, P. nutans, P. pubescens, P. Reinii, P. Sieboldii, Pulsatilla vulgaris, Ranunculus alpestris, R. amplexicaule, R. glacialis, R. gramineus, R. pyrenaeus, Sanguinaria canadensis, Saxifraga Arco-Valleyi, S. aretioides, S. Boydii, S. caesia, S. decipiens* in var. (mossy saxifrages), *S. diapensioides, S. hypnoides* (mossy saxifrages), *S. kewensis, S. lilacina, S. marginata, S. Obristii, S. oppositifolia* and vars., *S. Petraschii, S. sancta, S. tombeanensis, S. valdensis, Shortia galacifolia, S. uniflora, Soldanella alpina, S. montana, Synthyris reniformis, Tiarella cordifolia, Townsendia Wilcoxiana, Viola biflora, V. gracilis* and vars.

Hardy Aquatics and Bog Plants. *Caltha palustris* and vars., *C. polypetala, Cardamine pratensis plena, Chrysosplenium oppositifolium, Dodecatheon Meadia* and vars., *Primula Cockburniana, Saxifraga peltata.*

Hardy Evergreen Shrubs. *Arctostaphylos Manzanita, Berberis buxifolia, B. Darwinnii, B. hakeoides, B. replicata, Ceanothus rigidus* (wall), *Choisya ternata,*

VIBURNUM BURKWOODII

This is a most attractive and easily grown evergreen shrub, with white flowers. It reaches a height of 6 to 8 feet but flowers when young.

Coronilla glauca (shelter), *Daphne Dauphinii, Erica arborea, E. australis* Mr Robert, *E. carnea* and vars., *E. darleyensis, E. mediterranea, Euphorbia Wulfenii, Kalmia glauca, Mahonia aquifolium, M. japonica* and vars., *Osmanthus Delavayi, Osmarea Burkwoodii, Phillyrea Vilmoriniana, Photinia serrulata, Pieris floribunda, P. japonica, Rhododendron arboreum* (shelter), *R. agrophyllum, R. Augustinii, R. calophytum, R. campanulatum, R. campylocarpum* and hybrids, *R. cephalanthum, R. Falconeri, R. fastigiatum, R. hippophaeoides, R. impeditum, R. neriiflorum, R. racemosum, R. rubiginosum, R. scintillans, R. spinulosum, R. Valentinianum, R. Williamsonianum, Skimmia Fortunei S. japonica, Viburnum Burkwoodii, V. Tinus, Vinca minor.*

Hardy Deciduous Shrubs. *Azalea amoena, A. Rhodora, A. Vaseyi, Cassandra calyculata, Colletia infausta, Corylopsis Veitchiana, C. Willmottiae, Cydonia japonica, C. Maulei, Cytisus praecox, Elaeagnus multiflorus, Enkianthus campanulatus, Exochorda Korolkowii, Forsythia intermedia* and vars., *F. suspensa, F. viridissima, Fothergilla Gardenii, Genista radiata, Magnolia obovata, M. salicifolia, M. stellata, Prunus dehiscens, Rhodora canadensis, Ribes aureum, R. sanguineum* and vars., *R. speciosum, Rosa Hugonis, Spiraea arguta, S. prunifolia, S. Thunbergii, Ulex europaeus plenus, Viburnum Carlesii, Xanthorrhiza apiifolia.*

Hardy Evergreen Trees. *Arbutus Andrachne, A. hybrida.*

Hardy Deciduous Trees. *Acer circinatum, A. macrophyllum, A. Opalus, A. platanoides* (Norway maple), *A. rubrum, Alnus firma, Amelanchier canadensis, A. grandiflora, A. vulgaris, Magnolia Campbellii* (shelter), *M. conspicua, M. Lennei, M. Sargentiana, M. Soulangiana, Prunus Amygdalus* (bitter almond), *Prunus Avium, P. Cerasus* (wild cherry), *P. incisa, P. Lannesiana* (Japanese cherry), *P. Mahaleb* and vars., *P. Padus* (bird cherry), *P. Persica* and vars. (peach), *P. Sargentii, P. serrula, P. serrulata* and vars. (Japanese cherry), *P. subhirtella, Pyrus aldenhamensis, P. baccata* (Siberian crab), *P. communis* (pear), *P. Eleyi, P. floribunda, P. theifera, P. spectabilis, Robinia pseudoacacia.*

Hardy Climbing Plants. *Akebia lobata, Clematis alpina, C. Armandii, Ercilla volubilis, Schizandra chinensis, Stauntonia hexaphylla.*

Greenhouse Plants. Abutilons, acacias, arum lilies, astilbes, azaleas (Indian, mollis, etc.) *Boronia megastigma*, bougainvilleas, *Callistemon speciosus*, calceolaria (herbaceous), *Cantua dependens*, carnations (perpetual - flowering),

BOUGAINVILLEA
BUTTIANA

The bougainvilleas are among the most beautiful climbers for the warm greenhouse where they reach 10 to 15 feet. Hybrids are available in many shades of pink, red, crimson, and purple.

chorizemas, cinerarias (hybrids), clivias, *Coronilla glauca, Deutzia gracilis, Dicentra spectabilis Dillwynia floribunda*, eriostemons, freesias, *Genista fragrans*, hippeastrums, *Hydrangea Hortensia* in var., hyacinths (large-flowered) kennedyas, *Leucocoryne ixioides, Lilium Harrisii*, pelargoniums (show and regal), rhododendrons (Javanese), roses, schizanthus and other annuals (see list, September, First Week), stephanotis, tulips (Cottage, Darwin), wallflowers.

Vegetables in Store. Same as March.

Vegetables Outdoors. Broccoli (late), sprouting broccoli, cabbage (sown July, August), kale, leeks, lettuce, spring onions, rhubarb, seakale, spinach beet, turnip tops.

Vegetables under Glass. French beans, carrots, cucumbers, lettuces, mustard and cress, radishes.

Fruits in Store. *Apples:* Allan's Everlasting (D), Annie Elizabeth (C), Barnack Beauty (CD), Belle de Boskoop (CD), Bramley's Seedling (C), Brownlees' Russet (D), Cornish Gillyflower (D), Crawley Beauty (C), D'Arcy Spice (D), Duke of Devonshire (D), Easter Orange (D), Edward VII (C), Encore (C), King George V (D), King of Tompkin's County (D), Laxton's Pearmain (D), Lord Burghley (D), Lord Hindlip (D), May Queen (D), Monarch (C), Newton Wonder (C), Ontario (CD), Sanspareil (CD), Stark (D), Sturmer Pippin (D), Wagener (C). *Grapes:* Mrs Pince, Prince of Wales. *Pears:* Bergamotte d'Esperen (D), Catillac (C), Joséphine de Malines (D), Uvedale's St Germain (C).

Fruits under Glass. Strawberries.

May

GENERAL WORK

Thin and Stake Herbaceous Perennials. It is usually a mistake to allow herbaceous perennials to retain all the growth they produce. Much better results can be obtained by thinning out the shoots a little at this time of the year. Delphiniums and Michaelmas daisies in particular repay rather drastic thinning. Retain some of the sturdiest shoots and nip off the rest. Before the stems get too long and begin to flop about, place bamboo canes in position and loop the stems to these. Usually it is best to have several canes per plant, thrust in close to the clump but leaning outwards towards the top so that, as growth extends and is tied to the canes, it will be spread out and get its full ration of light and air.

Thin out Rose Growth. It is an excellent plan to examine rose bushes and standards occasionally during the month and to pinch out any badly

THINNING A ROSE
A young shoot growing inwards is being pinched out to prevent overcrowding.

placed or overcrowded shoots. Those growing inwards and so tending to crowd the centre of the plant are the ones most likely to cause trouble later on.

Keep a Watch for Greenfly. Greenfly is likely to make its first appearance during the month. Keep a sharp look out for this pest especially on the young growths of roses and plum trees. At the outset it is easy enough to kill all the insects by spraying once or twice at short intervals

ROSE PESTS

A. *Greenfly.The young shoots are attacked first and should be sprayed before this pest spreads to the leaves.*

B. *A bloom damaged by thrips. Dusting with* DDT *as soon as the buds form will control this pest and prevent damage to the blooms.*

with nicotine, malathion, derris, or lindane, but if you neglect to do this the leaves will very soon cockle and curl to such an extent that the aphides (greenflies) will be almost completely protected within their folds, when the most effective insecticide is menazon, which is systemic.

Kill Slugs. Slugs are also likely to be much in evidence now and may do a lot of damage to tender seedlings, lettuces, delphiniums, etc., unless you take measures against them. There are numerous proprietary powders which may be sprinkled round plants to protect them. An effective home-made slug killer can be prepared by mixing 1 ounce of metaldehyde with 3 pounds of bran. Place this in small heaps where slugs have been feeding.

A well-manured trench being prepared for celery.

Left: Well-rooted fuchsia cuttings ready for potting. *Right:* Fuchsia cuttings separated to show extent of roots.

Above, left: Side shoot of tomato being removed.
Above: A spray is used to help to set the tomato fruits.
Left: Placing a rooted dahlia cutting in a pot.

Use Lawn Sand on Weedy Lawns. May is a good month for using lawn sand or finely powdered sulphate of ammonia to kill small, broad-leaved weeds on the lawn. What actually happens is that the chemical lodges on broad leaves and scorches them but slips harmlessly off the upright narrow blades of grass. It is most effective in dry weather. If you use sulphate of ammonia, be certain to distribute it as evenly as possible and not to use more than ½ ounce per square yard. You can give a second application a few weeks after the first provided there has been some rain meanwhile to wash the former dose away. Commercial lawn sand should always be used strictly according to manufacturer's instructions.

An alternative and even more effective method is to use one of the selective hormone weed killers such as MCPA or 2, 4-D. These are sold under various trade names and for lawn use are generally offered in liquid form (see p. 16).

Feed Plants that are in Full Growth. It is a very good plan to feed plants that are growing fast. At this time of the year most herbaceous plants are making a big effort and many of them are forming their flower stems. Spring-sown vegetables are also growing freely and need plenty of nourishment. Early in the month give all such plants a small top dressing of a compound, quick-acting fertilizer and hoe this in. There are plenty of good fertilizers on the market for this purpose or, if you prefer, you can make your own mixture with seven parts of superphosphate of lime, three parts of sulphate of ammonia, two parts of sulphate of potash, and one part of steamed bone-flour well mixed and applied at the rate of 3 ounces per square yard. Repeat the application after about three weeks. The mixture mentioned above is suitable for a great variety of plants, but for vegetables grown principally for their leaves, and also peas, you can increase the proportion of sulphate of ammonia to five parts with advantage. An occasional thorough soaking with weak liquid manure, made by soaking a small sack of well-rotted farmyard, stable, or sheep manure, or old soot in a tub of water, will also do these vegetables a lot of good.

Plant Aquatics. May is the best month of the year for planting water lilies and other aquatic plants. These may either be planted direct in soil, spread on the bottom of the pool to a depth of at least 6 inches, or they may be planted in baskets or pots which are then sunk into position. If you adopt the former method, empty the pool first, place the soil in position and plant the roots with a trowel exactly as if you were dealing with herbaceous perennials. Then run a little water into the pool, but only a few inches at first. Add more as the plants grow, the idea being to

H

keep the leaves of water lilies just floating on the surface. If the plants are placed in boxes or pots these may stand on bricks temporarily to keep the crowns near the surface. When growth is well started the bricks are removed.

HOW TO PLANT A LILY POOL

The inset sketch shows the method of spreading soil to form a bed and covering with clean gravel to prevent water discolouration.

Harden off Bedding Plants in Frames. During the early part of May bedding plants in frames must receive as much ventilation as possible, though it is still unwise to expose any of them to frost. Take the lights right off by day if the weather is fine, but replace them in the afternoon should there be a threat of frost. A clearing sky in the afternoon is to be regarded with suspicion at this time of the year, as, more often than not, it is an indication that there will be a sharp frost at night. Geraniums, fuchsias, and marguerites, also almost all half-hardy annuals sown in February (see February, Third Week), should be fully hardened off and ready for the open ground by the last week in May; but it is advisable to give dahlias, heliotropes, scarlet salvias, and cannas a further week as they are more susceptible to cold.

General Greenhouse Management. As sun heat gains still more in power you will have to be increasingly careful in shading plants. Foliage plants in general, and particularly many ferns, suffer a lot if exposed too long to intense light and heat. Tuberous-rooted begonias also take it badly, and gloxinias appreciate a measure of shade.

Another consequence of the increased sun heat is that plants will require considerably larger supplies of water. This is particularly so with cucumbers and tomatoes. The earlier raised plants should be growing very freely and will transpire a lot of water on a warm day. You must certainly examine all the plants in your greenhouse daily. It does not follow that all the plants will require water every day, though it is quite possible some will, but you should examine the soil carefully to make quite certain how things are. Where plants in pots are concerned, rap these with a hard piece of wood or the leg bone of a chicken. If the pot gives a ringing note the soil within it is dry, but if it has a dull heavy sound the soil is probably moist enough. I say 'probably' because the test is valueless if the pot happens to be cracked. Broken pots always give a dull note, so see that you are not misled.

More ventilation can be given by day and usually it is safe to give a little ventilation at night, but I still prefer to rely exclusively on the top ventilators, except with plants that have been grown under cool conditions from the outset—trees in the unheated orchard house, for example. Side ventilators are well enough in the summer, but in the spring they are liable to cause damaging draughts. One thing that you must particularly guard against from now onwards is a sudden rise of temperature early in the morning. As soon as direct sunlight first strikes the greenhouse, this quick rise in temperature is likely to take place, and the wise gardener will be at hand to increase ventilation and so steady the thermometer. A vast amount of damage in amateurs' greenhouses must be done every year during the spring and summer on bright mornings between about 5 and 8 a.m.

Pot on Spring Rooted Pelargoniums, etc. If you struck cuttings of fuchsias and pelargoniums in March (see March, General Work) and you wish to grow on some of the plants in pots for autumn and winter flowering, they will need potting now into 5-inch pots. Use the compost described on page 62. Pinch the points out of fuchsias to encourage bushy growth. Return the plants to the greenhouse for a week or so after potting. At the end of the month they may go to a sunny frame for the summer. Similar remarks apply to rooted cuttings of coleuses and other greenhouse plants. Some of the later cuttings of all these plants will be in need of first potting into 3-inch pots.

Cuttings of winter-flowering begonias rooted last month (see April, General Work) must be potted as soon as they are well rooted. Pot them singly in 3-inch pots, using the compost described on page 62. Place them on the staging in the greenhouse with an average day temperature of 65°, not falling below 55° at night, and shade from direct sunshine.

Allow Nerines, Arums, etc., to go to Rest. Gradually reduce the amount of water given to nerines, and place the plants in the sunniest part of the greenhouse. The object of this is to ripen the bulbs and allow them to go to rest. The foliage will gradually turn yellow and die down. Freesias and lachenalias (see April, General Work) will benefit from a similar thorough baking on a shelf near the glass or in some such sunny place. Once their foliage dies down no water need be given until July or August. Arum lilies must also be allowed to go to rest (see April, General Work). This now applies to the later batches that have flowered in a cool house as well as to the earlier forced roots. Do not attempt to bake them in the sun after the fashion of nerine bulbs, but simply reduce the water supply gradually and then, when the foliage dies down, lay the pots on their sides and give no more water until August.

Pot and Stop Perpetual-flowering Carnations. Carnations grown from cuttings taken during the winter and early spring are all likely to be ready for their final shift into pots 6 or 7 inches in diameter some time during the month. Do the work as soon as the 3-inch pots are comfortably filled with roots but before they show the slightest tendency to become pot-bound. Use a compost of twelve parts of good yellow loam, two parts of well-rotted manure, one part of wood ashes, one part of old mortar rubble, and from one to two parts of coarse sand, according to the nature of the loam. Pot firmly and then arrange the plants in a frame, keeping the lights on if it freezes or the wind is very cold, but removing them altogether when it is mild.

From time to time break out the ends of the first side shoots resulting from the earlier stopping (see March, General Work). The ideal time to do this is when the shoot has made about eight joints, and two complete joints should be broken out. Do not deal with more than one shoot per plant at a time but spread the work over a period so that the plant does not suffer any severe check to growth.

Thin out Chrysanthemum Growths. During the month chrysanthemums that were stopped during March and April will be making new growths —'breaks' the chrysanthemum expert terms them. You will have to decide just how many of these you require per plant and then rub the rest out as soon as possible. The actual number retained will depend upon the type of chrysanthemum and the purpose for which you are growing it. With exhibition Japanese chrysanthemums that are being grown for the very biggest flowers possible, only one shoot must be retained per plant. If prize winning is not the main object you may be satisfied to leave three stems per plant, and this is usually the ideal number to leave on incurved varieties that are being grown for exhibition. The reason for leaving more with these is that great size is not desirable, quality and form are the imperative points and these are best obtained by having several blooms per plant. Decoratives that are being grown for cutting may also have three stems from the present stopping. They will be

EXHIBITION CHRYSANTHEMUMS

After stopping only three shoots have been retained, all others having been rubbed out at an early stage.

DECORATIVE CHRYSANTHEMUMS

As the flowers had not to be of great size, three shoots were retained after the first stopping, and from two to three further shoots on each of the first 'breaks' after the second stopping.

allowed to carry still more when they break again (see June, General Work).

Make Successional Sowings. Once again there will be a number of sowings to be made during the month to provide a succession of vegetables after those raised from earlier sowings. Lettuces, spinach, turnips, radishes, and mustard and cress should be sown exactly as explained in the notes for April, General Work, with the one exception that it is now more than ever advisable to sow the three first-named in a partially shaded position. They will not stand a great amount of summer heat, as this makes them run to seed. You should make a couple of sowings of maincrop peas to give you a chance of continuing the crop well on into the autumn. Make a further sowing of endive (see April, Fourth Week) towards the end of the month, and another sowing of kohl rabi about the middle of the month (see April, First Week).

Stake Culinary Peas. Successional batches of culinary peas will be growing freely during the month and these must be staked as soon as they are a couple of inches in height. Even the dwarf peas should have small brushy twigs to keep them erect. At the same time draw a little soil into a ridge on each side of the row. This will serve to protect the young plants and will also make a trough into which you can pour water and liquid manure later on.

Earth up Early Potatoes. As the earlier crops of potatoes push their shoots through the ground draw more soil around them for protection.

EARTHING UP POTATOES
The sectional drawing shows the way in which tubers are formed in the mounded soil.

A few degrees of frost will injure these shoots and there can be no certainty about the weather until May is well advanced. The very earliest outdoor crops, on sheltered borders (see February, Fourth Week) will be well advanced in growth and it will not be possible to protect them with soil alone. Keep some dry straw, bracken, or evergreen boughs at hand and strew these thickly over the bed when frost threatens.

Potatoes in frames must be ventilated as freely as possible on all mild days, but be sure to place the lights in position again early in the afternoon if frost threatens. Incidentally, it is wasteful to lift whole roots of frame potatoes when the tubers form. Scrape away the soil from them as they grow, remove the biggest tubers and then return the soil once more. The smaller tubers will continue to swell and you can collect them later on. You should get some tubers early this month.

Thin Onions, Root Crops, etc. Various crops sown in drills out of doors will be in need of thinning during the month. The sooner this can be started the better, once the seedlings can be clearly seen, but I do not advise you to complete the thinning all at one operation as there may be some casualties yet. Your ultimate object is to leave onions from 6 to 9 inches apart, turnips 5 or 6 inches apart, kohl rabi 9 inches apart, short-horn carrots 3 inches and long or intermediate carrots 6 inches apart, lettuces 6 inches to 1 foot apart according to the size of the variety, and leeks 4 inches apart (they will be transplanted in July). If you sowed globe artichokes and asparagus last month (see April, First Week) the seedlings will also need thinning, the former to 6 inches and the latter to 1 foot apart. It is always advisable to increase these distances if you wish to have big produce for exhibition. Seedlings of lettuce may be transplanted elsewhere if you water them in well. The seedlings of root crops are not of any value for transplanting. Pull out the weakest and least promising seedlings first, and be careful not to disturb those you leave more than you can help. Make the loosened soil firm again with the knuckles. This is particularly important with onions, as the dreaded onion fly frequently lays its eggs in the loose soil caused by careless thinning.

As a further precaution against this pest sprinkle 4% calomel dust along the rows of onions, keeping it as far as possible in a narrow band on each side of the plants.

Dust Brassica Seedlings with D D T. Lightly dust all seedlings of cabbage, broccoli, cauliflower, brussels sprouts, kale, turnip, swede and other brassicas with DDT to kill flea beetles before they have a chance to do any harm. The treatment can be repeated occasionally if any flea beetles are seen or if small holes appear in the leaves.

Feed, Disbud, and Pollinate Tomatoes. Tomatoes will be in various stages of growth. The earliest will have set some fruits by this time, later batches may be just coming into flower, while yet others from March sowings will be ready for potting on into 5-inch pots early in the month. With all these you must remove side shoots regularly.

It is advisable to continue to fertilize flowers by hand either by tapping the plants or by scattering dry pollen from flower to flower with a camel's hair brush. This is most effective if done about midday when the sun is shining.

The earliest plants will benefit from a top-dressing of old, well-rotted manure thoroughly broken up and spread evenly all over the existing compost to a depth of about 1 inch. You can give additional food in liquid form once a week. There is nothing better than a good proprietary fertilizer for this purpose—only be sure to use it weak. I prefer to dilute

METHOD OF TRAINING TOMATOES IN A SPAN HOUSE

Each plant is stopped—that is to say, the growing tip is pinched out—as soon as it reaches the ridge of the house

with twice as much water as the manufacturers recommend and then give the feed rather more frequently. If you prefer to make your own mixture use three parts of superphosphate of lime, two parts of sulphate of ammonia, and two parts of sulphate of potash well mixed and dissolved in water at the rate of 1 teaspoonful per gallon.

Keep the main stems tied up regularly and pinch out the points of the most forward plants as soon as they reach the ridge.

Train and Feed Melons. You will now be able to see the result of your pollination last month (see April, General Work). If sufficient fruits have set per plant, well and good; but if only one or two have set, remove them and start all over again, fertilizing the requisite number of female flowers all on the same day. As soon as white rootlets appear on the surface of the bed, top dress with an inch of well-rotted manure thoroughly broken up. Water very freely. Continue to pinch out points of side shoots so that the house does not get overcrowded with foliage. Maintain a rather moist atmosphere and a day temperature averaging 70°.

Train and Feed Cucumbers. Cucumbers in heated greenhouses and in frames on hotbeds will be in various stages of growth. All will require regular training and stopping as already described (see April, General Work), and all must be watered freely and ventilated very sparingly. A damp, warm atmosphere is what the cucumber likes, and only on really mild days should a little air be admitted. From this time onwards a

LIQUID MANURE
This is prepared by soaking a small sack of manure in a tub of water. The simplest method is to attach the sack to a stick long enough to span the tub easily.

permanent shading of lime wash will be needed on the glass to prevent sun scorch.

The earliest plants in full bearing will need regular feeding with very dilute liquid manure (horse, cow, and sheep dung steeped in water are all good, and so is old soot); while if you note white rootlets on the surface of any of the beds, top dress at once with an inch-thick layer of old manure, well broken up.

Mulch Fruit Trees. Spread a fairly thick layer of well-rotted farmyard or stable manure, or failing this spent hops (not hop manure, which contains chemicals), around fruit trees and bushes of all types, also raspberries. This is known technically as a mulch, and it is very valuable for two reasons: it provides the trees with much-needed nourishment while they are in growth, and helps to retain moisture in the soil by preventing surface evaporation.

Disbud and Thin Peaches, Nectarines, etc., Outdoors. During the month peaches, nectarines, and apricots on walls will be growing freely, and you must continue to disbud them in the same way as those grown under glass (see February, General Work). The fruits must also be thinned a little, but do not complete this process until the stones are formed (see April, General Work).

Management of Orchard House. Peaches and nectarines that were started into growth in January will be ripening their fruits during May and you must no longer syringe them. Ventilate as freely as possible without letting the temperature fall below 60° by day or 50° by night. Later trees will be in various stages of growth and will require thinning, disbudding, etc., as described in my notes for General Work during March and April. Apricots should be thinned moderately if overcrowded, and laterals must be pinched from time to time to prevent unnecessary formation of wood.

Treatment of Vines. Outdoor vines will be growing freely now and you must regulate their growth in much the same manner as that of indoor varieties. Reduce the number of laterals to one per spur, retaining those that are showing flower trusses. Stop them beyond the truss but before

SIDE VENTILATION IN THE VINERY

The arrows show the currents of air caused by using both side and top ventilators and emphasize the danger of causing cold draughts with this dual ventilation.

they have grown so far as to interfere with neighbouring vines or the laterals from other rods.

Indoor vines will be in various stages of growth according to the time at which you started them, and I refer you to my notes in the General Work for February, March, and April for information on such matters as pollination, stopping, thinning, etc. The earliest vines started in January will now be starting to ripen, and you must give increased ventilation, using side ventilators as well as those at the ridge. This, of course, applies in measure to all vineries now that the weather is getting warmer, but in particular to the earliest house, because a heated, stagnant atmosphere is a certain cause of cracking. There is no need to keep the evaporating trays filled with water any longer in the forward house as a rather dry atmosphere is an advantage. Keep the top ventilators a little open throughout the night, even though this necessitates the use of a little more artificial heat when the weather is cold.

FIRST WEEK

Plant Dahlia Tubers Outdoors. If you have not been able to start dahlia tubers into growth in either a greenhouse or frame you can plant them outdoors now. Cover the tubers with 3 inches of soil and then they will be quite secure against frost. It will be some weeks before shoots appear above ground.

Sow Hardy and Half-hardy Annuals. If you want flowers of hardy and half-hardy annuals outdoors in early autumn, now is the time to sow them. The seeds should be scattered broadcast where the plants are to flower and should be covered lightly with soil exactly as described for earlier sowings (see March, Third Week, and April, Second Week).

Sow Cinerarias. Sow a few seeds of cinerarias if you want to have plants in flower by December. The seeds will want a little warmth to encourage germination so early, but the ordinary greenhouse temperature of 55° to 60° will be ample. Sow very thinly in well-drained sand, using the usual seed compost (see p. 26). Cover lightly with fine soil and sand, and shade until germination begins.

Stop Exhibition Chrysanthemums. Japanese chrysanthemums which should be stopped during this week if you require blooms for a mid-November show are Amethyst, Charles Woolman, Jean Ricardo, Jessie Habgood and Majestic and all its sports.

Plant out Winter Greens. Winter green crops from early sowings, and particularly cauliflowers and brussels sprouts sown in March (see March, First Week) should be planted outdoors in their permanent quarters at the first opportunity. Of course, they must be properly hardened off first, but it should be easy to accomplish this by early May.

It is better to plant with a trowel rather than with a dibber, even though the work is done more rapidly with the latter tool. Usually it is sufficient to plant 2 feet apart in rows 2½ feet apart, but these distances may need to be varied a little according to the size of the varieties you are growing. Seed packets usually give adequate information on these points.

Sow Dwarf French Beans. It should be safe to make a sowing of dwarf french beans in the open, if you were not able to raise any plants under glass last month. Sow the seeds singly about 6 inches apart in drills

2 inches deep. An economical method is to have two drills about 9 inches or 1 foot apart, then an alleyway about 2½ feet wide, then another couple of rows, and so on.

Sow Maincrop Beetroot. Early May is the time to sow the main crop of beetroot. For this you should choose a long-rooted or tankard beet rather than a globe variety, unless your ground happens to be very shallow. Sow the seeds in drills 2 inches deep and 18 inches apart. If you space the seeds, which are quite large, at about 2 inches apart it will be a very simple matter to thin the seedlings to about 6 inches later on.

Blanch Leeks. If you planted leeks in trenches during April (see April, Second Week) you must start to blanch them as soon as they are well established and growing freely. The best method is to make tubes out of stiff brown paper, slip one of these over each plant, fastening it to a bamboo cane and drawing a little soil up around its base. The tubes should be about 6 inches in length and about 3 inches in diameter.

Start to Cut Asparagus. From now onwards, for something like six weeks, you should be able to cut good asparagus from established beds. It is, however, a great mistake to cut any shoots at all until the roots are well established. I certainly do not advise you to cut a single shoot until the second year after planting, and it may even be worth waiting until the third year.

It is an excellent plan to give established asparagus beds a dressing of salt at the rate of 3 ounces per square yard. A second application can be given a fortnight later.

Straw the Strawberry Beds. Place clean straw around and between strawberry plants. The object of this is twofold: mainly to protect the fruits later on from mud splashings, but also to provide a mulch and so conserve soil moisture, a most important point in the cultivation of good strawberries.

Ring Unfruitful Apples and Pears. Apple and pear trees that persistently refuse to blossom and bear fruit can often be made fruitful by checking the flow of food from the leaves to the roots. This is done by removing a ring of bark around the main trunk or low down on each main branch. Now is the time to do it, and the method is to cut out a strip of bark, ¼ inch wide, down to the wood and right round the branch or trunk. You should understand, however, that ringing will only be of assistance if the trees are failing to flower as well as to fruit. If they bloom freely but yet bear no crop the cure must be sought elsewhere. It may be that the trees lack suitable 'mates' for cross pollination, that the position is too exposed, or that the trees are under-nourished.

RINGING A FRUIT TREE

A strip of bark ¼ inch wide is removed right round the main trunk of the tree or near the base of each of the main branches. A handy tool made from a ¼-inch thick iron bar and two razor blades, is shown in the inset.

CUTTING THE RING

In some instances the bark may be only partially removed round the tree trunk when ringing so as to prevent the tree suffering too great a check.

Spray Apple Trees against Scab. It is at just about this time that the expanding blossom buds on apple trees reach the point of development described by growers as 'pink bud stage'—*i.e.*, the first trace of pink petal colouring can be seen. This is the ideal moment for applying a second application of lime sulphur, dispersible sulphur, or captan as a preventive of scab disease. You must not delay beyond this stage or the disease may spread rapidly, particularly in warm, humid weather. The actual details of application are exactly the same as for the earlier spraying (see April, Second Week).

SECOND WEEK

Plant Early-flowering Chrysanthemums. By this time early-flowering chrysanthemums raised from cuttings taken in February and March should be sufficiently hardened off to be planted outdoors in the beds in which they are to flower. Choose a good open place and well-manured, deeply cultivated ground if you want blooms of the highest quality. For cutting it is best to have the plants in beds by themselves, 15 inches apart in rows 2 to 2½ feet apart; but they can also be used to fill up spaces in the herbaceous border, in which case they should be spaced 15 inches apart each way. Plant with a trowel, taking care to make holes large

STAKING BORDER CHRYSANTHEMUMS

This is a very handy method. A square of string netting is stretched between four canes arranged around the plants while they are still young. As they grow the shoots pass through the netting and get all the support they require.

enough to accommodate all roots without doubling or twisting. Make moderately firm and water freely if the soil is dry.

Plant out Seedlings of Hardy Perennials, etc. If you were able to sow hardy perennials and alpines in a greenhouse or frame in March (see March, Second Week) you may now plant the seedlings outdoors. Place them in a nursery bed where they can grow on undisturbed throughout the summer. The soil should be good but not heavily manured—indeed, it is better that it should have no manure at all for alpines. Set the plants in lines about 1 foot apart leaving from 3 inches to 1 foot between the plants according to the nature of their growth. Violas, primroses, and polyanthuses succeed best in a partially shaded place, but the other plants mentioned in my March notes prefer a reasonably sunny position. Similar remarks apply to herbs raised from seed and also to hardy perennials raised from root cuttings (see January, General Work).

Remove Greenhouse Plants to Frame. You can further clear the greenhouse by removing a good many of the winter and spring-flowering plants to frames; but keep plenty of sacks at hand for use at night during the first week or so, as we often have treacherous weather about the middle of May. In addition to forced bulbs, shrubs, and bedding plants, about which I have already given advice (see April, General Work and Third Week), you can now clear out arum lilies, freesias, vallottas, and any perpetual-flowering carnations that have for the time being finished flowering. It is not worth keeping the various greenhouse primulas, cinerarias, and calceolarias for another year after they have finished flowering. All these should be raised annually from seed.

Greenhouse cyclamens, both seedlings raised last August (see August, Second Week) and old flowering plants, will also be better in a shady frame during the summer. The old corms must be kept practically dry from now onwards until the middle of August, but the seedling plants should be maintained in growth all the time, and that means an ample water supply.

Prick out Winter Greens. It is a mistake to let winter green crops get overcrowded in the seed beds. Prick out all the seedlings from the April sowing (see April, Second Week) into a nursery bed in the open. This should be well broken down on the surface and fairly rich. Plant the seedlings 3 inches apart in lines 8 inches apart. Do the same to any seedlings left over from the March sowings, but give these rather more room.

Prick off and Plant Celery. Celery sown last month (see April, Second Week) will require to be pricked off into a frame. Give the seedlings plenty of space for they will be growing fast now. Planting 4 inches apart in rows 6 inches apart will not be overdoing it. Ventilate carefully at first but very freely after a week or so.

It will not be possible to keep the earliest celery (see February, Third Week) in boxes or frame beds any longer without risk of checking them severely in transplanting, so get them out into the trenches now (see April, General Work). There is still danger of frost sufficient to kill the plants, so you must keep some protection at hand. The simplest and best method is to draw up some soil to form a ridge on each side of the shallow trench and then to rest some ordinary frame lights on this, so converting the whole trench into a temporary frame. Set the plants 1 foot apart in a single line down the middle of the trench if it is a narrow one, or in two lines, one at each side of the trench, if it is a wide one. Water in really freely. Celery loves moisture and will fail if allowed to get dry.

Sow Sweet Corn. Sweet corn may be sown out of doors where the plants are to grow. Drop the seeds in pairs 2 feet apart each way and thin out later to one plant at each station.

Sow Chicory. Chicory is often neglected by amateurs, but it is a most useful vegetable and a welcome change from seakale and endive in the winter and spring. It is blanched and eaten raw or cooked. Sow seeds now in a sheltered place and on rich, deeply dug ground. Sow sparingly in drills $\frac{1}{2}$ inch deep and 1 foot apart.

Plant Tomatoes in Unheated Greenhouses. When you have cleared the greenhouse sufficiently you can plant it with tomatoes for a late summer crop. Little or no artificial heat will be needed for these from now onwards if you are careful with ventilation and you have stout canvas blinds that can be lowered over the glass on frosty nights. The tomatoes can be grown in pots as advised for the early crops (see March, Second Week), or you can have them in boxes, on a bed of soil made up on the staging, or in a border on the floor. In any case the plants should be at

A BED FOR TOMATOES

This sectional impression of a tomato bed shows the method employed when the staging is of the open lath type. This is covered with galvanized iron sheets, which are in turn covered with a thick layer of coarse cinders or gravel for drainage before the soil is placed in position.

least 1 foot apart in rows which should themselves be quite $2\frac{1}{2}$ feet apart. An alternative method, which certainly makes working easy, is to have two rows quite close together (say 15 inches apart) and then an alleyway 3 feet wide. Make the soil very firm around the roots. The best compost is good fibrous loam, with a little well-rotted manure, leafmould, bonemeal, etc. (see the mixture recommended for potting, March, Second Week). Water the plants in freely after planting or potting, and provide each with a small bamboo cane for support.

Spray Pear Trees. By this time most of the blossom will probably have fallen from pear trees, and it will be necessary to spray again, this time with captan, if there is much danger of scab attacking the trees during the summer. The ideal period is between a week and ten days after blossom can first be shaken from the topmost branches. The details of

Above: Gloxinias may be propagated by seed or cuttings. With leaf cuttings the veins should be cut, as shown, and the leaves pressed into a sandy compost.
Right: Sowing peas broadcast in a wide drill taken out with a spade.
Below: Stopping vine laterals by pinching out the growing point at one leaf beyond the second bunch of grapes.

Left: Sweet peas trained on the single stem system. *Right:* Delphiniums should be staked at an early stage of their growth.

Left: Twiggy stakes being positioned to keep early dwarf peas erect. *Right:* Planting cabbages in a narrow drill, with a dibber.

application are exactly the same as before flowering (see April, Second Week). If caterpillars have been troublesome in previous years, it is also an excellent plan to spray with a good insecticide, such as derris, or to mix derris powder at the rate of 2 ounces to 5 gallons of fungicide or to use DDT.

Dust Strawberries with Flowers of Sulphur. If you had any trouble last season with mildew on strawberries, now is the time to take preventive measures this year by dusting the leaves thoroughly with flowers of sulphur or with dinocap. You can either place the sulphur or dinocap in a small muslin bag, hold this over the plants and hit it with a stick, or else purchase a small powder blower from any dealer in horticultural sundries. This latter is a very handy implement to have about the place, for it can also be used to apply any of the dry powder insecticides and fungicides that have become so popular, particularly for use in greenhouses.

THIRD WEEK

Clear Beds for Summer Bedding. Next week it will be time to make a start at planting the summer bedding subjects and so some time this week you must clear the beds of their spring occupants. Lift daffodils,

HEELING IN TULIPS
The plants have been removed from the flower garden to make room for summer bedding, and are being planted temporarily in an out-of-the-way border so that the bulbs may complete their growth and ripen properly.

I

hyacinths, and tulips as carefully as possible and with all the roots that you can get and heel them in temporarily in any out of the way, but preferably sunny, place. Heeling in simply means making a trench about 6 inches deep, laying the bulbs in this with their leaves exposed to sun and air and covering the roots and bulbs with soil which should be made moderately firm. It is useless to take the bulbs up and dry them straight away, for they have not yet finished their growth and would be too weak to do any good another year, but if heeled in as described, some, at least, will give flowers next season.

Remove Side Shoots from Sweet Peas. Early sweet peas that are being grown on the single stem (cordon) system will need regular attention from now on in the way of removal of all side shoots and tendrils. Be

REMOVING SIDE SHOOTS FROM A SWEET PEA

The tendrils should also be nipped back, as indicated by the black line, so that the whole strength of the plant is concentrated on a single stem. This method of training is not necessary for garden display, but only when big flowers are required.

careful not to pinch out flowering stems by mistake; it is quite easy to tell these, as the flower buds are evident even at an early stage.

The later peas will be in need of staking and tying in (see April, Third Week).

Stop Chrysanthemums. If early-flowering chrysanthemums required for specimen blooms and planted out last week are not showing a break bud—that is to say, a flower bud—at the extremity of the central growth, stop them now by pinching out the tip and first pair of leaves. Note well that this instruction applies only to plants that are being grown for large specimen blooms. If your object is to have a big number of comparatively small flowers, two stoppings are necessary, one in April (see April, General Work) and the other in June (see June, General Work).

Indoor exhibition varieties and incurves grown for natural breaks should be stopped now if they have failed to break. These include such varieties as Albert Barnes, Albert Shoesmith, Harold Habgood, and Piccadilly, also Monica Winterton if it had a mid-March stop, in the exhibition section and Pink Cloud and Yellow Marvel in the incurved section, if they had a first stop in March.

THE NATURAL DEVELOPMENT OF A CHRYSANTHEMUM

This plant has been left to grow naturally, producing a break bud and first and second crown buds.

Pot Late-flowering Chrysanthemums. It should now be possible to get most of the late-flowering chrysanthemums, including Japanese exhibition varieties, incurves, decoratives, and singles, into their final flowering pots. Exception, of course, must be made for late cuttings, some of which may as yet be barely rooted. Flowering pots for the early-rooted cuttings should be 8 or 9 inches in diameter according to the strength of the plants, while for late March cuttings, 6-inch pots should prove adequate. Use a good coarse compost with about three parts of fibrous loam, pulled apart by hand and not sifted, one part of dried cow manure, one part of coarse sand, and a 7-inch pot full of bone-meal added to each barrowload of compost. This soil must be made quite firm round the plants, and it is advisable to use a wooden rammer to force it down round the sides of the pots. After potting, remove the plants to a sheltered place in the open.

Pot Begonias, Gloxinias, etc. Begonias, gloxinias, and streptocarpuses from an early sowing (see January, Third Week) should be ready for removal to their flowering pots. Do not be in a hurry, however, if roots are not showing freely around the sides of the present balls of soil. Overpotting does no good—but then neither does overcrowding. The flowering pots should be 5 or 6 inches in diameter. Use the same soil mixture as before (see April, Second Week). Water freely, place in the greenhouse, and shade from direct sunshine.

POTTING LATE-FLOWERING
CHRYSANTHEMUMS
Right; A correctly crocked pot.
Left; This illustrates the ideal
position for the plant in the pot,
allowing space for top dressing
later.

Sow Runner Beans Outdoors. It is now time to make a good sowing of runner beans in the open. Sow the seeds individually or in pairs about 8 inches apart in two lines 10 inches apart. If you require more than one double row, have an alleyway of at least 8 feet wide between each set. Cover the seeds with 2 inches of soil. If you sow the seeds in pairs and they all germinate you will need to single the seedlings out later on.

Plant out Celeriac. Celeriac raised from seed in March (see March, Fourth Week) may now be planted outdoors. Choose an open position and reasonably rich soil and plant 15 inches apart in rows 18 inches apart.

Plant Melons and Cucumbers in Frames. Melons raised in the greenhouse last month (see April, Third Week) may be planted in frames. Prepare a compost as described for cucumbers (see March, First Week) and allow one plant for each full-sized garden light (6 feet by 4 feet). Plant on a small mound of compost in the centre of the space covered by the light. Pinch out the point of each plant when it has made about five leaves.

Cucumbers raised from seed last month (see April, Third Week) for cultivation in unheated frames may also be planted in exactly the same way as melons (see above). Subsequent training is the same as for cucumbers in frames on hotbeds (see April, General Work).

Spray Raspberries, Loganberries, etc. Raspberries and loganberries, and also to a smaller extent blackberries, sometimes suffer severely from a disease known as cane spot. Purplish patches of decayed tissue appear on the canes, gradually encircling them and cutting off the supply of sap. If you have had any of this trouble in former years, spray now with lime sulphur wash at twice the ordinary summer strength or with thiram.

Start to Pick Green Gooseberries. It is usually possible to get a first picking of green gooseberries at about this time. The fruits will still be very small and immature and it would be foolish to strip the branches as yet, but if you remove a few here and there where they are overcrowded it will give the remainder a chance to develop more fully and will give you the opportunity of enjoying an early gooseberry pie. This thinning can be repeated from time to time as the fruits increase in size until eventually they are spaced out evenly two or three inches apart for ripening.

FOURTH WEEK

Plant out Bedding Plants and Half-hardy Annuals. If the weather appears reasonably settled and you have followed out instructions regarding hardening off, now is the time to plant out the majority of bedding plants and half-hardy annuals. As I mentioned in the General Notes for this

REMOVING PLANTS FROM BOXES
It is important to keep as much soil as possible around the roots when removing plants from boxes.

month, I make exception for dahlias, heliotropes, scarlet salvias, and cannas, all of which are very susceptible to the cold and are better kept where they can be protected easily until the first week in June. Plant with a trowel, giving roots plenty of room and firming the soil thoroughly round them. Water in liberally if the soil is dry.

Plant Window Boxes, Hanging Baskets, etc. This is also the time to fill window boxes, hanging baskets, and ornamental vases with their summer occupants. To hang over the edge you can have ivy-leaved pelargoniums, *Lobelia tenuior, Campanula isophylla, Lysimachia Nummularia aurea,* and *Asparagus Sprengeri,* while good plants of erect habit for this purpose are zonal pelargoniums, marguerites, fuchsias, petunias, and bedding calceolarias. Give the plants a thorough watering after planting. The hanging baskets must be well lined with sphagnum moss to prevent the soil from washing through.

PLANTING OUT SUMMER BEDDING PLANTS
Make a hole of ample width with a trowel and be certain to make the soil really firm around the roots.

Plant out Chrysanthemums for Lifting. It is possible to grow many of the late decorative chrysanthemums without keeping them in big pots all the summer. Plants from 4- or 5-inch pots are planted outdoors now exactly like the early border varieties (see Second Week) and are allowed to grow on in the open ground until September or early October, when they are lifted, carried into the greenhouse, and either placed in big boxes or planted in beds of soil. One great advantage of this method is that plants do not need constant watering during the summer.

Start Last Batch of Achimenes. A last batch of achimenes (see February, First Week), started now, will carry the display of flowers well on into the autumn.

Prick off Primulas. Greenhouse primulas sown in April (see April, Fourth Week) will need to be pricked off in other boxes or seed pans by this time. Use the same compost as for seed sowing and space the seedlings about 1½ inch apart each way. Water them in well and then place them in a sheltered frame. The plants will be better in frames for the rest of the summer. Ventilate rather sparingly at first, but freely once the seedlings take hold of their new soil.

Sow Vegetable Marrows and Ridge Cucumbers Outdoors. Vegetable marrows and ridge cucumbers can now be sown outdoors where the plants are to grow. Sow the seeds singly or in pairs about 3 feet apart, cover them with 1 inch of soil, and then invert flower pots over them as an additional protection. It is common practice to prepare vegetable marrow beds by building up a mound of turves, but in view of the fact that the plants can do with any amount of moisture, it is really much better to dig out a large hole and fill this with the chopped turves, or, better still, a mixture of turfy loam and manure. It is then a comparatively simple matter to flood the bed from time to time with water. Ridge cucumbers are better on low mounds of turf and dung, for they need all the sun they can get to make them grow rapidly. Still, do not build up the mounds too steeply or watering will be a problem.

Plant out French Beans. If you were able to raise some french beans in boxes last month (see April, Second Week), and have hardened the plants carefully in a frame, you may now plant them out with safety. Choose a

PROTECTION FOR
SEEDLING FRENCH
BEANS
The plants are liable to be injured by frosts, so if nights are cold it is advisable to give some protection, as shown.

reasonably sheltered place and be ready to cover the plants at night with some sheets of brown paper should the weather turn suddenly frosty. Plant the beans 1 foot apart in rows 2 feet apart.

Spray Apples against Scab, Sawfly, etc. By this time the blossom will probably be falling freely from all save the latest-flowering apples. About ten days after it can first be shaken from the topmost branches is the ideal time to give yet one more spraying with lime sulphur wash, sulphur, or captan as a protection against scab disease (see April, Second Week, and May, First Week). Where lime sulphur is used, it should be applied at a weaker strength than before, otherwise there is danger of scorching the leaves, particularly on the sensitive varieties, such as Cox's Orange Pippin. You should consult manufacturer's instructions on this point, for different brands may vary in strength. If in former years maggots have been found in the young apple fruits during June and many of these fruits have fallen off in consequence the trees should be sprayed with nicotine or DDT insecticide now. The insecticide can be mixed with the fungicide used against apple scab if desired.

Thin out Raspberry Canes. Look over the raspberry plantation and reduce the number of new canes if these are very numerous. There is no point in having more than six canes per plant, and these should be quite close to the clump for preference. Raspberries have a habit of sending up suckers all over the bed, and unless you remove them from the alleyways it may be almost impossible to get between the canes to pick fruit later on.

FLOWERS, VEGETABLES, AND FRUITS IN SEASON
DURING MAY

Hardy Herbaceous Plants. *Adonis autumnalis, Anchusa officinalis, Aquilegia chrysantha, A. longissima, A. Skinneri, A. vulgaris* vars., aquilegias (long-spurred hybrids), *Aster subcaeruleus, Baptisia australis, Barbarea vulgaris plena, Bellis perennis* vars. (daisy), *Brunnera macrophylla, Centaurea montana, Cheiranthus Allionii, C. Cheiri* (wallflower), *Dicentra eximia, D. spectabilis, Doronicum plantagineum, Eremurus Elwesii, E. robustus, E. himalaicus, Euphorbia Cyparissias* (spurge), *E. pilosa major, Galax aphylla, Geranium armenum, G. Endressi, G. nepalense, Geum bulgaricum, G. coccineum* hybrids, *Heuchera tiarelloides, Incarvillea grandiflora, Iris florentina, I. germanica* vars. (Flag, German iris), *I. longipetala* and vars., *I. susiana, Lupinus polyphyllus* hybrids (lupins), *Meconopsis cambrica* and vars., *Mertensia virginica, M. laevigata, M. paniculata subcordata,* Myosotis hybrids (forget-me-nots), *Nepeta Mussinii, Paeonia albiflora* and vars. (Chinese peony), *P. officinalis* and vars. (peony), *P. tenuifolia* and vars., *P. Wittmanniana, Papaver orientale* and vars. (Oriental poppy), *Phlox divaricata* vars., *Polygonatum multiflorum* (Solomon's Seal), Pyrethrum hybrids, *Ranunculus aconitifolius plenus, Saxifraga umbrosa* (London Pride), *Smilacina racemosa, Trollius europaeus* and vars., *Verbascum Thapsus, Veronica gentianoides,* violas (bedding), *Viola tricolor* (pansy).

Hardy Bulbs and Tubers. *Allium albopilosum, A. caeruleum, A. giganteum, A. karataviense, A. Moly, A. neapolitanum, A. Ostrowskianum, A. Rosenbachianum, Anemone coronaria* and vars., *Calochortus albus, C. amabilis, C. Benthamii, C. clavatus, C. Kennedyi, C. lilacinus, C. Maweanus, C. venustus, C. Weedii, Camassia Cusickii, C. esculenta, C. Leichtlinii, C. Quamash, Convallaria majalis* (lily of the valley), *Cyclamen repandum, Endymion nonscriptus* and vars. (bluebell), *Erythronium americanum, E. californicum, E. Dens-canis, E. grandiflorum* and vars., *E. Hartwegii, E. Hendersonii, E. revolutum, Fritillaria camschatcensis, F. imperialis* and vars., *F. meleagris* vars., hyacinths (large-flowered hybrids), *Iris cristata, I. Hoogiana, I. Korolkowii, I. Lortetii, I. Sisyrinchium, I. stolonifera, I. tingitana, Ixiolirion montanum* and vars., *Leucojum aestivum, L. pulchellum, Muscari comosum monstrosum, M.* Heavenly Blue, *Narcissus Jonquilla* vars., *N. poeticus recurvus* and Double White, *Romulea rosea, Scilla amoena, S. hispanica* and vars. (Spanish bluebell),

Trillium erectum, T. grandiflorum, T. ovatum, T. recurvatum, T. sessile and vars., *T. stylosum, Tulipa Batalinii, T. Gesneriana, T. persica, T. saxatilis, T. Sprengeri, T. tubergeniana,* tulips (Cottage, Darwin, Rembrandt, and Parrot).

NARCISSUS POETICUS
There are many forms and varieties of the pheasant's eye or poet's narcissus. The white-petalled flowers are borne singly, and the short corona has a red edge.

Rock Plants. *Achillea tomentosum, Aethionema coridifolium, Ae. grandiflorum, Ae. pulchellum, Ae.* Warley Rose, *Alyssum saxatile* and vars., *A. spinosum, Androsace lactea, A. primuloides, A. sarmentosa* and vars., *A. sempervivoides, Anemone sylvestris* and vars., *Antennaria dioica* and vars., *Aquilegia caerulea, A. glandulosa, A. jucunda, Arabis albida* and vars., *A. alpina, A. aubrietioides, Arctostaphylos Uva-ursi, Arenaria balearica, A. laricifolia, A. montana, A. purpurascens, Armeria caespitosa, A. maritima* and vars., *Asperula hirta, Aster alpinus* and vars., *A. Forrestii, Astilbe simplicifolia, Astragalus tragacanthus, Aubrieta deltoidea* and vars., *Bellis rotundifolia caerulescens, B. sylvestris, B. bellidioides, Calceolaria polyrrhiza, Campanula alpestris, C. Aucheri, C. garganica* and vars., *C. Poscharskyana, Cheiranthus alpinus, Codonopsis ovata, Cornus canadensis, Cortusa Matthiolii, Corydalis cheilanthifolia, C. nobilis, C. tuberosa, Cotyledon Purpusii, C. simplicifolia, Cypripedium Calceolus, Delphinium nudicaule, Daphne Cneorum, D. retusa, Dianthus caesius, Eomecon chionantha, Epigaea repens,* epimediums (as April), *Erinacea pungens, Erinus alpinus* and vars., *Erodium chamaedryoides, E. corsicum, Gentiana acaulis, G. verna, Geranium argenteum, G. cinereum, G. Pylzowianum, Geum Borisii, G. montanum, Globularia incanescens, G. vulgaris, Haberlea Ferdinandi-Coburgii, H. rhodopensis, Helianthemum alyssoides, H. lunulatum, H. Tuberaria, H. vulgare* in var. (sun rose), *Houstonia caerulea, H. serpyllifolia, Hutchinsia alpina, Iberis correaefolia, I. gibraltarica, I. saxatilis, I. sempervirens, Iris Chamaeiris, I. flavissima, I. gracilipes, I. graminea, I. verna, Isopyrum thalictroides, Leucocrinum montanum, Linaria alpina, L. hepaticaefolia, L.*

pallida, Linnaea borealis, Linum arboreum, L. monogynum, Lithospermum prostratum and vars., *Lychnis alpina, L. Lagascae, Mazus Pumilio, M. reptans, Morisia hypogaea, Myosotis rupicola, Oenothera caespitosa, Omphalodes Luciliae, O. verna, Orobus vernus, Oxalis adenophylla, O. corniculata, O. enneaphylla, Penstemon Menziesii, P. Scouleri, Phlox divaricata Laphamii, P. Douglasii, P. subulata* and vars., *Potentilla ambigua, P. aurea, P. fragiformis, P. nitida, Primula Auricula* and vars., *P. capitata, P. chrysopa, P. farinosa, P. frondosa, P. Juliae, P. Mooreana, P. nutans, P. pubescens, P. Sieboldii, P. Veitchii, Ramonda pyrenaica* and vars., *R. serbica, Ranunculus alpestris, R. gramineus, Saponaria ocymoides, Saxifraga Aizoon* and vars., *S. Andrewsii, S. cochlearis, S. Cotyledon* and vars., *S. decipiens* vars. (mossy saxifrages), *S. hypnoides* vars. (mossy saxifrages), *S. granulata plena, S. ligulata* and vars., *S. longifolia Schizocodon soldanelloides, Sedum pilosum, Shortia uniflora, Silene acaulis*

RAMONDA PYRENAICA
(ROSETTE MULLEIN)

This interesting dwarf plant for the rock garden has deep lavender flowers on 4-inch stems in early summer. It prefers north-facing vertical crevices between rocks, and a soil containing plenty of humus.

Sisyrinchium angustifolium, S. Bermudiana, S. filifolium, S. striatum, Stachys corsica, Tanakaea radicans, Tiarella cordifolia, Trollius pumilus, Veronica catarractae, V. canescens, V. filiformis, V. fruticans, V, pectinata, V. rupestris, Viola biflora, V. bosniaca, V. calcarata, V. canadensis, V. cornuta and vars., *V. cucullata, V. gracilis* and vars., *V. hederacea, Wahlenbergia graminifolia, W. Pumilio, W. serpyllifolia.*

Hardy Aquatics and Bog Plants. *Caltha leptosepala, C. palustris* and vars., *C. polypetala, Cardamine pratensis plena, Dodecatheon Hendersonii, D. Meadia, D. radicatum, Geum rivale, Hottonia palustris, Iris laevigata, I. ochroleuca, I. Pseudacorus, Mimulus cupreus, M. luteus* and hybrids, *Myosotis palustris, Orchis latifolia, O. maculata, O. palustris, Primula Beesiana, P. Bulleyana, P. chionantha, P. Cockburniana, P. helodoxa, P. japonica, P. littoniana, P. microdonta* and vars., *P. pulverulenta* and vars., *P. rosea, P. secundiflora,*

P. sikkimensis, P. vittata, Ranunculus aquatilis, Villarsia (Limnanthemum) nymphaeoides.

Annuals. Hardy vars., sown September (see list, September, First Week).

Bedding Plants. *Cheiranthus Allionii,* double daisies, forget-me-nots, wallflowers.

Evergreen Shrubs. *Andromeda polifolia, Berberis Darwinii, B. empetrifolia, B. Gagnepainii, B. hakeoides, B. replicata, B. stenophylla, B. verruculosa, Buddleia globosa, Ceanothus dentatus, C. rigidus, C. thyrsiflorus, C. Veitchianus, Choisya ternata, Cotoneaster Franchetii, Erica cinerea* vars., *E. lusitanica, E. mediterranea, Fabiana imbricata, Gaultheria Shallon, Jasminum Giraldii, Kalmia glauca, Ledum latifolium, L. palustre, Leiophyllum buxifolium, Leucothoe Catesbaei, Mahonia aquifolium, Olearia Gunniana, O. nitida, Osmarea Burkwoodii, Photinia serrulata, Pieris Forrestii, P. formosa, Pyracantha coccinea* and vars., *P. Gibbsii, P. Rogersiana, Rhododendron argyrophyllum, R. calostrotum, R. cantabile, R. catawbiense, R. charitopes, R. chryseum,*

CHOISYA TERNATA (MEXICAN ORANGE)

This beautiful hardy, evergreen shrub produces its flowers in May and often flowers again in the autumn. It grows well on chalky soils and requires little pruning. It attains a height of 6 feet.

R. cinnabarinum, R. Falconeri, R. fastigiatum, R. Fortunei hybrids, *R. glaucum R. Griffithianum* hybrids, *R. haematodes, R. impeditum, R. intricatum, R. Keysii, R. lapponicum, R. Loderi, R. orbiculare, R. ponticum* hybrids, *R. racemosum, R. rubiginosum, R. repens, R. Sargentianum, R. sinogrande* (shelter), *R. Soulei, R. Smirnowii, R. vernicosum, R. Wardii,* also many fine hybrid rhododendrons, *Rosmarinus officinalis, Ulex europaeus plenus, Veronica Hulkeana, Viburnum Burkwoodii, V. rhytidophyllum, V. utile, Vinca major, V. minor, Yucca Whipplei.*

Hardy Deciduous Shrubs. *Aegle sepiaria, Amelanchier florida, Calycanthus floridus, Caragana arborescens, C. pygmaea, Ceratostigma Willmottianum, Colletia infausta, Cornus florida, C. Kousa, C. Nuttallii, Coronilla emeroides, C. Emerus, Cotoneaster multiflorus, Cytisus albus, C. Ardoinii, C. Beanii, C.*

Dallimorei, *C. decumbens*, *C. kewensis*, *C. praecox*, *C. purgans*, *C. purpureus*, *C. ratisbonensis*, *C. scoparius* and vars. (common broom), *C. versicolor*, *Deutzia gracilis*, *D. Wilsonii*, *Diervilla florida* and vars., *Dipelta floribunda* *Enkianthus campanulatus*, *Exochorda Giraldii*, *E. grandiflora*, *E. macrantha*, *Fothergilla major*, *Fremontia californica* (shelter), *Genista hispanica*, *G. pilosa*, *Halesia carolina*, *Jamesia americana*, *Kerria japonica*, *Kolkwitzia amabilis*, *Lonicera Maackii*, *L. syringantha*, *Magnolia obovata*, *M. Watsonii*, *M. Wilsonii*, *Neillia longiracemosa*, *Paeonia Moutan* and vars. (tree peony), *Piptanthus concolor*, *Pyrus arbutifolia*, *Rhodotypos kerrioides*, *Ribes aureum*, *R. sanguineum* and vars., *R. speciosum*, *Robinia hispida*, *Rosa Banksiae*, *R. Fargesii*, *R. Hugonis*, *R. sericea*, *R. spinosissima*, *Rubus deliciosus*, *Spiraea arguta*, *S. Van Houttei*, *Syringa chinensis*, *S. persica*, *S. vulgaris* in var. (lilac), *Tamarix tetrandra*, *Vaccinium corymbosum*, *Viburnum Carlesii*, *V. macrocephalum*, *V. tomentosum* and vars., *Xanthoceras sorbifolia*.

Evergreen Trees. *Arbutus Andrachne*, *A. hybrida*, *A. Menziesii*.

CLIANTHUS DAMPIERI
(PARROT'S BILL)
The clianthuses are greenhouse climbers with strikingly handsome flowers. This has scarlet flowers shaped like a lobster's claw, and fern-like foliage. It reaches 6 feet in height.

Deciduous Trees. *Acer Ginnala*, *Aesculus Hippocastanum* (horse chestnut) *Ae. indica*, *Ae. octandra*, *Ae. plantierensis*, *Amelanchier alnifolia*, *A. canadensis*, *A. vulgaris*, *Cercis Siliquastrum*, *Crataego-mespilus grandiflora*, *Crataegus coccinea*, *C. Crus-galli*, *C. monogyna* and vars. (hawthorn), *C. oxyacantha* and vars. (hawthorn), *Cydonia vulgaris*, *Laburnum Adamii*, *L. vulgare*, *Magnolia conspicua*, *M. Fraseri*, *M. Lennei*, *M. parviflora*, *M. Sargentiana*, *M. Soulangiana*, *M. tripetala*, *Meliosma Beaniana*, *Mespilus germanica* (medlar), *Paulownia imperialis*, *Prunus Avium* (gean), *P. Lannesiana* vars. (Japanese cherries), *P. Mahaleb pendula*, *P. Padus* (bird cherry), *P. serrulata* vars. (Japanese cherries), *P. Sieboldii*, *P. virginiana*, *Pyrus aldenhamensis*, *P. arnoldiana*, *P. Aria* (whitebeam), *P. Aucuparia* (mountain ash), *P. communis* (pear), *P. Conradiniae*, *P. coronaria*, *P. Eleyi*, *P. floribunda*, *P. Halliana*, *P. kansuensis*, *P. Lemoinei*, *P. Malus* vars. (apple), *P. Niedzwetzkyana*, *P. Sargentii*, *P.*

Scheideckeri, P. Sorbus, P. spectabilis, P. toringoides, P. Wilsoniana, P. yun-nanensis, Robinia Pseudoacacia (false acacia), *Staphylea colchica, Symplocos paniculata, Viburnum Lantana* (wayfaring tree), *V. Lentago.*

Hardy Climbing Plants. *Akebia quinata, Actinidia callosa, A. coriacea, Aristolochia Sipho, Clematis alpina, C. montana* and vars., *C. patens* and vars., *Schizandra chinensis, Trachelospermum divaricatum, Wisteria chinensis, W. multijuga, W. venusta.*

Greenhouse Plants. Abutilons, astilbes, beaufortias, begonias (tuberous-rooted), boronias, bougainvilleas, calceolarias (herbaceous), *Callistemon speciosus, Cantua dependens,* carnations (perpetual-flowering), chorizema, cinerarias (hybrids), *Clianthus dampieri,* clivia, correas, *Coronilla glauca, Dillwynia floribunda, Diplacus glutinosus, Epacris longiflora, Erica Cavendishi-ana, E. Spenceriana,* eriostemons, fuchsias, gloxinias, heliotrope, hippeastrums, *Hydrangea hortensis* and var., kennedyas, lantanas, *Lilium longiflorum, L. regale,* marguerites, pelargoniums (show, regal, zonal, and ivy-leaved), petunias, roses, schizanthus and annuals (as April), stephanotis.

Vegetables in Store. Jerusalem artichokes, carrots, onions, parsnips, potatoes, turnips.

Vegetables in Garden. Asparagus, broccoli (late), cabbage (sown July and August), leeks, lettuces (sown under glass Feb.), spring onions, mustard and cress, radishes, rhubarb, seakale, spinach (sown March).

Vegetables under Glass. French beans, carrots, cucumbers, lettuces, mush-rooms, mustard and cress, potatoes, radishes.

Fruits in Store. *Apples:* Allen's Everlasting (D), Annie Elizabeth (C), Cornish Gillyflower (D), D'Arcy Spice (D), Encore (C), May Queen (D), Newton Wonder (C), Ontario (CD), Sandling (D), Sanspareil (CD), Stark (D), Sturmer Pippin (D). *Grapes:* Mrs Pince, Prince of Wales.

Fruits Outdoors. *Gooseberries* (green).

Fruits under Glass. *Strawberries.*

June

GENERAL WORK

Spray against Pests. Greenfly is likely to become more of a nuisance this month unless you take appropriate measures to destroy it at the first sign of attack (see May, General Work). Caterpillars may also put in an appearance now. Usually they can be poisoned before they have done much damage by spraying with derris, which fortunately, is not poisonous either to human beings or to domestic animals. Use 2 ounces of derris powder and 4 ounces of soft soap to 5 gallons of water, or else purchase one of the proprietary derris insecticides and mix it according to manufacturer's instructions. Continue to use metaldehyde and bran against slugs (see May, General Work).

An alternative is to use DDT, which is a more powerful caterpillar killer than derris and one which retains its effect on plants for a longer period.

Red spider can become a nuisance on fruit trees at this time of year, infecting the under sides of the leaves and causing them to turn a mottled greyish-gold colour. If this occurs spray at once with derris and repeat after ten days or a fortnight. Alternatively use one of the modern controls containing malathion, according to manufacturer's instructions.

Trim Hedges. You can trim evergreen hedges lightly at any time during the month. If you grow *Berberis Darwinii* as a hedge, the best time to trim it is immediately the flowers fade. Cut the flowering shoots back sufficiently to give the hedge a neat appearance.

Continue to Feed Plants in Full Growth. Herbaceous plants and vegetables that are growing freely will be all the better for one or two more applications of a quick-acting fertilizer and some soakings with weak liquid manure (see May, General Work).

Remove Runners from Violets and Strawberries. If left to their own devices, violets will make innumerable runners during the summer and early autumn. You should remove these, cutting them off close to the main clump.

142

Similar remarks apply to the runners produced by strawberries, unless you require some for propagation (see July, First Week).

A VIOLET CLUMP THROWING OUT RUNNERS

These long thin shoots, growing out in all directions from the centre of the plant, must be removed, or they will take strength from the flowering crowns.

Disbud Roses for Exhibition. Hybrid tea, tea, and pernetiana roses will be forming their flower buds freely throughout the month, and if you want some big blooms for exhibition or cutting you must disbud them from time to time. This simply means that out of each cluster of buds only the big terminal one must be retained, all the side buds being nipped out at as early a stage as possible.

DISBUDDING A ROSE

If specially fine blooms are required, only the terminal bud on each stem should be retained, all the smaller side buds, as shown in the above sketch, being removed at an early stage of development.

Stake and Disbud Border Carnations. Border carnations will be forming their flower stems and these must be staked as necessary. Beginners often go wrong over this. The natural habit of the border carnation is to arch its flower slightly and not hold it stiffly erect. This you must allow it to do, and any ties you make must be sufficiently low down the stem not to interfere with its natural arching habit. If you make ties all the way up to the bud, rain will collect in the expanding flower and spoil the petals and hot sun will complete the damage.

Another important task if you want to have really fine blooms is to remove the side shoots that form on the flower stems and to remove all flower buds except the terminal one on each stem, exactly as advised before for roses.

Pot on Perpetual-flowering Carnations and Chrysanthemums. If you did not pot on all the young stock of perpetual-flowering carnations last month (see May, General Work) you should certainly complete the work before the end of June. Deal with the most forward plants first and gradually work through the whole batch. Continue to stop first laterals a few at a time as they make their eighth joint.

Backward or late-struck chrysanthemums should also be dealt with at the earliest opportunity (see May, Third Week). Very late cuttings of special varieties grown for forming dwarf specimens in 5- or 6-inch pots (see April, Fourth Week) must be placed in their flowering pots as soon as they have filled their first 3-inch pots with roots.

Stop Early-flowering and Decorative Chrysanthemums. If you are growing some early-flowering chrysanthemums with the object of getting a large number of comparatively small flowers (see April, General Work, and also May, Third Week), the plants will require a second stopping some time during this month. The ideal time is when the most forward side shoots caused by the first stopping are a foot in length; but stopping must be completed by the end of the month. Precisely similar remarks apply to the late-flowering decoratives and singles, except that these are almost always better for two stoppings, whether the object in view is to get a lot of medium-size blooms or only a few big ones. If the latter is your aim, then you must reduce the number of side shoots that grow after the stopping, keeping only from six to a dozen per plant according to its strength.

General Greenhouse Management. As the weather gets warmer ventilation must become even more free. Keep a sharp watch on the thermometer at the beginning of the month, however, and be ready to close the ventilators quite early if it shows a tendency to drop rapidly, for early June nights can be very treacherous. The night average at this time of the year for the majority of popular greenhouse plants should be 60°. Keep the top ventilators open a little at night when the weather is mild and ventilate really freely by day as soon as the thermometer registers 65°. Side ventilators and doors can be opened wide on hot, sunny days.

Plants that are still making growth or are producing flowers must be watered with increasing freedom as the days become hotter, but some

Above: Firming aquatics after planting them at the bottom of a pool. *Above, right:* When planting out early-flowering chrysanthemums firm them well and label the varieties clearly.

Right: Removing the old flowering stems of a forsythia.

The left hand is used to keep the remaining onions firm while thinning.

Planting celery, with a trowel, in a trench in which plenty of compost or farmyard manure has been incorporated.

greenhouse plants will be going to rest (see p. 115). It is advisable to examine pot plants daily during the summer. Watering is best done in the morning.

Earth up Potatoes. The earthing up of all March and April planted potatoes must be completed during this month. This is not a task to be finished at one operation. Better results are obtained by drawing the soil up round the potato stems a little at a time. Go over them about three times in all, eventually leaving the bed in a series of broad flat-topped ridges.

Continue to Blanch Leeks. The process of blanching leeks planted in trenches must be carried on during the month. As the plants lengthen gradually draw up the brown paper collars placed in position last month (see May, First Week), and draw more soil up around them. It is quite a good plan to place a board on edge down each side of the row and about 9 inches apart, and to fill the space between with dry soil instead of drawing up soil in a ridge.

Make Successional Sowings. Successional sowings are almost precisely the same as those for last month (see May, General Work). Lettuces, endive, radishes, mustard and cress, turnips, should still be sown at intervals. It is too late to sow maincrop peas, but it is not a bad plan to make a sowing at the beginning of the month of an early variety. Choose a fully open place for this last crop, for late peas in the shade are certain to be ruined by mildew. All the salad vegetables, and also turnips, will be better in a rather shady place.

Plant Winter Greens. Throughout June you should miss no opportunity of planting out all manner of winter greens, including brussels sprouts,

A BLIND CAULIFLOWER PLANT
All winter greens are liable to go 'blind,' losing their growing points. Such plants are useless.

broccoli, kale, and savoy. Usually these should be planted about 2 feet apart in rows 2½ feet apart, but, as different varieties grow to varying sizes, you should consult the seedsman's notes on the seed packet regard-

K

ing this. Make the soil really firm around the roots; none of the cabbage family does well in loose soil, and for this reason the beds should be well trodden before planting. Then after planting, run a hoe through the surface to leave a dust mulch.

Lift Autumn-sown Onions as Required. During June the bulbs of autumn-sown onions (see August, Fourth Week) will have attained sufficient size to be used. Do not lift the whole crop yet, however, for the bulbs will not be properly ripened. Simply dig up a few onions at a time as you require them.

Stake Culinary Peas. Peas sown last month must be staked in the same way as the earlier batches (see May, General Work).

Feed and Fumigate Tomatoes under Glass. The earliest tomatoes (see January, Second Week) will be ripening freely, while even the latest batches planted last month (see May, Second Week) will be setting fruits

TRAINING TOMATOES
IN A LEAN-TO HOUSE
*The back wall plants are
shown planted in a bed,
but they could equally
well be grown in pots.*

during the month. All must be watered freely—they will need supplies every day when the weather is warm—and should be fed regularly as I described in my notes for last month (see May, General Work). Plants in flower should be pollinated, as explained in the same place; while training, stopping at the apex of the house, and the removal of all side shoots must proceed as before. A top dressing of well-rotted manure will help the later plants.

White fly may become a nuisance now. If it does, fumigate at once with DDT or lindane smokes, putting the pellets or canister on the path in the evening, setting light to them, and then keeping the house closely shut up until the morning. Repeat twice, at intervals of fourteen days, to catch the adult flies as they emerge from the scales which are unaffected by the fumigant.

Ventilate very freely, keeping the top ventilators partly open during mild nights, and opening doors as well as side ventilators on very warm days. Cut back some of the lower leaves on early plants to expose the fruits to the light and so hasten ripening.

Train and Feed Melons. Melons in the heated greenhouse should be swelling well by now and you must sling the fruits up in special melon nets to take their weight off the stems. Gradually reduce the amount of atmospheric moisture and give increased ventilation, but without reducing the average day temperature of 70°. This will assist ripening.

Melons in frames (see May, Third Week) will be making side shoots as a result of having their points pinched out. Retain four per plant and train them to the four corners of the bed, pegging them down to its surface. Pinch out their points when they reach the limits of the bed. Sublaterals will be formed. Fertilize about half a dozen female flowers all at one time (see April, General Work). Keep the plants well watered and top dress the bed with an inch of well-rotted manure as soon as white rootlets appear on the surface.

Train, Feed and Renovate Cucumbers. Cucumbers in greenhouses and frames, both on and off hotbeds, will be in various stages of growth, and I refer you to my previous notes for details of treatment (April, General Work, and May, General Work). Some of the earliest plants in the hothouse will be getting past their prime, but they can be renovated a lot and induced to go on bearing for another month or so by cutting out old laterals that have borne fruit and training young laterals in their place. See that shading material does not get washed off the glass. Strong sunshine may do a lot of damage. Keep the atmosphere really moist by frequent syringeing and by wetting the paths.

Finish Thinning of Outdoor Peaches, Nectarines, etc. You will be able to complete the thinning of peaches, nectarines, and apricots on walls as soon as the stones are formed (see May, General Work). Continue to disbud the two first named and to pinch the laterals of apricots to encourage the formation of fruit spurs.

Management of the Orchard House. There is little to add to my remarks on this subject in May (see May, General Work). Ventilation can be very free whenever the weather is mild, and you may open side ventilators by day as well as those at the ridge. Ripening can be assisted by removing a leaf here and there to expose fruits to the sun, or propping them forward with the aid of ordinary wooden plant labels.

As soon as you have cleared the earliest trees of their fruits, recommence syringeing at least twice a day with clean water. There is no better preventive of red spider and thrips, two pests that always prove troublesome in a dry atmosphere.

Treatment of Vines. Continue to train outdoor vines and pinch out the tips of secondary laterals when they have made one leaf. This will prevent the vines from getting overcrowded with foliage. The earliest varieties will need thinning (see March, General Work).

Indoor vines will be in various stages of growth and once again I refer you to my notes in the General Work for March, April and May for particulars regarding stopping, thinning, etc. These tasks are the same for late as for early vines. You must be very careful about ventilation whatever the state of growth. The earliest vines will be approaching ripeness and must have a rather dry atmosphere. Excessive heat, however, is to be avoided. Late vines in unheated houses will require much more moisture in the atmosphere, which means that you must keep evaporating trays filled with water or thoroughly wet the paths two or three times a day. If red spider should appear, syringe the foliage with clear water once or twice daily. Otherwise do not syringe now.

Up till this month outside borders usually need little or no watering, but from now on they should be watched closely and watered freely if they show signs of getting really dry. In order to conserve moisture it is a good plan to spread a 3-inch thick mulch of strawy horse manure over the border after watering.

The earliest grapes will be ready for cutting some time during the month, and once you have done this you can syringe the rods and leaves freely several times a day.

FIRST WEEK

Plant Tender Bedding Plants. The few tender bedding plants that I advised you to omit from May planting (see May, Fourth Week) may now go outdoors into their flowering quarters. These plants include dahlias, begonias, scarlet salvias, heliotropes and cannas, also a few choice foliage plants, such as abutilons, cordylines, ricinus, *Zea Mays* and *Leucophyta (Calocephalus) Brownii*. Details for planting are exactly as for those plants put out in May.

Sow Perennials and Biennials. Most perennials and biennials, if sown out of doors now, will make good sturdy plants for placing in flowering quarters in the autumn. I make exception only with forget-me-nots and Brompton stocks, which I find are better sown rather later as they get too big if sown now, tending to flower before the winter; this is always a bad point. The most useful biennials are Canterbury bells, various verbascums and *Coreopsis grandiflora*. Perennials which are almost invariably

COVERING SEED DRILLS
This can be done very conveniently with the back of a rake drawn along the drill, as shown.

treated as biennials are wallflowers, *Cheiranthus Allionii*, foxgloves, Sweet Williams, double daisies, Iceland poppies and *Campanula pyramidalis*. These may also be sown now. Among the easiest perennials to raise from seed are aquilegias, lupins, oriental poppies, hollyhocks and delphiniums, also easy rock plants such as aubrietas, *Alyssum saxatile* and *Campanula carpatica*; but there are many other things that you can try if you can obtain the seeds. Sow thinly in drills 6 or 8 inches apart and cover with from ¼ to 1 inch of soil, according to the size of the seeds. Violas, pansies, primroses and polyanthuses may also be sown now outdoors, but it is preferable to choose a rather shady place for these.

Sow St Brigid Anemones. Anemones of the St Brigid and Du Caen types can also be raised quite readily from seed sown outdoors now and will flower next summer. Choose a sunny, sheltered position and sow the seed very thinly indeed in drills ½ inch deep and 9 inches apart. The reason that I stress the importance of thin sowing is that then no transplanting will be necessary and the plants can grow on unchecked in the seed bed until they have flowered next year.

Plunge Pot Shrubs and Roses Outdoors. From this time until the end of September, all the shrubs and roses that have been grown in pots for early flowering, and are either still in the greenhouse or have been removed to shelters and frames, will be much better in a sunny but not too scorchingly hot position outdoors. This also applies to greenhouse heaths, Indian azaleas, camellias and acacias. The ideal method is to prepare a deep bed of sifted boiler ashes or coarse sand, and to plunge the pots up to their rims in this. Watering will be considerably reduced

AN OUTDOOR PLUNGE BED

The planks, nailed on edge, serve to keep the plunging material from spreading about. Pot plants, plunged as shown, require much less watering than those that are stood in the open without any protection.

by this means and the soil in the pots will be maintained at a more even temperature. Do not on any account choose a position that is exposed to cutting draughts, as, for example, near an alleyway between buildings. Syringe daily with clear water throughout the summer to ward off attacks by red spider. This is particularly necessary with Indian azaleas.

Prick off Cinerarias. Cinerarias sown early in May must be pricked off 2 inches apart each way in seed boxes filled with the compost recommended for seed sowing. Stand in a frame and ventilate freely.

Place Chrysanthemums in Summer Quarters. Exhibition and decorative chrysanthemums grown in pots will also be better right out in the open from now onwards. If you have many of these plants I advise you to make a special standing ground for them in an out-of-the-way-place. The soil should be well covered with sharp sifted boiler ashes or gravel to give good drainage. The plants are then arranged in straight rows at least 2½ feet apart, so that you can move between them easily for watering, tying, bud staking, etc. Drive a good strong stake into the ground

SUMMER QUARTERS FOR CHRYSANTHEMUMS

The pots may be placed on boards to assist drainage and prevent worms from entering, or good drainage material such as sifted ashes, in an out-of-the-way place. Testing for watering is shown in the inset. The pots are struck sharply with a bone or a stick. If they give off a ringing sound they need water, but if there is only a dull note they are moist enough.

at each end of each row, stretch a couple of wires between the pairs of stakes and then attach each bamboo cane to the wires. This is the ideal method with exhibition chrysanthemums grown to a single stem. With big decorative plants the horizontal wires get in the way.

Stop Exhibition Chrysanthemums. Exhibition chrysanthemums to stop now are Shirley Masterpiece, and also Audrey Shoesmith, John Rowe, Keith Luxford, Oporto and Souvenir, if they had a first stop in April. Incurved varieties which should be stopped are Ivy Meredith, Lilian

Shoesmith, Onward and True Form. Onward should only be stopped if late cuttings were taken.

Thin out Vegetable Seedlings. Various vegetable seedlings from April and May sowings will still be in need of thinning (see May, General Work).

Plant Outdoor Tomatoes. Tomatoes that have been well hardened off in frames may be planted outdoors in a sunny, sheltered position. A border at the foot of a fence or wall with a southerly aspect is the best possible place for the plants, which should be 15 inches apart. If you have more than one row, space them 2½ feet apart. The soil should be in good condition, but not too richly manured, as it is wise to let tomatoes set a few fruits and then to feed regularly with any reliable tomato fertilizer.

Plant Vegetable Marrows and Ridge Cucumbers. Vegetable marrows and ridge cucumbers raised under glass and properly hardened off may be planted out on a prepared bed (see May, Fourth Week). If the weather

A BED FOR RIDGE CUCUMBERS

The low mound of soil and manure built above the normal level of the soil exposes the plants to the sun without making watering too difficult. This task is assisted by the shallow depressions in which each plant is set. The hoops support temporary night shelter until danger of frost is passed.

is cold and nights tend to be slightly frosty, keep some big flower pots at hand and invert one over each plant every evening, removing it in good time the next morning. The plants should be at least 3 feet apart each way in the beds. Pinch out the tip of each plant when it has made about six or seven leaves. Then train the laterals that form evenly around the plant to fill the bed and pinch the tip out of each as soon as it reaches the edge of the bed.

Plant Runner Beans. Runner beans that you raised in boxes under glass in April will be ready for planting out in double lines 10 inches apart, allowing 8 inches from plant to plant in the rows. If you have more than one row of beans they should be at least 8 feet apart, because when they grow up they cast a considerable amount of shade. For this same reason it is an advantage if all the rows can run north and south, as then each row does stand a chance to get some direct sunshine.

You must provide a stout stake for each plant. These stakes should be at least 8 feet long and must be thrust as firmly as possible into the ground. There are many ways of finishing the task, but none that is simpler than to cross the sticks at the top and then place other sticks horizontally in the forks so made. Bind all the sticks together where they meet and you will have a support for your beans that will stand any amount of wind.

If you cannot obtain stakes for all your runner beans you can grow some of them as bush plants by the simple process of pinching out the growing points of the shoots from time to time. Quite a good crop of beans can be obtained in this manner, though, of course, it will not be so heavy, nor will the beans be quite so fine, as those from plants grown in the more usual way on stakes.

Plant Celery. You can also plant out celery with safety and without the necessity for any protection. Details of work are the same as for the earliest crop (see May, Second Week). Get out all plants that are 3 inches in height or more. Backward seedlings and those from late sowings may wait for a few weeks yet. Water in freely.

Pinch Broad Beans. The earliest broad beans should now have set about three clusters of pods each, and it is wise to stop them growing any taller by pinching out the tip of each plant. This may prevent an attack by black fly, because this pest invariably goes for the young growing tips, and if there is no soft growth it will seek food elsewhere. Incidentally, the stopping will hasten the development of the pods.

SECOND WEEK

Repot Auriculas. If you grow auriculas in pots now is the time to repot them. Shake the old soil from the roots and make certain that these have no woolly aphis upon them. This, by the way, is the same pest that causes the white woolly patches on apples, and is often known as American blight. If it should be present wash the roots in a solution of any good petroleum emulsion insecticide or sprinkle them with nicotine powder. Then repot either in 3½- or 4-inch pots, reducing the size of the plants if necessary and using a compost of four parts of loam, one part of dried cow manure, one part of leaf-mould, and one part of mixed sand and crushed oyster shell. Pot firmly, water freely, and place in a frame or a sheltered place outdoors. You can remove offsets with roots if you wish and pot them separately.

Divide Auriculas, Polyanthuses, etc. Auriculas, polyanthuses and coloured primroses growing in the open may be lifted and carefully divided if they are particularly good selected varieties. With ordinary mixed strains, however, it is better to raise a new stock each year from seed, as the old plants tend to get weakened by attacks from greenfly, red spider, etc.

Lift Anemones in Frames. Anemones of the St Brigid and Du Caen types, grown in frames for winter and spring flowering, will have completed their growth by this time and should be lifted. Shake the tubers clear of soil and place them in trays, surrounding them with a little dry peat moss. Then stand the trays in a cool dry place. The corms will keep safely under these conditions until you wish to plant them again.

Dig Early Potatoes. The earliest potatoes planted at the end of February will probably be ready for digging. Lift one or two roots and see what kind of a crop there is. There is no point in waiting for the tubers to mature. So long as they are big enough to be used, lift them, but only as you actually require them for use. It is a great mistake to dig too many early potatoes at once for they lose quality rapidly when out of the ground.

Thin Chicory. Chicory sown last month (see May, Second Week) will require thinning. Leave the seedlings 9 inches apart.

Sow Shorthorn Carrots. Make a last sowing of shorthorn carrots outdoors (see March, Third Week). These will come in at about the same time as the maincrop carrots and will be more tender and delicately flavoured for immediate use. The maincrop is principally of value for storing for winter use.

Sow Parsley for Succession. Make a third small sowing of parsley for succession (see February, Fourth Week, and April, Third Week).

Expose Shallot Bulbs. Shallots will now be approaching their ripening period and you should draw the soil away from the bulbs a little in order to allow them to swell freely and get the full benefit of sunlight.

Start to thin Apples and Pears. You will now be able to see how many fruits have been formed on your apple and pear trees. It is no use leaving too many, or they will only get misshapen, small, and poor in

THINNING PEARS

(A) *Shows a cluster of pairs ready for final thinning and (B) the fruits have been reduced to one or two if quality is the first consideration.*

quality. Usually one per spur is enough, and two should be regarded as the maximum. If there are more than this the weakest or least satisfactory will have to be removed, and you can begin to do this now, but do not complete the work yet for there is usually a fairly heavy natural fall later in the month. Be content at the moment to thin the fruits to about four per cluster, removing any that are noticeably poor, badly shaped, or spotted. You will find a pair of pointed vine scissors most serviceable for this work.

SUMMER-PRUNING A GOOSEBERRY

The older fruiting wood is marked A. Current year's shoots, two of which are labelled B, must be shortened a few at a time, with the exception of shoots terminating branches, which are allowed to grow unchecked.

Start to Summer-Prune Gooseberries and Currants. You can save yourself a great deal of winter work, and incidentally improve the yield of your gooseberry and currant bushes by summer pruning. Start this now, but do not attempt to complete it all at once. The ideal is to spread the work over a period of about six weeks. Then the bushes will not suffer any check from sudden loss of foliage. Summer pruning, by the way, does not apply to black currants but only to the red and white kinds. It consists in cutting off the ends of all side shoots when they are 5 or 6 inches in length. Shorten them to about 3 inches.

THIRD WEEK

Prune Flowering Shrubs. Any shrubs that flowered during May or early June can be pruned now, but this is not to say that pruning is always necessary. Much depends upon the purpose for which the shrub is being grown and the amount of space that you can spare it. For example, evergreen ceanothuses must be pruned annually when grown against a wall, but there is no necessity to prune them at all if they are cultivated as bushes in the open. The method against walls is to cut back to within an inch or so of the main branches all laterals that are growing away from the wall.

Brooms may become very straggly if they are not pruned annually. You must never cut back into very hard, old wood, but it is quite safe to clip the bushes lightly now, shortening the young flowering shoots to within an inch or so of the older branches. Lilacs, rhododendrons, and azaleas need no regular pruning of a severe nature, but it is a great advantage to cut off the faded flower trusses and so prevent the formation of seed. *Clematis montana* may be cut back sufficiently to keep it within bounds. The popular *Chaenomeles speciosa* (*Cydonia japonica*) must be pruned when grown against a wall. The best method is to shorten laterals a few at a time, spreading the work over a period of several weeks.

Take Pink Pipings. Now is the time to propagate pinks by means of cuttings. Select healthy-looking, non-flowering shoots 4 or 5 inches in length and pull them out at a joint. This is known as taking a 'piping.' Insert these pipings firmly, 2 inches deep and about 4 inches apart each way, in sandy soil, preferably in a frame, but failing this in a shady border outdoors, and keep well watered. If in a frame shade from direct sunlight. They should be well rooted and ready for planting out by the end of September.

Cut back Aubrietas, etc. Aubrietas, arabis, and perennial candytufts may be cut back quite considerably as soon as they have finished flowering if you wish to prevent the plants from spreading very far. In any case, it is a good plan to remove the faded flowers before seed pods form. The work can be done very quickly with a large pair of scissors, or, where large clumps are concerned, with garden shears.

Pot Cyclamen into Flowering Pots. About this time cyclamen seedlings that were potted individually in April (see April, First Week) will be ready for their final potting into 5-inch pots. Use a similar compost to that mentioned before, but add a little well-rotted manure to it if possible. As before, be careful not to bury the corm. After potting, arrange the plants in an unheated frame and shade from sunshine for a few days. After this the plants may have more light, but should always be shaded from very hot sunshine and must be ventilated freely, indeed the lights may be removed altogether most of the time and only replaced when the weather is stormy or cold.

Sow Cinerarias and Primulas for Succession. To provide a succession of flowers after those from the May sowing (see May, First Week) you should now make a second sowing of cinerarias. The seeds are treated in exactly the same way as before, except that now no artificial heat will be needed to effect germination. You can even place the seed pans in a frame if you are short of space in the greenhouse.

It is also an excellent plan to make a second sowing of *P. sinensis* and its variety *stellata* to flower after the earliest plants (see April, Fourth Week). *P. malacoides* may be sown now for the first time. It grows more rapidly than the others, and there is nothing to be gained by sowing earlier.

Sow Greenhouse Calceolarias. Sow the large hybrid greenhouse calceolarias now. Seed should be sown in well-drained seed boxes and given the lightest possible covering of fine sand, for it is very small. Cover the boxes with brown paper and place the seeds in a frame to germinate. This is better than a greenhouse as it can be ventilated more freely. There is nothing more likely to harm greenhouse calceolarias than excessive heat.

Sow Coleworts. Coleworts are really small cabbages, and they are very useful as a catch crop. Sow a little seed broadcast now and you will be cutting useful heads all through the autumn and winter.

Sow French Beans. Make one more sowing of french beans in a sheltered place outdoors in exactly the same way as advised in the notes for May,

First Week. This will provide you with plants that will crop in September and continue until the first sharp frosts.

Stop Cutting Asparagus. It is most unwise to cut asparagus after the third week in June. Allow the plants to make foliage now so that new crowns may be formed for next year. Give the bed a small dressing of any good compound fertilizer. If you prefer to make your own mixtures, use three parts of superphosphate of lime, two parts of sulphate of ammonia and one part of sulphate of potash at the rate of 2 ounces per square yard.

Spray Apples against Codlin Moth. If in former years grubs have been found feeding inside apples during July and August it is probable that the codlin moth is responsible, and steps should be taken now to pre-

CODLIN MOTH
A section of an apple attacked by the larva of this moth.

vent further damage. Spray all apple trees at once with DDT or derris insecticide making sure that the fruitlets are covered. It would be advisable to spray again in about 3 weeks' time, to catch any later-hatching grubs.

FOURTH WEEK

Sow Brompton Stocks and Forget-me-nots. This is a good time to sow Brompton stocks to stand the winter and flower outdoors next May and June. It is possible to germinate the seeds in the open, but I find it better to sow in boxes and place these in a frame. Here the seeds can be shaded from strong sunshine and protected from rain storms until they germinate. Cover the seeds very lightly with sandy soil and water moderately. Forget-me-nots may be sown at the same time, but these germinate freely enough in a shady place in the open. Sow in drills $\frac{1}{2}$ inch deep and 6 inches apart.

Divide Mossy Saxifrages. Old clumps of mossy saxifrage may be divided, and this is a good policy if they are tending to get brown in the centre. Discard the brown pieces altogether, and replant the green clumps in a semi-shady place in soil that contains plenty of leaf-mould or moss peat. Water freely for a few weeks.

Lift and Divide June Flowering Irises. This is the ideal time for lifting and dividing all the May and June-flowering flag irises, as most of the plants will be starting to make new roots. Of course, it is not wise to lift and divide the clumps every year, but after four or five years they tend to

DIVIDING AND REPLANTING A GERMAN IRIS

Old woody ends of rhizome unprovided with roots are best cut off cleanly with a sharp knife. The rhizomes should be kept well up near the surface (A) when replanting and must never be buried deeply as at (B).

get overcrowded and to exhaust the soil. Then you should dig them up carefully with a fork, cut off the old central portions of bare rhizome, discarding them altogether, and replant the healthy outer growths with 3 or 4 inches of rhizome attached to each. Plant in well-prepared soil which has been dusted with superphosphate of lime at the rate of 2 ounces per square yard. If you use animal manure, work it in rather deeply, so that it does not come in contact with the rhizomes. These, by the way, should only just be covered with soil.

Start to Bud Roses. It is usually possible to start budding rose stocks at about this time, though much depends on the weather. If June is very dry, one may have to wait until well on into July, whereas if the weather is wet it is sometimes possible to start budding even earlier than this. The test is to make an incision in the stock and then attempt to lift the bark away from the wood. If it comes easily and cleanly budding can proceed at once, but if it drags away unwillingly it is better to wait awhile. The buds chosen should be from firm young shoots. A good test is to break off the thorns. If they come off easily, but leave moist-looking green scars, the wood is just right; if the scars are dry the wood is too ripe; but if the thorns refuse to break off easily, tearing instead, it is immature. Usually the tip of each shoot will have to be discarded as too young. There is no objection to using flower stems.

BUDDING A STANDARD ROSE

(A). *A suitable bud indicating the method of removal with a shield-shaped portion of bark.* (B). *Inside view of the bud after the thin strip of wood contained within the shield-shaped portion of bark has been removed.* (C). *Front view of the bud ready for insertion. Note that the leaf has been cut off, but the leaf stalk is retained to form a handle by which the bud can be held while it is being slipped into position beneath the bark of the stock.* (D). *T-shaped incisions made in young growths from the stock.* (E). *The bark is lifted with a scalpel and the bud is inserted and bound in place.* (F). *Bush roses are budded just below ground level.*

Pot Cinerarias. The first batch of cinerarias, sown early in May, will do better singly in pots now. Use the compost described on page 62 and return the plants to a frame after potting. Ventilate very freely.

Examine Grafted Fruit Trees. It is a good plan to examine any fruit trees that you grafted in March or April to make quite sure that all is in order. If the stock appears to have swollen a good deal, remove the grafting wax and make sure that the raffia tie is not strangling the scion.

Spray Raspberries with Derris. This is about the period to spray or dust raspberries with derris insecticide to kill the maggots that eat into the fruits and spoil them. The ideal time is when the most forward fruits of the variety Lloyd George begin to turn red.

A hanging basket is lined thickly with sphagnum moss to hold the soil.

A hanging basket being planted after it has been filled with soil.

Pelargoniums being hardened off in frames in preparation for planting out of doors.

Left: When trimming the top of a hedge the shears should be held as shown in the illustration. *Right:* After flowering it is advisable to remove the dead flowering shoots of lilacs.

Left: Take pink 'pipings' as shown in the illustration. *Right:* Pinching out the soft growing tips of broad beans encourages the formation of pods and reduces, and may even prevent, attacks by blackfly.

FLOWERS, VEGETABLES, AND FRUITS IN SEASON
DURING JUNE

Hardy Herbaceous Plants. *Acanthus mollis, Achillea millefolium* vars., *A. Ptarmica* and vars., *A. taygetea, Aconitum Napellus praecox, Anchusa italica* and vars., *Anthemis Cupaniana, A. Sancti-Johannis, A. tinctoria* and vars., *Anthericum Liliago, Aquilegia canadensis, A. chrysantha, A. longissima, A. Skinneri, A. vulgaris* vars., aquilegia hybrids (long-spurred), *Armeria latifolia* and vars., *Arnica Chamissonis, Asphodeline lutea, Asphodelus ramosus, Aster subcaeruleus, Astrantia carniolica, A. major, Borago laxiflora, Buphthalmum salicifolium, Calceolaria* John Innes hybrids, *Campanula Aucheri, C. glomerata dahurica, C. lactiflora, C. latifolia, C. latiloba, C. persicifolia* and vars., *C. rapunculoides, C. rhomboidalis, C. Trachelium, C. Vanhouttei, Centaurea dealbata, C. macrocephala, C. montana* and vars., *Centranthus ruber,*

INCARVILLEA DELAVAYI

This is a good plant for the centre of the border. The trumpet-shaped, rose-coloured flowers are produced in summer. The crowns need some protection in winter.

Chrysanthemum Leucanthemum vars., *Cichorium Intybus, Coreopsis grandiflora* and vars., *C. lanceolata* and vars., *Crambe cordifolia, Delphinium Belladonna* vars., *D. formosum,* delphiniums in var. (large-flowered hybrids), *Dianthus Allwoodii, D. plumarius* (common pink), *Dictamnus Fraxinella, Dicentra eximia, D. spectabilis, Digitalis ambigua, D. gloxinioides* vars. (foxglove), *D. lutea, Dracocephalum Ruyschiana, Eomecon chionantha, Eremurus Bungei, E. Elwesii, E. himalaicus, E. robustus, Erigeron aurantiacus, E. philadelphicus, E. speciosus* and vars., erigeron hybrids, *Filipendula hexapetala flore-pleno,* gaillardias, *Galega officinalis* and vars., *Gaura Lindheimeri, Geranium armenum, G. Endressii, G. grandiflorum, G. ibericum, G. nepalense, G. pratense* and vars., *Geum coccineum* vars., *G. Heldreichii, Helenium Hoopesii, Hemerocallis Dumortieri, H. flava, H. fulva, H. Middendorfiana,*

L

hemerocallis hybrids, *Heuchera brizoides, H. sanguinea* and vars., *H. tiarelloides, Hosta glauca, Incarvillea Delavayi, I. grandiflora, Inula glandulosa, Iris aurea, I. Bulleyana, I. fulva, I. germanica* and hybrids (flag, German iris), *I. hexagona, I. longipetala, I. Milesii, I. setosa, I. spuria, I. susiana, I. versicolor, I. Wilsonii, Kniphofia Tuckii, Libertia formosa, L. grandiflora, L. ixioides, Linaria dalmatica, Lindelofia longifolia, Linum narbonense, L. perenne, Lupinus arboreus* (tree lupin), *L. polyphyllus* hybrids (lupin), *Lychnis coronaria, L. Haageana, L. Viscaria* and vars., *Lysimachia clethroides, L. japonica, Macleaya cordata, M. microcarpa, Malva moschata, Meconopsis betonicifolia, M. cambrica* and vars., *M. Regia, Mertensia virginica, Nepeta macrantha, N. Mussinii, Oenothera fruticosa* and vars., *Oe. glauca, Paeonia albiflora* and vars. (Chinese peony), *P. decora, P. Delavayi, P. officinalis* and vars. (peony), *P. tenuifolia, P. Wittmanniana, Papaver nudicaule* (Iceland poppy), *P. orientale* and vars. (Oriental poppy), *Paradisea Liliastrum, Phlox divaricata* vars., and hybrids, *P. suffruticosa* hybrids, *Polemonium carneum, P. caeruleum* and vars., *P. pauciflorum, Polygonatum multiflorum* (Solomon's Seal), potentillas (hybrids), *Foterium obtusum,* pyrethrums in var., *Ranunculus aconitifolius plenus, R. acris plenus, Saxifraga umbrosa* (London Pride), *Smilacina racemosa, Spiraea Aruncus, Stachys grandiflora, Thalictrum aquilegifolium* and vars., *T. glaucum, Thermopsis montana, Trollius europaeus* and vars., *T. Ledebourii* and vars., *Tropaeolum polyphyllum, Verbascum densiflorum, V. olympicum, V. phoeniceum,* verbascum hybrids, *Veronica gentianoides,* violas (bedding), *Viola tricolor* (pansy).

Hardy Bulbs and Tubers. *Allium albopilosum, A. Moly, A. neapolitanum, A. Ostrowskianum, A. sphaerocephalum, Anemone coronaria* and vars., *Brevoortia Ida-Maia, Brodiaea grandiflora, B. laxa,* calochortuses and camassias (as in May), *Convallaria majalis prolificans, Gladiolus byzantinus, G. Colvillei* hybrids, *Hippeastrum pratense* (shelter), *Iris juncea, I. xiphioides* (English iris), *I. Xiphium* (Spanish iris), *Ixiolirion montanum, Lilium cernuum, L. croceum, L. elegans, L. Hansonii, L. Martagon* and vars., *L. parvum, L. philadelphicum, L. pomponium, L. pyrenaicum, L. Roezlii, L. rubellum, L. tenuifolium, L. testaceum, L. umbellatum* hybrids, *Nomocharis Mairei, N. pardanthina, Ornithogalum narbonense, O. umbellatum,* ranunculus (turban and French), *Scilla peruviana.*

Rock Plants. *Acantholimon venustum, Achillea Clavenae, A. rupestris, A. tomentosa, Aethionema coridifolium, Ae. grandiflorum, Ae. pulchellum, Ae. Warley Rose, Alyssum montanum, A. saxatile* and vars., *A. spinosum, Androsace lanuginosa* and vars., *A. sarmentosa* and vars., *Antennaria dioica, Anthyllis montana, Aquilegia alpina, A. caerulea, Arenaria montana, A. purpurascens, Armeria maritima* and vars., *Asperula suberosa, Aster Farreri, Astilbe simplicifolia, Bruckenthalia spiculifolia, Calamintha alpina, C. grandiflora, Calceolaria polyrrhiza, Callianthemum anemonoides, Calopogon pulchellus, Campanula abietina, C. Allionii, C. barbata, C. cochlearifolia, C. Elatines, C. garganica* and vars., *C. Portenschlagiana, C. Poscharskyana, C. pulla, C. pulloides, C. rotundifolia, C. Waldsteiniana, Cerastium tomentosum, Codonopsis ovata, Conandron ramondioides, Convolvulus mauritanicus, Coreopsis rosea, Corydalis cheilanthifolia, C. lutea, Cotyledon simplicifolia, Cypripedium humile, C. japonicum, C. spectabile, Cytisus decumbens, Daphne* *petraea, Delphinium nudicaule, Dianthus alpinus, D. caesius* and vars., *D. deltoides* and vars., *D. fragrans, D. glacialis, D. Knappii, D. subacaulis, Diplarrhena moraea, Dryas octopetala, Erinus alpinus* and vars., *Erodium chamaedryoides, E. corsicum, Erythraea Massonii, Genista pilosa, G. sagittalis, Geranium cinereum, G. Pylzowianum, G. sanguineum* and vars., *G. Wallichianum, Geum Borisii, G. montanum, Globularia bellidifolia, G. cordifolia, G. incanescens, G. nudicaulis, G. vulgaris, Gypsophila cerastioides, G. prostrata, G. repens, Habenaria ciliaris, H. conopsea, Helianthemum vulgare* hybrids, *H. lunulatum, H. Tuberaria, Heiracium aurantiacum, H. villosum, Helichrysum bellioides, Horminum pyrenaicum, Houstonia caerulea, Hutchinsia alpina, Hypericum Coris, Leontopodium alpinum, Lewisia Columbiana, L. Cotyledon, L. Heckneri, L. Howellii, L. Tweedyi, Linaria aequitriloba, L. alpina, L. pallida, Linnaea borealis, Linum alpinum, L. arboreum, L. flavum, L. salsoloides, Lippia canescens, Lithospermum graminifolium, L. prostratum* and vars., *L. purpureocaeruleum, Lysimachia Nummularia* and vars., *Lychnis alpina, L. Lagascae, Matthiola fenestralis, Mazus Pumilio, M. reptans, Mitchella repens, Myosotis*

CONVOLVULUS MAURITANICUS

A pleasant dwarf, creeping plant for the rock garden, C. mauritanicus bears blue flowers in summer. It has none of the faults of our native bindweeds.

rupicola, Oenothera acaulis, Oe. caespitosa, Oe. missouriensis, Onosma alboroseum, O. tauricum, Orchis maculata, O. militaris, Ourisia coccinea, Oxalis adenophylla, O. enneaphylla, Papaver alpinum, Parochetus communis, Penstemon Menziesii, P. rupicola, P. Scouleri, Phlox Douglasii, P. subulata and vars., *Phyteuma Halleri, P. Scheuchzeri, Polemonium confertum, Potentilla ambigua, P. aurea, P. fragiformis, P. nepalensis* and vars., *P. nitida, P. Tonguei, Primula capitata, P. farinosa, P. Mooreana, P. Sieboldii, P. spectabilis, P. Veitchii, Prunella incisa, Ramonda pyrenaica, Ranunculus alpestris, R. crenatus, Rhodohypoxis baurii, Roscoea cautleoides, Rosa Roulettii, Saponaria ocymoides, Saxifraga Aizoon* and vars., *S. cochlearis, S. Cotyledon* and vars., *S. ligulata* and vars., *S. longifolia, Scabiosa graminifolia, Schizocodon soldanelloides, Silene acaulis* and vars., *S. alpestris* and vars., *Sisyrinchium angustifolium, S. Bermudiana, Stachys corsica, Thymus nitidus, T. Serpyllum* and vars., *Trollius pumilus, Tunica Saxifraga, Veronica Bidwillii, V. carnosula, V. fruticans, V. pectinata, V. rupestris,* violas (as May), *Wahlenbergia tenuifolia, W. vincaeflora, Waldsteinia trifoliata.*

Hardy Aquatics and Bog Plants. *Acorus Calamus, Alisma Plantago, Anemone rivularis, Bletia hyacinthina, Butomus umbellatus,* dodecatheons (as May), *Filipendula ulmaria flore-pleno, Geum rivale, Hottonia palustris, Iris Kaempferi* and vars., *I. laevigata, I. Monnieri, I. ochroleuca, I. Pseudoacorus, I. sibirica, Limnanthemum nymphaeoides, Limnocharis Humboldtii, Lychnis Flos-cuculi* vars. (Ragged Robin), *Lysimachia vulgaris, Mimulus cardinalis, M. luteus, M. ringens, Menyanthes trifoliata, Myosotis palustris, Orchis latifolia, O. laxiflora, O. palustris, Primula Beesiana, P. Bulleyana, P. burmanica, P. Florindae, P. helodoxa, P. involucrata, P. japonica, P. Littoniana, P. microdonta* and vars., *P. Poissonii, P. prionotes, P. pseudosikkimensis, P. pulchella, P. pulverulenta, P. secundiflora, P. sikkimensis, P. vittata, P. Wardii, Ranunculus aquatilis, Rodgersia pinnata, R. podophylla, Veronica Beccabunga.*

Annuals. Hardy vars. (as list March, Third Week).

Bedding Plants. Ageratums, antirrhinums (autumn-sown), calceolarias, Canterbury bells, fuchsias, geraniums (zonal and ivy-leaved pelargoniums), lobelias, marguerites.

Hardy Evergreen Shrubs. *Abelia floribunda* (shelter), *Andromeda polifolia, Berberis Gagnepainii, Carpenteria californica* (shelter), *Ceanothus cyanus, C. dentatus, C. thyrsiflorus, C. Veitchianus, Cistus albidus, C. corbariensis, C. crispus, C. cyprius, C. ladaniferus, C. laurifolius, C. Loretii, C. obtusifolius, C. purpureus, C. salvifolius, C.* Silver Pink, *Cotoneaster Henryana, C. lactea, C. pannosa, Crinodendron hookerianum* (shelter), *Daboecia azorica, D. cantabrica, Daphne acutiloba, Erica Stuartii, E. Tetralix, Escallonia langleyensis, E. macrantha, E. punctata, Gaultheria Shallon, G. Veitchiana, Hebe anomala, H. balfouriana, H. buxifolia, H. cupressoides, H. hectori, H. hulkeana, Jasminum Giraldii, Kalmia angustifolia, K. latifolia, Leucothoe Davisiae, L. racemosa, Olearia Gunniana, O. macrodonta* (shelter), *Phlomis fruticosa, Pieris Mariana, Pyracantha coccinea* and vars., *P. Gibbsii, P. Rogersiana, Phyllodoce caerulea, Raphiolepis japonica, Rhododendron azaleoides, R. catawbiense, R. discolor* and hybrids, *R. ferrugineum, R. Fortunei* hybrids, *R. Griersonianum* (shelter), *R. hirsutum, R. lapponicum, R. lepidotum, R. ponticum* hybrids, *Salvia Grahamii* (shelter), *Sophora tetraptera, Stranvaesia Davidiana, S. glaucescens, Telopea truncata, Viburnum rhytidophyllum, Vinca major, V. minor, Yucca Whipplei.*

Hardy Deciduous Shrubs. *Abelia triflora* (shelter), *Abutilon vitifolium, Adenocarpus decorticans, Aesculus Pavia, Anthyllis Hermanniae, Buddleia alternifolia, B. Colvillei* (shelter), *B. globosa, B. paniculata, Calycanthus floridus, C. occidentalis* (Allspice), *Carmichaelia grandiflora, Ceratostigma Willmottianum, Chionanthus retusa, C. virginica, Colutea arborescens, Cornus capitata* (shelter), *C. Kousa, Cytisus scoparius* and vars., *C. sessilifolius, Deutzia corymbosa, D. crenata, D. discolor, D. longifolia, D. purpurascens, D. scabra* and vars., *D. taiwanensis, D. Vilmoriniae, D. Wilsonii, Diostea juncea, Dipelta floribunda, Discaria serratifolia, Fremontia californica, Gaylussacia frondosa, Genista cinerea, G. dalmatica, G. germanica, G. hispanica, G. radiata, G. virgata, Halimodendron argenteum, Hedysarum multijugum, Hydrangea Bretschneideri, H. Hortensia, Indigofera Potaninii, Jamesia americana, Kolkwitzia amabilis, Lonicera chrysantha, L. Ferdinandi, L. hispida, L. Maackii, L. syringantha, Magnolia glauca, M. obovata, M. parviflora,*

M. sinensis, M. Wilsonii, Meliosma myriantha, Menziesia pilosa, Neillia bracteata, N. longiracemosa, N. opulifolia, Notospartium Carmichaeliae, Paulownia Fargesii, Pettaria ramentacea, Philadelphus coronarius, P. Delavayi, P. grandiflorus, P. inodorus. P. insignis, P. Lemoinei hybrids, *P. microphyllus, P. purpurascens, Plagianthus Lyalli, Potentilla fruticosa, Pterostyrax hispidum, Rhodotypos kerrioides, Robinia hispida, R. Kelseyi, Rosa alba, R. alpina, R. bracteata, R. carolina, R. filipes, R. Helenae, R. Hugonis, R. macrantha, R. moschata, R. Moyesii, R. multibracteata, R. nitida, R. nutkana, R. omeiensis, R. rubiginosa* (sweet brier), *R. rugosa, R. sericea, R. Willmottiae, R. xanthina,* hybrid roses (tea, hybrid tea, hybrid perpetual, pernetiana, polyantha),

MAGNOLIA SINENSIS

Magnolias are not difficult to grow. They prefer a deep, rich, sandy peaty loam and many will flower when young. This one bears fragrant, white, saucer-shaped flowers with a central boss of rosy-crimson stamens.

Rubus deliciosus, Sophora viciifolia, Spiraea bracteata, S. canescens, S. discolor, S. Menziesii, S. Sargentiana, S. trichocarpa, S. Vanhouttei, S. Veitchii, Styrax Wilsonii, Syringa chinensis, S. emodi, S. japonica, S. villosa, S. vulgaris and vars., (lilac), *Vaccinium stamineum, Viburnum cassinoides, V. dilatatum, V. pubescens, V. tomentosum* and vars., *Weigela coraeensis, W. floribunda* and vars., *W. florida* and vars., *Zenobia speciosa.*

Hardy Evergreen Trees. *Prunus lusitanica* (Portugal laurel).

Hardy Deciduous Trees. *Aesculus californica, Ae. carnea, Ae. indica, Ae. octandra, Castanea sativa* (sweet chestnut), *Crataego-mespilus grandiflora, Fraxinus Mariesii, F. Ornus* (flowering ash), *Laburnum alpinum, L. anagyroides, L. Vossii, Magnolia Fraseri, M. tripetala, M. Watsonii, Paulownia Fargesii, Pyrus Aria* (Whitebeam), *P. Aucuparia* (mountain ash), *P. coronaria, P. Hartwegii, P. hupehensis, P. ioensis, Robinia pseudoacacia* (false acacia), *Styrax japonica, S. obassia, Viburnum Lantana* (wayfaring tree), *V. Lentago.*

Hardy Climbing Plants. *Aristolochia californica, A. heterophylla, A. moupinensis, A. Sipho, A. tomentosa, Bignonia capreolata* (shelter), *Berchemia Giraldiana, Clematis azurae* hybrids, *C. Durandii, C. florida* and vars., *C. lanuginosa* and vars., *C. montana rubens, C. patens* vars., *C. Pitcheri, Hydrangea petiolaris, Jasminum officinale* (jessamine), *J. stephanense, Lonicera Brownii,*

L. caprifolium, L. Giraldii, L. glaucescens, L. Heckrotti, L. Henryi, L. japonica and vars., *L. Ledebourii, L. Periclymenum belgica* (early Dutch honeysuckle), *L. plantierensis, L. Tellmanniana, L. tragophylla, Passiflora caerulea* (passion flower), *Periploca sepium, Rosa arvensis* (Ayrshire rose), *R. Banksiae* (Banksian rose), *R. cerasocarpa, R. laevigata,* hybrid roses (climbing hybrid tea and tea, also Carmine Pillar), *Solanum crispum, S. jasminoides, Trachelospermum divaricatum, Wisteria chinensis, W. formosa, W. frutescens, W. venusta.*

**PASSIFLORA CAERULEA
(PASSION FLOWER)**
A good climber for a sheltered wall or pergola, the passion flower has curious flowers of pale pink, white and purple. It will quickly reach 20 to 25 feet.

Greenhouse Plants. Achimenes, *Adenandra fragrans, A. amoena, Agapanthus umbellatus,* annuals, hardy and half-hardy (see February, Third Week, and March, First Week), balsam, beaufortias, begonias (tuberous-rooted), boronias, bougainvilleas, callistemons, cannas, carnations (perpetual-flowering and border), celosias, *Cestrum elegans,* celsias, *Clianthus Dampieri, C. puniceus,* correas, *Cuphea ignea,* daturas, *Epacris longiflora, Erica Cavendishiana, E. Spenceriana, E. ventricosa,* eriostemons, *Erythrina Crista-galli, Francoa ramosa* (bridal wreath), fuchsias, gloxinias, heliotrope, *Hibbertia dentata,* hippeastrums, hydrangeas, lantanas, *Lapageria rosea, Lasiandra macrantha,* lilies in var., *Mandevilla suaveolens,* marguerites, *Mitraria coccinea, Oxalis tetraphylla,* passifloras, pelargoniums (regal, show, zonal, and ivy-leaved), *Plumbago capensis, Rehmannia angulata,* streptocarpus (old plants), *Streptosolen Jamesonii,* tropaeolums (including double vars.).

Vegetables in Store. Onions, potatoes.

Vegetables in the Garden. Asparagus, broad beans, broccoli (late), shorthorn carrots, cauliflowers (sown September), lettuces, mustard and cress, spring onions, onions (sown August), peas (early vars.), potatoes (early vars.), radishes, rhubarb, spinach, turnips (sown March).

Vegetables under Glass. French beans, cucumbers, mushrooms (cool cellars and sheds), tomatoes.

Fruits in Store. *Apples:* Allen's Everlasting (D), Annie Elizabeth (C), Encore (C), Sandling (D), Stark (D), Sturmer Pippin (D), Wagener (C).

Fruits Outdoors. *Cherries:* Early Rivers (D), Guigne D'Annonay (D), May Duke (D), Olivet (C), Schrecken Bigarreau (D), Waterloo (D). *Gooseberries* (green). *Raspberries:* Red Cross, Lloyd George, Malling Jewel, Malling Promise. *Strawberries:* George V, Huxley Giant, Royal Sovereign, Sir Joseph Paxton, Talisman, The Duke, Western Queen.

Fruits under Glass. *Grapes, Peaches,* and *Nectarines* (early varieties started in January and forced steadily; see list, July, Fruits under Glass).

July

GENERAL WORK

Cut off Faded Flowers, etc. From time to time during the month you should examine all the flowering plants in the garden and remove any blooms or flower spikes that are so faded as to be no longer decorative. This applies to roses, to early-flowering herbaceous plants, and also to bedding plants and annuals. The object is to prevent seed formation, which weakens the plant unnecessarily. Exception may be made if one wants some seeds of any special thing, but then the best plan is to reserve one particular plant of this variety for seed bearing.

Thin and Disbud Dahlias, etc. If you want some extra fine dahlias for exhibition, you must thin out the plants and only allow them to bear a restricted number of flowers. A good strong plant of one of the large-flowered varieties may carry three stems, but no more. Remove others, keeping only the sturdiest. Then, when the flower buds appear, remove all except the central terminal one on each stem. Plants that are only grown for garden decoration do not need this drastic restriction and may be allowed to grow naturally. All will benefit from liberal soakings of weak liquid manure every few days.

It will also be necessary to continue the disbudding of roses as described in the notes for June, General Work.

Continue to Trim Hedges, etc. You can continue to trim evergreen hedges and topiary specimens as necessary to keep them neat and tidy.

Take Cuttings of Shrubs, Alpines, etc. A great many hardy shrubs, and also shrubby alpines, such as helianthemums, penstemons, etc., can be increased during July and August by cuttings prepared from firm young sideshoots and the ends of non-flowering stems. Select pieces from 1 inch to 4 inches in length, according to the nature of the plant. Prepare them by cutting the base of each cleanly through just below a joint and removing the lower leaves. Then insert them firmly in a suitable compost, burying them just sufficiently deep to keep them erect. If you can attend to the cuttings at any time during the day, use pure silver sand as the rooting medium; but if you are away from home most of the day, use a mixture of sharp sand, moss peat, and good loam in equal parts.

The compost may either be placed in a frame or else prepared in the open and covered with a handlight. If you can watch the cuttings frequently, no shading will be necessary; but if they have to be left for hours on end, it is advisable to shade from strong direct sunlight. Cuttings unshaded and in pure sand may need watering every hour or so on a hot day, but those that are shaded and in compost are not likely to need water more than once in 2 days. Keep the frame or handlight quite tight until the cuttings begin to grow, but then begin to admit a little air,

A FRAME FOR CUTTINGS
This sectional view of a frame shows a drainage layer of stones covered by sifted cinders, then turfy loam, with a bed of fine sandy soil on top for the cuttings.

increasing the amount daily. If desired all these cuttings can be treated with a root-forming hormone as described on page 56.

Mist propagation is a recent innovation which automatically maintains a humid atmosphere so that the cuttings never have a chance to dry out or wilt. Under this system they root very much more quickly and satisfactorily. Briefly the system consists of an electronic 'leaf' which is placed among the cuttings, and as this dries out so an electrical circuit is broken, and water is turned on, to spray in a fine mist over the cuttings through jets fixed above them. As soon as the 'leaf' is sufficiently wet contact is 'made' again and the water stops. Non-electric models are now available.

Continue to Bud Rose Stocks. You can continue to bud rose stocks throughout the month so long as the bark parts readily from the wood of the stock (see June, Fourth Week). Sometimes, if the weather gets very hot and dry, the stocks refuse to work properly and then the work should be discontinued for the time being.

Continue to Spray against Foes. Caterpillars, red spider, thrips and greenfly are still sources of danger. Take prompt measures to destroy these pests as soon as they put in an appearance (see June, General Work). Fungal diseases, such as mildew, rust, and black spot, are likely to be on the increase as the weather gets warmer. Occasional spraying with Bordeaux mixture or some other good fungicide is the only certain method of keeping them down. It is wise to spray roses every fortnight or so as a precautionary measure, for it is much easier to prevent diseases than it is to cure them. Good modern remedies for black spot of roses and rose mildew are captan and dinocap respectively which should be sprayed on the leaves according to the manufacturer's instructions.

ROSE BLACK SPOT
DISEASE
This is a very troublesome disease, but it can be checked by regular summer spraying with captan

Continue to Feed Plants in Growth. You should continue to feed all plants that are making rapid growth as I advised in my notes for May and June (see General Work, May and June). For winter green crops planted during May and June, nitrate of soda may well be used in place of a compound fertilizer. Give two applications, each of $\frac{1}{2}$ ounce per square yard, at an interval of about 3 weeks.

Remove Grass Box from Lawn Mower. During this month and August, when the weather is likely to be hot, it is an excellent plan to remove the grass box from the lawn mower and let the tiny clippings fall on to the lawn. They will act as a mulch and will protect the roots from scorching.

General Greenhouse Management. There is really little to add to my remarks in the June notes on this subject. Fire heat for all ordinary greenhouse plants will now be quite unnecessary. Indeed, the problem usually will be to keep the house sufficiently cool by day. This is particularly so in very small houses, which must, in consequence, be ventilated freely and shaded carefully. Shading for a few hours per day may even be necessary for such a sun-loving crop as tomatoes. Occasional damping down of paths and walls will also help matters, but the syringe must be used cautiously on plants themselves when the sun is shining brightly on them.

Pot on Zonal Pelargoniums, etc. Spring-struck cuttings of zonal pelargoniums required for autumn flowering in the greenhouse are almost sure to need potting on into 6-inch pots during July. Similar remarks apply to other greenhouse plants raised from spring cuttings (see March, General Work), except that sometimes even bigger pots may be required. In this connexion I refer you to my general remarks on potting in the notes for April, General Work, and would remind you that it is rarely wise to shift plants into pots more than two sizes larger than those in which they are already growing. Use the same compost as before but coarser in texture, and press it more firmly around the roots.

Continue to Thin Seedlings. Various vegetables sown last month for succession must be thinned out before they become overcrowded (see June, General Work).

Cut Globe Artichokes. From now onwards you can cut the heads of globe artichokes as they become available. On no account leave any on the plants so long that they begin to flower. The ideal time to cut them is when they are nice and plump, but before the scales begin to open out too much.

Continue to Plant Winter Greens. Continue to plant out all manner of winter green crops as you clear ground of early crops, such as dwarf peas, early potatoes, and the first sowings of turnips and salad vegetables. So far as possible, choose showery weather for this work, but do not delay long on this account. If July is persistently dry, push on with the planting and then water freely for a few days.

Plant March-sown Leeks. Leeks from the March sowing (see March, Third Week) may also be planted, as opportunity occurs, on similar ground to the winter greens. Plant with a large dibber in holes 9 inches deep, dropping the leeks right down into these, but not refilling the holes with soil. Simply water in thoroughly. This deep planting will blanch the stems without need for earthing up. The leeks should be 1 foot apart in rows 18 inches apart.

Continue to Blanch Leeks. The process of blanching leeks grown in trenches must be continued gradually, as explained in my notes for June, General Work.

Plant Celery for Succession. During the month you can make further plantings of celery as plants from late sowings become available. It is not wise to shift the plants to the trenches while they are very small. Wait until they are at least 3 inches in height and can be lifted with a nice ball of roots (see June, First Week).

Make Successional Sowings. These are in the main the same as for last month (see June, General Work). Sow turnips for the last time about the middle of the month. You can be rather more generous with the seed, as this crop will supply roots for storing. One more sowing each of lettuce, endive, and summer spinach should meet all requirements. It is necessary to choose a shady place for all these crops, for heat and drought will make them run to seed prematurely. Mustard and cress and radishes can be sown as before, also in a cool position.

Feed, Train, and Fumigate Tomatoes. Outdoor tomatoes will be growing freely and forming their flower trusses. Keep each plant to a single stem

TOMATO DEFOLIATION
As the lower trusses ripen a few leaves can be removed, as indicated, to let in more sunlight.

and nip out all side shoots at the earliest opportunity. Water freely during dry weather and, as soon as the bottom truss is set and you can see the tiny fruits swelling, spread a 2-inch layer of well-rotted manure round the plants. From that time onwards feed every week with small doses of any good tomato fertilizer.

There is really nothing to add to my remarks on indoor tomatoes last month (see June, General Work). Cut back more foliage as you clear the lower trusses of fruit. Free ventilation, steady feeding, and ample watering are the all-important points to watch.

Feed and Train Cucumbers. Nor is there much to add to my notes on cucumbers in the same place. Plants in frames will now be tending to take the place of those in greenhouses, though even the latter may be kept going for a surprising time by frequent removal of all side growths that have ceased to bear and their replacement by young growth. Syringe and watering pot must be used constantly to keep up the necessary moisture in soil and air. Ventilate rather more freely, especially when the temperature shows signs of rising above 80°, but do not allow the air to get dry on this account or you are sure to have trouble with red spider and thrips. Heavier shading will help to keep the temperature down. Continue to stop and train the plants in frames and on outside ridges, and regulate growth in such a manner that the beds are never overcrowded but you are continually getting a new supply of laterals with flowers. Be very careful to cut the cucumbers directly they are fit to use. If a few hang and ripen, the plants will soon stop bearing.

Management of the Orchard House. Peaches, nectarines, and apricots under glass must be treated according to their state of growth (see General Work, May and June). As trees are cleared of ripened fruits daily (or even twice daily) syringeing should be recommenced, for there is no better way of keeping down that commonest of orchard house foes, the red spider. Ventilate freely by day, but do not let the temperature fall below 55° at night. Even July nights can be chilly occasionally.

Protect Vines from Mildew. Thinning of the fruits will now become general with outdoor vines, and as the process is exactly the same as

VINE MILDEW

In outward appearance this disease is very similar to the mildew that attacks roses. It is encouraged by dry soil, a wet atmosphere, and overcrowded foliage.

for indoor varieties I refer you to my earlier notes on that subject (see March, General Work). A thick mulch of well-rotted manure spread over the border will help the vines a lot at this season. Indoor vines in various stages of growth will also require treatment as before (see General Work for April, May, and June).

Mildew may become troublesome from now onwards, covering leaves and grapes with a white, mealy growth. If there is the slightest sign of this disease, give increased ventilation and dust foliage and fruits with flowers of sulphur. Make certain that the border is not short of water, for dry soil combined with damp, unventilated atmosphere are sure causes of mildew.

Shanking sometimes occurs at this time of the year. This is a physiological disorder which causes the footstalks of the berries to die, with the result that the berries themselves suddenly collapse. It is caused by poverty of soil or a cold, wet subsoil, and remaking of the border the following autumn is the best remedy.

FIRST WEEK

Lift Tulips, Hyacinths, etc. Tulips and hyacinths will now have completed their growth and may be lifted and cleaned. Lay the bulbs in shallow trays and stand them in a dry, cool, airy place, but not in full sun. Dead tops can be removed and the bulbs sorted out into two sizes, the biggest for flowering again next year (though do not rely on them for the most important beds) and the smaller ones to be planted in good soil in an out-of-the-way place to grow on. If your garden is only small it will be best to throw these small bulbs away, for they will scarcely be worth the space they take up. Anemones of the St Brigid and Du Caen types, and also turban ranunculuses are treated in much the same way, the tubers being lifted as soon as foliage has died down. Store in a dry, cool place until planting time. Crocuses can also be lifted now, but only if they are overcrowded or you need the ground for something else. If you do have them out, get them replanted quite soon; they gain nothing from being out of the ground.

Complete Stopping of Carnations. By this time you should complete all the second stopping of perpetual-flowering carnations (see May, General Work). If the plants are stopped later than this they will not start to flower until well on in the new year, and carnations are much in demand at Christmas and even before. Roughly speaking, five months must elapse before a stopped growth can produce any flowers.

Stand out Regal and Show Pelargoniums. Show and regal pelargoniums will have practically finished flowering by this time and will be better out of the greenhouse. Stand them in the open in any sunny, fairly sheltered place and gradually decrease the water supply, practically witholding it for the last fortnight in July. If it rains a lot, lay the pots on their sides. The object is to check and ripen growth and give the plants a rest.

Sow Carrots. A small sowing of shorthorn or intermediate carrots made now is often amply justified, especially if the season happens to be a bad one for carrot fly. This fly does all its damage early in the summer, and seedlings from a July sowing usually escape. In any case, young carrots in the autumn are very welcome.

Spray Potatoes with Bordeaux Mixture. Do not wait until disease attacks your potatoes, but spray them now with Bordeaux mixture. The potato late blight disease is so common that some of your plants are almost sure to get infected unless you take this precaution, and in any case spraying is repaid because it lengthens the season of growth and so indirectly increases the weight of the crop. You can purchase Bordeaux mixture in powder or paste form from any dealer in horticultural sundries and it is only necessary to dissolve this in water at the strength stated on the package. When spraying, be very careful to cover the under as well as the upper sides of the leaves.

Make an Outdoor Mushroom Bed. In sheds, pits, etc., mushrooms can be grown throughout the year, but unprotected outdoors they are only satisfactory in late summer and early autumn. Now is the time to make such a bed. First you will need to get a good quantity of fresh stable manure. This you must turn and shake with a fork two or three times, at intervals of a day or so, until the first heat of fermentation has died down and the manure is decaying steadily. Then build it up into a ridge-shaped heap in the open, or a more or less flat-topped bank against a wall. Beds made against a north wall at this time of the year are usually very satisfactory. Tread the manure firmly layer by layer as you build it up into the mound. When finished, the bed should be $2\frac{1}{2}$ feet deep; it can be of any width, but 3 feet is usual and convenient. Plunge a soil thermometer into the bed and, when the temperature falls to 70°, insert sterilized mushroom spawn in small pieces at intervals of 10 inches all over the bed. Simply make a hole about 1 inch deep in the manure, push a piece of spawn in, and cover it with manure. Then cover the whole bed with a foot-thick layer of straw. You can purchase sterilized mushroom spawn in bottles. A quart bottle contains enough spawn to plant a bed from 30 to 40 square feet in area. After 2 or 3 weeks scrape away a little of the manure and see how things are getting on. If there are white filament-like growths penetrating the bed freely, the spawn is 'running' and the bed is ready for casing. This is done by covering the manure evenly with a 1-inch thick layer of loam, beaten smooth with the back of a spade. Then replace the clean dry straw to keep the bed at an even temperature. If the weather is dry, the bed must be watered occasionally with tepid water, but too much moisture is not desirable.

Begin to Summer-prune Cherries and Plums. You can now begin to summer-prune cherries and plums growing on walls. It is not worth while trying to apply this method of pruning to large bushes and stan-

SUMMER-PRUNING A
SWEET CHERRY

A typical fruiting lateral showing the way in which ends of laterals are removed (see black lines) to encourage production of further fruit buds.

dards, for these are better allowed to grow rather freely. With the one exception of the Morello cherry, the method is the same for all varieties. Side shoots which have been growing during May and June should be udding roses. *Above, left:* A suitable bud is cut from the stock. *Above, right:* The ood is removed from behind the selected bud. *Below, left:* A T-shaped slit is made the bark of the stock. *Below, right:* The bud is tied with raffia after insertion.

Leeks may be planted by being dropped into holes made with a dibber and then watered in.

The tops of onions bent over to help to ripen off the bulbs.

shortened by about one-third each, but leaders terminating main branches are left unpruned. Do not do all the work on any one tree at once, but spread it over a period of about six weeks. In this way the trees will not suffer any check to growth. Morello cherries bear their best fruits on young wood, and so are disbudded just like peaches and nectarines. Side shoots growing on the fruiting laterals are gradually rubbed off or pinched back a few at a time with the exception of two per lateral, one near its base and one at its tip. The former will replace it after the winter pruning, while the latter serves to maintain a good flow of sap to swell and ripen the fruits.

Complete Thinning of Apples and Pears. It is now the time to complete the thinning of apples and pears (see June, Second Week). Reduce the fruits to one, or at most two, per spur.

Burn Straw on Strawberry Beds. If you have had any mildew or other disease on your strawberries or the plants have been badly attacked by greenfly, set fire to the straw on the beds as soon as you have gathered all the fruits. This will burn up all the foliage and leave the bed looking very bare and sad for a week or so, but the crowns themselves will not be damaged and will soon produce healthy new growth. Of course, you must not do this to any plants around which you intend to peg down runners (see below).

Peg Down Strawberry Runners. Strawberry plants tend to deteriorate after a few years, and so it is advisable to raise a few new plants every year to take the place of old, worn-out ones. To do this it is only neces-

PROPAGATING STRAWBERRIES

Runners from the parent plant are pegged down into pots sunk to their rims in the strawberry bed.

sary to peg down, at this time of the year, some of the plantlets that form on the runners. Each runner will form a number of plantlets if allowed to do so, but for propagation that nearest the parent plant is the best, and the tip of the runner may be pinched out beyond this. It is not usually wise to peg down more than three or four plantlets round each old plant. There are two methods of doing the work: one is simply to press

M

the plantlet down on to the soil in the strawberry bed and hold it in position with a wooden or wire peg; and the other is to fill a 3-inch flower pot with a mixture of loam, leaf-mould, and sand, plunge this into the strawberry bed at any convenient point, and peg the plantlet into it. The second method is the better of the two because, when the rooted runners are severed from their parent plant later on and are removed to a new bed, there need be no serious root disturbance. The pot, complete with roots, is simply lifted from the strawberry bed and the ball of soil tapped out intact. But rooting in pots does mean a little more watering. If you can get all the runners you require now, so much the better, for early rooting gives the best results, but if there are not enough runners at the moment you can continue to peg down throughout the month as the runners develop.

Cut off any runners you do not need, because they only weaken the plant. Continue to do this throughout the summer.

SECOND WEEK

Prick out Perennials and Biennials. Perennials and biennials sown in June (see June, First Week) will be in need of pricking out into a nursery bed. This should be in an open position except for violas, pansies, primroses, and polyanthuses, which grow more quickly in partial shade. The ground must be well forked and reasonably rich, but not recently manured with dung. If it needs feeding, give a very light dressing of hop manure and fork this in. Get the seedlings up as carefully as possible (if the ground is dry it is a good plan to give it a thorough watering the day before you intend to move the seedlings) and replant them with a trowel. Plant in rows about 9 inches apart. The bigger growing plants, such as hollyhocks, delphiniums, and lupins, should be 9 inches apart in the rows, but 6 inches will be sufficient for wallflowers, double daisies, *Cheiranthus Allionii*, primroses, etc., while violas and pansies may be as close as 4 inches. Pinch out the tips of wallflowers and cheiranthuses to make them branch freely.

It is possible that Brompton stocks and forget-me-nots from the late June sowing may also be far enough advanced to prick out in the same manner. If they are not, the work should be done at the first favourable opportunity.

Prune Mock Oranges and Weigelas. Most mock oranges (Philadelphus) and weigelas (Diervilla) will have finished flowering by now, and you can prune them if you do not want the bushes to get very big. The method is to cut out all the stems that have just flowered, leaving younger shoots from lower down to take their place.

Gather Herbs for Winter Use. This is the time to gather most herbs for winter use. Do not delay until they have flowered or you will lose much of the flavour. Tie the stems into small bundles and suspend these head

DRYING OFF HERBS
When cut, the herbs should be tied up in small bundles and suspended head downwards to dry.

downwards from a beam or hook in a cool, dry and airy shed or room. When thoroughly dry the leaves can be stored in tightly stoppered jars or tins in any reasonably cool, dry place.

Start to Earth up Early Celery. If you want to have some sticks of celery for a late August show, you must start to earth up now. This is not a task that can be completed in one operation. At first content yourself by drawing 3 or 4 inches of soil round the base of each plant. Remove basal offshoots as a preliminary, and tie the stems together with raffia so that soil does not find its way into the hearts of the plants. Then, about ten days later, draw up a further 4 inches or so of soil, and keep on in this manner at short intervals until only the blades of the leaves can be seen. A further method of ensuring that the plants are kept clean and that soil does not percolate into their hearts is to tie brown paper collars round them before earthing up.

Finish Planting Celery. All remaining celery seedlings should now be planted out in the trenches as soon as possible (see June, First Week). The last plants to be dealt with will be those from the April sowing in a frame (see April, Second Week).

Mulch and Syringe Runner Beans. Runner beans will benefit from a fairly thick mulch of well-rotted manure spread on the ground for a distance of at least a couple of feet on either side of the row. When the plants begin to flower, syringe them every evening with tepid water. This will help the flowers to 'set' and so ensure a good crop of beans. Keep this up all through the month and on into August.

Remove Plum Branches Attacked by Silver Leaf. Silver leaf is a disease caused by an organism that actually infects the sap of plums and occasionally apples and pears. It cannot be counteracted by spraying, and the only method of preventing its spread is to cut off and burn affected branches, afterwards painting wounds with Stockholm tar. By law wood killed by silver leaf must be removed before July 15. The leaves of diseased branches have a distinctive silvery appearance. The only other disease which may be confused with this is mildew, but the latter produces a white, mealy outgrowth on the leaves. With silver leaf there is no outward fungal growth until a later date, and then it is on the dead wood. At this time of the year there is just the tell-tale silvery sheen. The variety Victoria is particularly susceptible to attack, while Blaisdon Red, Yellow Pershore, and River's Early Prolific are resistant to it.

Spray apples against Codlin Moth. Repeat the spray recommended in June (see June, Third Week), using D D T or derris.

THIRD WEEK

Layer Border Carnations. Border carnations can be increased by cuttings like perpetual-flowering carnations, but it is much more satisfactory to increase them by layers. This means that you select young non-flowering shoots that can readily be bent down to soil level and make an incision with a sharp knife through a joint near the base of each. Then the slit portion of stem is bent down to open the slit, covered with fine sandy soil and is held firmly in position with a wooden or wire peg. If the layers are kept well watered, roots will soon be formed from the sides of the cut. In late August or early September the rooted layers can be cut completely from the parent plant and be planted elsewhere or potted up.

Summer-prune Wisterias. Wisterias that have filled their allotted space can be induced to flower freely year after year without making a lot of new growth by summer and winter pruning. Now is the time for the first of these operations. Shorten to about six leaves each all side growths formed on the main branches.

Summer-prune Roses. Bush and standard roses of the hybrid, tea and pernetiana types will pay for a light summer pruning now that the first flush of flowers is over. Cut back to about two leaves all stems that have flowered, but have no promising buds on them at the moment. Then give the beds a dusting of any good compound flower-garden fertilizer and hoe this in.

LAYERING A CARNATION

A suitable non-flowering shoot is slit near a joint and pegged down, with a galvanized wire peg as shown, into finely broken soil. When the required number of shoots have been layered a little fine soil is placed over them, as shown on the right, and watered freely.

Prick Off and Pot Primulas, Calceolarias, and Cinerarias. Greenhouse primulas sown in mid-June will now need pricking off exactly like the earlier batch (see June, First Week). These first primulas will also in all probability require a shift. Do not let them get crowded in their boxes or pans, but move them on singly into 3-inch pots, using the compost described on page 26. Return to the frame after potting and give a little shade from strong, direct sunshine.

Calceolarias and cinerarias sown in June (see June, Third Week) are almost certain to be forward enough for pricking off in exactly the same manner as the primulas, except that the cinerarias should be spaced a good 2 inches apart each way.

Sow Spring Cabbage. This is the time to make a first sowing of cabbages for use in the spring and early summer. Do not sow all the seed now, however, but keep some for a further sowing during the second week in August, as sometimes the later seedlings do best in the long run. Choose a suitable variety, such as Ellam's Early Dwarf, Flower of Spring, or Harbinger. Scatter the seed thinly in a bed of finely broken soil and cover lightly. Water freely if the weather happens to be dry.

Lift and Store Autumn-sown Onions. Autumn-sown onions should now have completed their growth and ripened their bulbs, so you may just as well lift them and have the ground free for some other crop as, for example, winter greens. Lift the onions carefully with a fork and lay them out in a sunny place for a few days to dry off. Then shake the soil from them and store in shallow boxes in a cool dry place.

Start to Summer-prune Apples and Pears. You can now start to shorten the laterals of apples and pears exactly as I described for cherries and

SUMMER PRUNING AN APPLE BRANCH

The side shoots should be shortened by about a third of their length to encourage spur formation. This may be carried out on pears, plums and sweet cherries.

plums earlier in the month (see First Week). The method is worth applying to all trained specimens, and also to small bushes, pyramids, and half-standards, but involves too much labour with full standards or very big bushes.

Start to Pick Apples and Pears. The earliest apples, such as Mr Gladstone and Early Victoria, and also the pear Early Market, should be ripe by now, and you can begin to pick, but only as you actually require the fruits for use. These early varieties do not keep at all well off the tree, and no attempt must be made to store them. The test for ripeness with apples is to lift a typical fruit without actually wrenching or twisting it off its branch. If it comes away easily with its stalk it is ready for picking, but if it parts unwillingly, tearing off part of the spur or breaking in the middle of its stalk, it is not yet ripe. With pears the best test is to press one or two of the fruits very gently near the stalk; if yielding they are ready.

A LADDER FOR PICKING FRUIT

This special ladder, narrowing at top, can be inserted between branches with much less risk of causing damage than the normal type.

FOURTH WEEK

Plant Madonna Lilies. This is the ideal time to plant *Lilium candidum*, the Madonna lily. It differs from almost all other lilies in making quite a lot of new growth in late summer, and it should be planted before this starts. Another peculiarity is that the bulbs grow practically on the surface. You should only cover them with 2 inches of soil. After a while they will probably work themselves out until they show; make no attempt to cover them again. The bulbs should be 8 inches apart. This lily prefers a sunny position and reasonably good, but not freshly manured, ground.

Plant Colchicums, Autumn Crocuses, etc. You should also plant colchicums, autumn-flowering crocuses, and sternbergias if you can obtain supplies. General bulb merchants rarely have them so early, but specialists will be able to supply. Plant the crocuses 3 inches deep and 3 inches apart; the colchicums and sternbergias 6 inches deep and 4 inches apart. All should be in well-drained soil and a rather sheltered but sunny position.

Lift Daffodils and Bulbous Irises. Daffodils and narcissi, also the various bulbous irises, will now have completed their growth and may be lifted and cleaned off if they are overgrown or you need the ground for something else. Otherwise leave them undisturbed for another year. They do not gain anything by annual lifting and drying, as do tulips and hyacinths. If you do lift them, get them replanted as soon as possible and certainly before the end of September.

Cut Back Helianthemums. Sun roses tend to get rather straggly if left to their own devices, but if cut back a little each year at about this time they can be kept quite neat and tidy. You can do the work with a large pair of scissors or even the garden shears.

Start to Feed Chrysanthemums. It is a mistake to begin to feed chrysanthemums of any type too early, but you can start now with safety. The more varied the 'feed' the better. Give very small doses every five days or so mixed with plenty of water and used in place of the ordinary water. Liquid manure, made by steeping a small sack of cow, horse, or sheep droppings in a tub of water, can be varied with soot water and any good chemical fertilizer made especially for chrysanthemums and used strictly in accordance with manufacturer's instructions.

'Take' Early-flowering Chrysanthemum Buds. This term requires some explanation. It is virtually the chrysanthemum grower's equivalent to disbudding, for it means that the flower buds required for producing big blooms are retained, while all smaller buds or shoots surrounding or below them are rubbed out. It is only necessary to do this if you want big flowers borne singly on long stems. If your object is to have sprays of comparatively small flowers, let the plants grow on naturally. In any case you will not be able to complete all the disbudding at once, but look over the plants now, for some at least should be showing flower buds.

Sow Parsley for Autumn and Winter Use. Make a final sowing of parsley for autumn and winter use. If you sow the seeds in a very sheltered place, you can leave some of the plants undisturbed and keep on cutting from them as long as possible, but a portion of the seedlings will have to be transplanted into a frame in September if you wish to have a Christmas supply.

Sow Hardy Green Colewort. If you wish to have a really full supply of green vegetables right through the autumn months, make a small sowing of hardy green colewort now to supplement the supply of rosette colewort made last month (see June, Third Week). Details of sowing are exactly as before. This variety will be available after the rosette colewort is over.

Start to Bud Fruit Stocks. Stocks of various fruit trees, such as apples, pears, plums, and cherries, can usually be budded at about this time. You can apply the same tests to the stocks as those suggested for rose stocks (see June, Fourth Week). Of course, there are no thorns by which you can test the shoots selected as scions, and as it is most important that they should be in just the right condition, you must examine them carefully. You should be able to peel the bark easily from the wood. If it tears, growth is either too young or too dry. The buds should be well

BUDDING A FRUIT TREE

1. *A suitable young but firm growth from which to take buds.* 2. *A bud as cut from the stem.* 3. *Removing the strip of wood contained within the bark carrying the bud.* 4. *T-shaped incision made in the bark of the stock.* 5. *The bark is raised carefully.* 6. *The shield-shaped piece of bark carrying the bud is slipped into position.* 7. *The top of the shield-shaped piece of bark is trimmed level with the top of the T-shaped incision.* 8. *The bud is bound firmly in position with soft raffia.*

developed and clearly visible. The actual details for budding are just the same as for roses, except that instead of inserting them as low down on the dwarf stocks as possible, they should be put in about 8 inches above soil level. It is desirable that the union of rose stock and scion should be covered with soil, but this is not advisable with fruit trees, for the scions might then make roots of their own, which would upset the particular effect, dwarfing or otherwise, of the stock chosen.

Buds can only be inserted into stocks that have thin, supple bark. Some form of grafting in spring (see March, Fourth Week) must be used for old, hard-barked trees that are being reworked.

FLOWERS, VEGETABLES, AND FRUITS IN SEASON
DURING JULY

Hardy Herbaceous Plants. *Acanthus mollis, Achillea filipendulina, A. mille-folium* vars., *A. Ptarmica* vars., *A. sibirica, A. taygetea, Aconitum Lycoctonum, A. Napellus* vars., *Adenophora Bulleyana, A. latifolia, Althaea rosea* vars. (hollyhock), *Alstroemeria aurantiaca, A. chilensis, A. haemantha, A. ligtu, A. Pelegrina, A. pulchella, Anaphalis margaritacea, Anthemis cupaniana, A. nobilis, A. Sancti-Johannis, A. tinctoria* and vars., *Anthericum ramosum, Armeria latifolia* and vars., *Arnica sachalinensis, Artemisia lactiflora, Asclepias tuberosa, Asphodeline lutea, Asphodelus ramosus, Aster ptarmicoides, A. subcaeruleus* vars., *A. Thomsonii, Astilbe Arendsii* hybrids, *Astrantia carnio-lica, A. major, Baptisia australis, Borago laxiflora, Calceolaria* John Innes, *Buphthalmum salicifolium, Campanula alliariaefolia, C. glomerata dahurica, C. lactiflora, C. latifolia, C. persicifolia* and vars., *C. pyramidalis, C. rapun-culoides, C. rhomboidalis, C. Trachelium, C. Vanhouttei, Centaurea babylonica, C. dealbata, C. macrocephala, C. montana, C. pulcherrima, C. ruthenica, Centranthus ruber, Cephalaria alpina, C. tartarica, Chrysanthemum leucan-themum* vars., *C. maximum* vars., *Chicorium Intybus* vars., *Cimicifuga dahurica, Clematis integrifolia, C. recta, Coreopsis grandiflora* vars., *C. lanceolata* vars., *Delphinium Belladonna* vars., *D. cardinale, D. formosum, D. sulphureum,* delphiniums in var. (large-flowered hybrids), *Dianthus Allwoodii, D. barbatus* vars. (Sweet William), *D. Caryophyllus* vars. (border carnations), *D. plumarius* Cyclops, *Dicentra eximia, D. spectabilis, Dictamnus Fraxinella, Digitalis ambigua, D. gloxinioides* vars. (foxgloves), *D. purpurea* (wild foxglove), *Dracocephalum Ruyschiana, Echinacea purpurea* and vars., *Echinops bannaticus, E. Ritro, E. sphaerocephalus, Eremurus Bungei* and vars., *Erigeron aurantiacus, E. Mesa-grande, E. speciosus* and vars., erigeron hybrids, *Eryngium alpinum, E. amethystinum, E. Bourgatii, E. giganteum, E. Oliverianum, E. planum, E. spinalba, E. Violetta, Euphorbia Myrsinites, Filipendula hexapetala flore-pleno,* gaillardia hybrids, *Galega officinalis* and vars., *Gaura Lindheimeri, Geranium armenum, G. Endressii, G. eriostemon, Geum coccineum* vars., *G. Heldreichii, Gypsophila paniculata* and vars., *Helenium autumnale* and vars., *H. Bigelovii* and vars., *Heliopsis laevis, H. scabra, Hemerocallis aurantiaca, H. Forrestii, H. fulva, H. multiflora, H. Thunbergii,* hemerocallis hybrids, *Heracleum villo-sum, Heuchera brizoides, H. sanguinea* and vars., *Hosta Fortunei, H. glauca, H. lancifolia, H. ovata, Inula glandulosa, I. Helenium, I. Oculus-Christi, I. Royleana, Iris dichotoma, Isatis glauca, Kniphofia caulescens, K. Macowanii, K. Nelsonii, K. rufa, K. Tuckii, K. Uvaria* vars., *Lavatera Olbia, Liatris pycno-stachya, Linaria dalmatica, L. purpurea, Linum narbonense, L. perenne, Lychnis chalcedonica, L. coronaria, L. Flos-jovis, L. Haageana, L. Viscaria* and vars., *Lupinus arboreus, Lysimachia clethroides, L. thyrsiflora, Lythrum Salicaria* and vars., *L. virgatum* vars., *Macleaya cordata, M. microcarpa, Malva moschata, Meconopsis betonicifolia, M. cambrica* and vars., *M. napaul-ensis, M. quintuplinerva, M. Regia, Mertensia sibirica, Monarda didyma* and vars., *Morina longifolia, Nepeta grandiflora, N. Mussinii, Oenothera biennis* vars., *Oe. fruticosa* and vars., *Oe. glauca, Oe. odorata, Oe. speciosa, Papaver nudicaule* vars. (Iceland poppy), *Penstemon barbatus, P. gentianoides* hybrids (shelter in winter), *P. isophyllus, Phlox Arendsii* hybrids, *P.-*

decussata hybrids, *P. suffruticosa* hybrids, *Phygelius capensis, Physostegia virginiana* and vars., *Platycodon grandiflorum, Polemonium carneum, P. caeruleum, P. humile, P. pauciflorum, Polygonum amplexicaule, P. bistorta* vars., *P. campanulatum,* potentilla hybrids, *Poterium obtusum, P. tenuifolium, Romneya Coulteri, R. trichocalyx, Rudbeckia amplexicaule, R. californica, R. speciosa (Newmanii), R. subtomentosa, Salvia argentea, S. Przewalskii, S. Sclarea* and vars., *S. virgata, Scabiosa caucasica* and vars., *Sidalcea candida, S. malvaeflora* and hybrids, *Solidago Virgaurea praecox, Spiraea Aruncus, S. lobata, S. palmata, Statice bellidifolium, S. eximia, S. Gmelinii, S. incana, S. latifolia, Thalictrum adiantifolium, T. dipterocarpum, Tradescantia virginica, Trollius Ledebourii* and vars., *Tropaeolum polyphyllum, Verbascum bombyciferum, V. Chaixii, V. nigrum* (vernale), *V. olympicum, V. phoeniceum, V. thapsiforme (densiflorum), V. Weidmannianum,* verbascum hybrids, *Veronica longifolia* and vars., *V. spicata, V. virginica* and vars.

Hardy Bulbs and Tubers. *Allium azureum, A. Beesianum, A. sphaerocephalum, Crocosmia masonorum, Galtonia candicans, Gladiolus Colvillei* vars., *Iris xiphioides,* (English irises), *Lapeyrousia cruenta Lilium amabile, L. Brownii, L. Burbankii, L. canadense, L. candidum* (Madonna Lily), *L. cernuum, L.*

LILIUM CHALCEDONICUM
This beautiful, easily grown, hardy lily bears red flowers on stems 3-4 feet tall. It likes some lime and plenty of leaf-mould in the soil.

chalcedonicum, L. columbianum, L. concolor, L. croceum, L. Duchartrei, L. elegans (Thunbergianum), L. giganteum, L. Grayi, L. Humboldtii, L. japonicum (Krameri), L. Martagon and vars., *L. Maxwillii, L. monadelphum Szovitsianum, L. pardalinum, L. parviflorum, L. parvum, L. philadelphicum, L. princeps* and vars., *L. regale, L. superbum, L. sutchuenense, L. testaceum, L. Willmottiae, Ostrowskia magnifica, Tigridia Pavonia.*

Rock Plants. *Acantholimon glumaceum, Achillea ageratifolia, A. Clavenae, A. tomentosa* and vars., *Androsace lanuginosa* and vars., *Antennaria dioica* and vars., *Armeria maritima* and vars., *Asperula suberosa, Astilbe simplicifolia, Calandrinia umbellata, Calceolaria polyrrhiza, Campanula Allionii, C. barbata, C. carpatica* and vars., *C. garganica* and vars., *C. Porten-*

schlagiana, C. Poscharskyana, C. pulla, C. pulloides, C. pusilla, C. Raddeana, C. Raineri, C. rotundifolia, C. sarmatica, C. Stansfieldii, C. Tommasiniana, C. Wockii, C. Zoysii, Chrysogonum virginianum, Conandron ramondioides, Convolvulus althaeoides, C. Cneorum, C. mauritanicus, Coreopsis rosea, Crucianella stylosa, Dianthus alpinus, D. caesius, D. deltoides and vars., D. Freynii, D. Knappii, D. neglectus, D. superbus, Epilobium Fleischeri, Erodium chamaedryoides, E. chrysanthemum, E. corsicum, E. guttatum, E. macradenum, E. Manescavii, E. trichomanifolium, Erythraea Massonii, Frankenia laevis, Genista sagittalis, G. tinctoria plena, Gentiana Freyniana, G. lagodechiana, G. Purdomii, G. septemfida, Geranium argenteum, G. cinereum, G. Pylzowianum, G. sanguineum and vars., Geum Borisii, G. montanum, Globularia cordifolia, G. nudicaulis, Gypsophila cerastioides, G. repens and vars., Helichrysum belli- dioides, Hieracium aurantiacum, H. villosum, Hypericum Coris, H. fragile, H. nummularium, H. olympicum, H. repens, H. reptans, Inula acaulis, I. ensi- folia, Jasione Jankae, J. perenne, Lavandula vera nana, Leontopodium alpinum,

GENTIANA SEPTEMFIDA

One of the easier gentians to grow, this is a somewhat sprawling plant with purplish- blue flowers. It likes a sunny position and a peaty soil.

Lewisia Columbiana, L. Cotyledon, L. Heckneri, L. Howellii, Linaria aequitri- loba, L. alpina, L. hepaticaefolia, L. pallida, Linum alpinum, L. arboreum, L. flavum, L. monogynum, L. salsoloides, Lychnis Lagascae, Lysimachia num- mularia, Matthiola fenestralis, Oenothera acaulis, Oe. caespitosa, Oe. missouri- ensis, Oe. riparia, Onosma albo-roseum, O. tauricum, Othonopsis cheirifolia, Papaver alpinum, Parochetus communis, Penstemon Davidsonii, P. heterophyllus, P. Menziesii, P. Scouleri, Phyteuma comosum, P. Halleri, P. hemisphaericum, P. orbiculare, P. Scheuchzeri, Potentilla ambigua, P. aurea, P. fragiformis, P. nepalensis and vars., P. nitida, P. Tonguei, Primula anisodora, P. capitata, P. Mooreana, Prunella incisa, Ranunculus alpestris, R. crenatus, Rosa Roulettii, Rhodohypoxis baurii, Scabiosa graminifolia, S. Pterocephala, Sedum acre, S. album, S. anglicum, S. dasyphyllum, S. Ellacombianum, S. Ewersii, S. hispani- cum, S. kamtschaticum, S. Lydium, S. Middendorfianum, S. pulchellum, S. reflexum, S. rupestre, S. spathulifolium, S. spurium, Sempervivum Allionii, S.

arachnoideum and vars., *S. calcareum, S. Funkii, S. globiferum, S. Hookeri, S. montanum, S. tectorum, S. triste, S. violaceum, Senecio tyrolensis, Silene alpestris, S. Schafta, Sisyrinchium angustifolium, Solidago Buckleyi, Stachys corsica, Statice minuta, Thymus Serpyllum* and vars., *Tunica Saxifraga, Verbena chamaedryfolia, Veronica Bidwillii, V. carnosula, V. catarractae, V. Hectori, V. pimeleoides, V. pinguifolia, Viola bosniaca, V. cornuta* and vars., *V. gracilis* and vars., *V. hederacea, Wahlenbergia vincaeflora.*

Hardy Aquatics and Bog Plants. *Acorus Calamus, Alisma Plantago, Anemone rivularis, Aponogeton distachyon,* astilbes in var., *Butomus umbellatus, Epipactis palustris, Filipendula ulmaria flore-pleno, Iris aurea, I. fulva, I. Kaempferi* and vars., *I. ochroleuca, I. sibirica* and vars., *Ligularia clivorum, Limnanthemum nymphaeoides, Limnocharis Humboldtii, Lysimachia vulgaris, Menyanthes trifoliata, Mimulus cardinalis, M. luteus* and vars., *M. ringens, Myosotis palustris, Nuphar luteum,* nymphaeas in var., *Orchis foliosa, Parnassia palustris, Pontederia cordata, Primula Beesiana, P. Bulleyana, P. Florindae, P. Littoniana, P. microdonta* and vars., *P. Poissonii, Ranunculus Lingua, Rodgersia aesculifolia, R. pinnata, R. podophylla, R. sambucifolia, R. tabularis, Sagittaria sagittifolia* and vars., *Stenanthium robustum, Stratiotes aloides, Typha angustifolia, T. japonica, T. latifolia, T. Laxmannii, T. minima.*

Annuals. Hardy vars. (as June); half-hardy vars. (as list February, Third Week).

Bedding Plants. As June, but also dahlias (bedding and charm) and begonias (tuberous-rooted and semperflorens).

Hardy Evergreen Shrubs. *Abelia grandiflora, Bupleurum fruticosum* (seaside), *Calluna vulgaris* and vars., *Carpenteria californica* (shelter), *Ceanothus Burkwoodii,* cistus (as June), *Cotoneaster lactea, C. serotina, Daboecia polifolia, Daphne acutiloba, Desfontainea spinosa, Erica ciliaris* and vars., *E. cinerea* and vars., *E. Mackeyi, E. stricta* and vars., *E. Tetralix, E. vagans* and vars., *E. Watsonii, Escallonia exoniensis, E. floribunda* (shelter), *E. Ingramii, E. Iveyi, E. langleyensis, E. macrantha* (shelter), *E. pterocladon* (shelter), *E. punctata, E. rubra, Hebe angustifolia, H. anomala, H. balfouriana, H. buxifolia, H. cupressoides, H. leiophylla, H. obovata, H. salicifolia, H. traversii, H. vernicosa, Hypericum calycinum, Jasminum revolutum, Kalmia cuneata, K. latifolia, Lavandula Spica* (English lavender), *L. vera* (Dutch lavender), *Leucothoe Davisiae, Magnolia glauca, M. grandiflora, Myrtus communis, Olearia Gunniana, O. Haastii, O. nummularifolia, Osmanthus fragrans, Phlomis fruticosa, Salvia Grahamii* (shelter), *Santolina Chamaecyparissus, Senecio Greyi, S. laxifolius, Teucrium fruticans, Ulex nanus, Vinca major, V. minor, Yucca filamentosa, Y. gloriosa.*

Hardy Deciduous Shrubs. *Abelia Schumannii, Abutilon vitifolium, Aesculus parviflora, Amorpha canescens, Buddleia alternifolia, B. variabilis* and vars., *Calycanthus floridus, Caragana decorticans, Carmichaelia grandiflora, Ceanothus americanus, C. azureus* and hybrids, *Ceratostigma Willmottianum, Clerodendrum trichotomum, Clethra alnifolia, Colutea arborescens, Cotinus coggygria, Cytisus leucanthus, C. nigricans, C. purpureus, C. virgata, Deutzia corymbosa, D. crenata* and vars., *D. scabra* and vars., *D. taiwanensis, Escallonia Phillipiana, Fremontia californica* (shelter), *Fuchsia macrostemma* and vars., *F. Riccartonii,*

*Gaylussacia frondosa, Genista aethnensis, G. cinerea, G. dalmatica, Halimoden-
dron argenteum, Hedysarum multijugum, Hydrangea arborescens grandiflora,
H. Bretschneideri, H. macrophylla* vars., *Hypericum patulum* and vars., *Indigo-
fera Gerardiana, Itea virginica, Jamesia americana, Leycesteria formosa,
Lupinus arboreus, Lyonia ligustrina, Magnolia parviflora, Meleosma cuneifolia,
M. myriantha, Nandina domestica, Notospartium cerasiformis, Philadelphus
grandiflorus, P. incanus, P. insignis, P. microphyllus, P. Satsumi, Plagianthus
Lyallii, Potentilla fruticosa, Rhodotypos kerrioides, Robinia Hartwegii,
Rosa alba, R. anemonaeflora, R. Beggeriana, R. bracteata, R. carolina
Nuttaliana, R. filipes, R. Moyesii, R. multibracteata, R. rugosa,* hybrid
roses (tea, hybrid tea, hybrid perpetual, pernetiana, polyantha), *Rubus
odoratus, R. thyrsoideus plenus, R. ulmifolius bellidiflorus, Spartium junceum,
Spiraea Aitchisonii, S. arborea, S. assurgens, S. discolor, S. japonica* and
vars., *S. Margaritae, S. Menziesii* and vars., *S. sorbifolia, S. Veitchii,
Stewartia pentagyna, S. pseudocamellia, Tamarix pentandra, Zenobia speciosa.*

LEYCESTERIA FORMOSA
(HIMALAYAN
HONEYSUCKLE)

*A shrub of unusual appearance,
this reaches 4 to 8 feet and
bears short trails of chocolate
and white flowers. It will grow
almost anywhere in sun or
shade.*

Hardy Evergreen Trees. *Eucryphia nymansensis, Koelreuteria paniculata.*

Hardy Deciduous Trees. *Aesculus californica, Castanea sativa, Catalpa
bignonioides, Cladrastis sinensis, Lagerstroemia indica* (shelter), *Oxydendrum
arboreum, Tilia cordata, T. euchlora, T. petiolaris, T. platyphyllos, T. tomentosa,
T. vulgaris* (common lime).

Hardy Climbing Plants. *Berberidopsis corallina* (shelter), *Clematis Durandii,
C. Fargesii, C. florida* and vars., *C. Hendersonii, C. Jackmannii* and vars., *C.
lanuginosa* and vars., *C. montana Wilsonii, C. Pitcheri, C. Viticella* and vars.,
Jasminum officinale (jessamine), *J. stephanense, Lathyrus latifolius* and vars.
(everlasting pea), *Lonicera caprifolium, L. etrusca, L. Heckrottii, L. japonica*
and vars., *L. Periclymenum* and vars. (honeysuckle), *L. plantierensis, L.
tragophylla, Passiflora caerulea, Periploca graeca, P. sepium, Polygonum bald-*

schuanicum, hybrid roses (climbing hybrid tea, tea, pernetiana, and polyantha, also multiflora, wichuraiana, noisette, hybrid bracteata, and hybrid rugosa), *Schizophragma hydrangeoides, Solanum crispum, S. jasminoides, Trachelospermum divaricatum, Tropaeolum speciosum, Wisteria frutescens, W. japonica, W. macrostachya.*

Greenhouse Plants. Achimenes, *Agapanthus umbellatus,* annuals (as June), *Asclepias curassavica*, balsam, begonias (tuberous-rooted), boronias, bougainvilleas, *Campanula pyramidalis*, cannas, carnations (perpetual-flowering and border), *Cassia corymbosa*, celosias, celsias, *Cestrum elegans, Clianthus Dampieri, C. puniceus, Cobaea scandens*, correas, *Crassula coccinea*, crinums, *Cuphea ignea*, daturas, *Didiscus caerulea, Diplacus glutinosus, Erica insignis, E. praestans rosea, E. ventricosa, Erythrina Crista-galli, Francoa ramosa*, fuchsias, gloxinias, heliotrope, *Hibbertia dentata, Hoya carnosa, Humea elegans*, lantanas, *Lagerstroemia indica, Lapageria rosea, Lasiandra macrantha*,

LAPAGERIA ROSEA (CHILEAN BELLFLOWER)

This is one of the most attractive evergreen climbers for the cool greenhouse. It has large, bell-shaped, rose-coloured flowers with waxy petals. There is a white form.

Lilium auratum, L. longiflorum, L. speciosum, Mandevilla suaveolens, marguerites, *Maurandya Barclaiana, Mitraria coccinea, Nerium Oleander*, pancratiums, passifloras, zonal pelargoniums, *Plumbago capensis, Rehmannia angulata, Rhyncospermum jasminoides*, streptocarpus (old plants), *Streptosolen Jamesonii*, swainsonas, tacsonias, tecomas, tropaeolums (including double vars.).

Vegetables in the Garden. Globe artichokes, broad beans, french beans, runner beans, shorthorn carrots, cauliflowers, lettuces, vegetable marrows, mustard and cress, onions, peas, potatoes (early vars.), radishes, spinach, turnips.

Vegetables under Glass. Cucumbers, mushrooms (cool cellars and sheds), tomatoes.

Fruits Outdoors. *Apples:* Beauty of Bath (D), Early Crimson (D), Early Victoria or Emneth Early (C), Gladstone (D), White Transparent (C). *Blackberry:* Bedford Giant. *Cherries:* Archduke (D), Bedford Prolific (D), Blackheart

(D), Black Tartarian (D), Early Amber (D), Elton (D), Flemish Red (C), Frogmore Bigarreau (D), Governor Wood (D), Kentish Bigarreau (D), Kentish Red (C), Knight's Early Black (D), Ludwig's Bigarreau (D), Peggy Rivers (D), Schrecken Bigarreau (D), Ursula Rivers (D), Whiteheart (D). *Currants, Black:* Boskoop Giant, Laxton's Giant, Mendip Cross, Seabrook's Black, Wellington XXX. *Currants, Red:* Earliest of Fourlands, Cherry, Fay's Prolific, Laxton's No. 1, Laxton's Perfection, The Comet. *Currants, White:* White Dutch, White Versailles. *Gooseberries:* Careless, Golden Drop, Early Sulphur, Keepsake, Leveller, Langley Gage, Lancashire Lad, Whinham's Industry, Whitesmith. *Loganberry. Pears:* Doyenne d'Eté (D), Early Market (D). *Phenomenal Berry. Plums:* Black Prince (C), Early Laxton (C), Rivers' Early Prolific (C). *Raspberries:* Lloyd George, Pyne's Imperial, Pyne's Royal, Red Cross, Yellow Antwerp. *Strawberries:* Baron Solemacher, Red Gauntlet, Sans Rivale, St Claude, Talisman. *Veitchberry.*

Fruits under Glass. *Apricots:* Early Moorpark, Frogmore Early, Luizet, New Large Early, Precoce de Boulbon. *Grapes:* Buckland's Sweetwater, Foster's Seedling, Royal Muscadine. *Nectarines:* Cardinal, Early Rivers, Joan Rivers. *Peaches:* Duke of York, Amsden's June, Hale's Early, Waterloo.

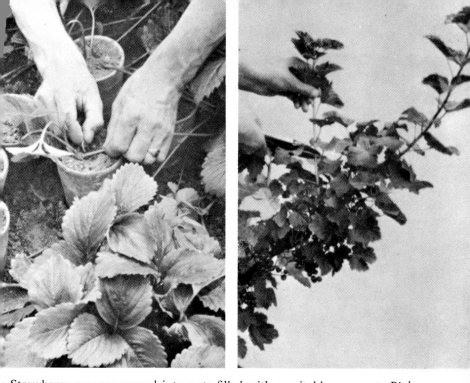

*: Strawberry runners pegged into pots filled with a suitable compost. *Right:*
side growths of red currants may be shortened to about 3 inches to encourage
formation of spurs.

cuttings of heaths ready for trimming before insertion in a sandy compost.

Layering suitable side shoots of a border carnation.

Left: When pruning raspberries only the new, vigorous canes are retained and tied in. *Right:* Disbudding dahlias, leaving the centre bud only.

August

GENERAL WORK

Take Geranium Cuttings. You can take cuttings of both zonal and ivy-leaved bedding geraniums (pelargoniums) at any time during the month. Choose shoots, 4 or 5 inches long, that are not carrying flowers. Sever them cleanly just below a joint and insert the cuttings around the edge of well-drained 4- or 5-inch flower pots filled with sandy compost. The cuttings will root most rapidly if you stand them in a frame and shade them from direct sunshine, but they can also be rooted in any reasonably sheltered place indoors or out. Water moderately until the cuttings commence to grow, after which they will need increasing supplies.

If you want a batch of greenhouse zonal pelargoniums for late spring and summer flowering, take a batch of cuttings now and treat them in exactly the same way as the bedding varieties.

Continue to Bud Fruit and Rose Stocks. You can continue to bud both fruit and rose stocks throughout the month provided the stocks work well (see note on Rose Budding, July, General Work). As a rule, however, it is wise to complete rose budding as early in the month as possible, as late buds do not give such good results.

Examine the early buds put in during June and July and loosen any ties that are cutting into the bark. It is advisable to replace such ties with new ones, as the buds may not have made a very secure union yet.

Continue to Remove Faded Flowers, Runners, etc. Throughout the month continue to remove faded flowers from roses, bedding plants, etc.; also runners from violets. Disbud roses and dahlias if you require some big flowers (see June and July, General Work).

Complete Trimming of Hedges, etc. Evergreen shrubs grown as hedges or topiary specimens can still be trimmed during August, but it is wise to complete the work for the season at the end of the month. Late trimming may result in soft autumn growth which will get damaged by frost.

Continue to Secure Shrub Cuttings. You can continue to take shrub cuttings during the month, as described in my notes for July (see July, General Work). Hydrangeas usually root very freely during this month, and do best if inserted singly in 2½-inch pots, so that there need be no subsequent root disturbance. They must be kept in a shaded frame without ventilation until rooted and should be watered very freely.

Keep an eye on the cuttings of shrubs, etc., taken last month and as soon as these start to grow remove them very carefully from the frames or hand lights and pot them up separately in 2½-inch pots, using the usual compost (see p. 44). Keep them in a frame or cool greenhouse for the time being, shading them from strong, direct sunshine and syringeing them with tepid water every day, but as they get hardened and root out into the new soil, accustom them to outdoor conditions, and eventually, after a few weeks, remove them to a plunge bed in a sheltered place outdoors. Plant them in a sheltered nursery bed in October or March.

HOW TO PROPAGATE A HYDRANGEA

In order to obtain strong young plants each carrying a fine truss of bloom such as that shown on the right, cuttings of young growth trimmed just below a joint (above) should be kept in a shaded frame.

Keep down Foes. Most of my July notes on the subject of pests and diseases (see July, General Work) apply with equal force to August. One foe that is likely to be on the increase is the earwig. Sprays are not effective against this, but a reliable poison bait can be made by thinning 1 pint of black treacle with a little water, adding ½ pound of sodium fluoride dissolved in a small quantity of water, and then mixing with about 4 pounds of bran to form a moist but not wet mash. Another method of ridding the garden of earwigs is to trap them in small flower pots, filled with hay and inverted on sticks among dahlias, chrysanthemums, and other plants commonly attacked. Examine the traps every morning. Earwigs will hide in them by day, for they dislike the light.

'Take' Chrysanthemum Buds. Continue to 'take' early-flowering chrysanthemum buds—*i.e.*, to secure the good buds you need for flowering and to remove all shoots and buds below them, as I explained in my notes

EARWIG TRAP

A small flower pot filled with hay and inverted on top of a dahlia stake. The earwigs hide in the pot by day and can be collected and destroyed.

BEFORE
SECURING
THE BUD

TAKING A CHRYSANTHEMUM BUD

This means that the flower bud is retained and all small side growths lower down the stem are rubbed out.

AFTER
SECURING
THE BUD

for July, Fourth Week. A little later in the month exactly the same process must be applied to late-flowering chrysanthemums that are being grown for large blooms. Exhibition varieties are usually needed about the middle of November, and it is desirable that they should show their buds from the middle to the end of August. However, if some do show up early you must keep them (or 'take' them, as the chrysanthemum grower confusingly puts it) now, for it is too late to remove them and wait for the next lot. Sometimes early buds can be retarded quite a bit by leaving the sideshoots to grow up around them for a week or so before pinching them out, but you must not overdo this, or you may starve the bud too much.

General Greenhouse Management. All the remarks in the June and July notes on this subject still apply with as much force as ever. Ventilation will be needed both day and night: top and side most days, but top only at night unless conditions are exceptional. Always be ready with shading at the first sign of scorched foliage, and damp down paths, stages, and walls with increased freedom if red spider or thrips put in an appearance. August is generally the peak month for these drought-loving pests.

The earliest batches of achimenes, begonias, and gloxinias will have finished flowering by this time, and their water supply should be very gradually reduced so that they ripen their growth and go to rest. Similar remarks apply to early hippeastrums, which will also be coming towards the close of their season of growth.

Make Successional Sowings. There are still a few successional sowings to be made. Mustard and cress and also radishes should be sown as before. A small sowing of shorthorn carrots made early in the month in a very sheltered place will continue the supply of young roots well into the autumn, while endive and lettuce sown about the middle of the month, also in a sheltered border, will provide you with seedlings some of which can be left to grow on undisturbed, while others are transferred to a frame.

Start to Blanch Endive. By this month endive from the first sowing (see April, Fourth Week) should be ready for blanching. Only do a few plants at a time, however, as blanching stops growth. There are several ways of accomplishing this task, but none, I think, better than the very simple plan of covering each plant with an inverted flower pot or a saucer. If you use flower pots, you must be careful to cover the hole in the bottom of each to secure perfect blanching. It usually takes about a fortnight to get a complete blanch.

Continue to Blanch Leeks. This work must be continued as I have already described (see June, General Work) until a sufficient length of blanched stem—usually about a foot—is obtained.

Lift Second Early Potatoes as Required. When you come to the end of the first early potatoes make a start on the second early or mid-season varieties such as Catriona and Arran Banner, but only lift a few roots at a time as you require them.

Plant Coleworts. You can continue to plant coleworts as ground becomes available (see July, General Work), but other winter greens should all be planted by this time.

Thin Vegetable Seedlings. Do not neglect to thin out seedlings of lettuce, spinach, etc., made last month. Do the work as soon as you can conveniently handle the seedlings and water those you leave if the soil is dry.

Feed and Train Tomatoes. In the main, treatment of tomatoes this month is exactly the same as during July (see July, General Work). As soon as the outdoor plants have made four trusses of flowers, stop them from growing further by pinching out the tips of the main stems.

Clear out Spent Cucumbers. It is probable that the early cucumbers will not be worth keeping any longer, especially if you have a good supply of plants in frames. Clear them out when they cease to bear freely, and take the opportunity to give the house a thorough clean out and scrub down. If you have been troubled with thrips and red spider, fumigate with naphthalene or sulphur while the house is empty. Use one of the lamps specially manufactured for vaporizing these chemicals. They can be purchased from any dealer in horticultural sundries. If the house cannot be emptied use azobenzene in the form of a smoke. Specially prepared canisters can be purchased for this purpose. Other effective preparations, containing derris, can be used for dealing with red spider. Manufacturer's instructions should be followed.

Kill American Blight on Apples. This is a suitable time to take steps to destroy American blight (also known as woolly aphis) on apples. This is an insect pest which infests cracks in the branches and twigs and protects itself with a white, cotton-wool-like covering. Go over the trees carefully and brush methylated spirits or a solution of BHC into the woolly patches. For larger attacks overall spraying with BHC or malathion may be carried out.

Pick and Summer-prune Apples and Pears. During this month and also throughout September you should continue to pick apples and pears as they ripen, applying the tests already described (see July, Third Week). You should also continue to summer-prune the trees (see July, Third Week), but strive to complete the work by the end of the month.

Management of the Orchard House. There is nothing to add to my remarks on this subject in the notes for July, General Work, except that ventilation can be even freer and syringeing of cleared trees more thorough than before.

Treat Vines according to Growth. Vines, both indoors and out, will be in various stages of growth, according in part to the time at which they were started and in part to the variety. Regarding actual treatment, there is nothing to be added to my former remarks (see notes on General Work, May, June, and July). Early vines from which you have gathered the crop should be ventilated freely and syringed fairly frequently if there is any sign of red spider on the leaves.

DESTROYING
AMERICAN BLIGHT
This pest is really a species of aphis which protects itself with a white, cotton-wool-like covering. It attacks the bark and eventually causes cracks and wounds, left. On the right methylated spirit is being brushed on to the the woolly patches to destroy the pest. BHC *may also be used.*

FIRST WEEK

Sow Stocks and Mignonette for the Greenhouse. Make sowings of both Beauty of Nice and Brompton stocks for flowering in pots in the greenhouse. The former will bloom from Christmas until February or March, while the Brompton stocks will follow on in late spring. Sow all very thinly in well-drained pans or boxes filled with the usual compost (see p. 26), and germinate in a frame, shading until the seedlings appear, but thereafter giving full light and free ventilation. Prick off or pot separately in 2½-inch pots as soon as the seedlings have two true leaves each.

Pot Freesias for Early Flowering. Provided the corms are properly ripened, the earlier freesias can be potted the better. The beginning of August is usually about as soon as one can purchase the corms, so if you want a supply of flowers for Christmas, pot up some now in 5- or 6-inch pots. You can place six corms in a 5-inch pot or ten in a 6-inch pot. Use a compost of three parts of loam, one part of moss peat, and one part of dry cow manure and sand in about equal proportions. Bury the corms 1 inch deep in this and then stand the pots in a frame. Water moderately and shade from direct sunshine, but do not use the lights as yet. Old corms from last year that have been resting during the summer (see May, General Work) should also be shaken out and repotted now.

Pot Lachenalias. Lachenalias for winter flowering in the greenhouse should also be potted or be placed in hanging baskets (a very delightful method of growing these beautiful South African bulbs). The method of culture in pots is exactly the same as for freesias (see above). If to be grown in hanging baskets, the latter must be well lined with moss and then some of the bulbs should be placed at the bottom and around the sides of the basket, as well as on top. Use the same compost as for freesias in pots and cover the top bulbs to a depth of 1 inch. Hang the baskets up in a cool place for the time being and water moderately until growth starts. Purchase new corms now, or shake the old ones out of the dry soil in which they have been resting and repot them (see May, General Work).

Repot and Start Arum Lilies. The arum lilies that have been resting during the summer (see May, General Work) should now be started into growth. If they have been more than one year in their present pots, repot them

AN ARUM LILY OFFSET
A sturdy young growth detached from a large root and potted on its own.

first. Shake the old compost off the tubers and place them in 6-, 8-, or 10-inch pots, according to their size. If they have made any sturdy offsets, these can be detached and potted separately. Use a compost of three parts of loam, one part of dried cow manure, and one part of sharp sand, with a sprinkling of bone-meal. Stand the pots in a sheltered place in the open and water very moderately at first, but gradually give more as growth proceeds.

Ripen off Onions. Onions from the January and March sowings will now be approaching ripeness, and you can hasten this by bending over the leaves just above the neck of each bulb.

Pot Winter-flowering Begonias. If you were able to root cuttings of winter-flowering begonias in late winter (see April, General Work) the plants should now be about ready for potting on into their flowering pots. These should be 5 or 6 inches in diameter. Use a compost of three parts of loam, one part of moss peat, one part of sharp sand, and one part of dried cow manure and wood ashes, or, failing this, the general compost recommended on page 62. Place the plants on a shelf in the greenhouse and shade from direct sunshine.

Sow Tomatoes and Cucumbers for Winter. This is the time to sow both tomatoes and cucumbers for cropping during the winter months. I do not recommend either crop to the amateur, however, for the tomatoes must have an average temperature of 65° and the cucumbers nearer 75° if they are to be satisfactory. That means more artificial heat than most amateur gardeners have at their command. In addition there is the difficulty of maintaining growth and getting the tomatoes to ripen when the days are short and light is poor. However, if you do decide to have a shot at either or both these crops, sow the seeds at once and follow the directions given for the early crops under glass.

SECOND WEEK

Cut Back Violas and Pansies for Propagation. It is an excellent plan to cut back a few plants of any good violas and pansies one may have with a view to encouraging basal growth which will provide cuttings next month. Scissor off the present flowering shoots to within 1 inch of the roots. Then scatter a little fine soil mixed with sand and sifted leaf-mould over the plants.

Pot Greenhouse Calceolarias and Cinerarias. As soon as greenhouse calceolarias begin to touch in the boxes in which they were pricked off last month (see July, Third Week) they must be pricked off a second time, leaving 3 inches from plant to plant, or, alternatively, potted up singly in 2½-inch pots. For this use the general potting compost (see p. 62) and return the plants to the frame, treating them as before and being very careful to keep them cool by free ventilation and shading. Also, keep a sharp eye on cinerarias in frames. The first batch sown in May (see May, First Week) is likely to require a move on into 5-inch pots, while the later batch, pricked off last month (see July, Third Week) will certainly very soon require first potting into 3-inch pots. This I have already described in the notes for June, Fourth Week. Syringe the plants daily with clear water.

ENCOURAGING THE FORMATION OF VIOLA CUTTINGS
This old plant has been cut back and is being top-dressed with a light compost. Later on an abundance of young growths will be produced, many of which may be pulled out with a few white rootlets, left.

Sow Cyclamen. It is possible to raise cyclamen from seed sown very early in the year and flower the plants the following winter, but very much better results are obtained by sowing about the middle of August and keeping the seedlings growing steadily, but slowly, throughout the following autumn, winter, spring, and summer so that they make fine big corms for flowering the following autumn and winter. Sow in well-drained pans in the usual seed compost (see p. 26), and space the seeds individually ½ inch apart each way. Cover with ¼ inch of the same soil and then with a pane of glass and a sheet of brown paper, and germinate in any frame or greenhouse in which you can maintain a steady temperature of 60° or rather more. Very high temperatures are not necessary or advisable.

Restart Old Cyclamen Corms. Old cyclamen corms that have been resting in a shady frame since May (see May, Second Week) may now be repotted and started into growth. Clean off all the old foliage, shake most of the soil off the roots and repot in the smallest pots that will accommodate the roots comfortably, without any doubling up. Use the same compost as for the final potting of seedlings (see p. 157). Return the plants to a shady frame for a few weeks, ventilate rather sparingly,

water very moderately at first, but syringe the corms daily with tepid
water to encourage them to make new growth.

Cut Back Pelargoniums and Insert Cuttings. Show and regal pelargoniums that were stood outdoors last month (see July, First Week)
should now be cut back. Shorten all growths to about 1 inch and then
begin to spray the plants daily with tepid water, continuing this daily

TAKING GERANIUM
CUTTINGS

*The prepared cuttings are
placed in 4- or 5-inch, well-
drained pots, filled with a
sandy compost. Keep them
shaded and water sparingly
until well-rooted.*

throughout the month. The shoots that you cut off can be inserted as
cuttings if you need some more plants. The method of preparing and
rooting cuttings is exactly the same as for bedding geraniums (see
General Work).

Sow Spring and Pickling Cabbages. Make a second sowing of spring
cabbages now in exactly the same way as I described in my notes for
July, Third Week. The reason for this is that in some seasons the earlier
seedlings grow thin and spindly and eventually run to seed instead of
forming hearts.

   If you also want to have some big red cabbages for pickling next year,
sow a few seeds in exactly the same manner as for ordinary spring
cabbages (see above).

Lift Early Beetroot. Beetroots do not improve by getting very big, so lift
the early globe varieties rather before they average the size of tennis balls
—which will probably be about this time. Twist off the tops without
injuring the skin of the beetroot in any way (bleeding is very easily
caused and, if severe, may spoil the colour of the roots) and store them
in any cool shed, cellar, or room. They will keep all the better if surrounded by sand that is just moist.

Prune Summer-fruiting Raspberries. By this time the summer-fruiting
raspberries will have quite finished cropping, and the sooner they are

pruned the better. Cut out, right to ground level, all the canes that have just fruited, and train in the young canes in their place. This treatment will also suit the variety Lloyd George, for though this raspberry is sometimes described as perpetual-fruiting, any late summer or autumn fruits it may carry will be on the current year's canes, not on last year's canes.

THIRD WEEK

Start Nerines. Give a little water to nerines that have been resting all the summer and increase the amount as soon as growth appears. The pots should stand on the staging in a sunny greenhouse. Ventilate freely and do not shade at all.

Sow Schizanthus for Spring Flowering. In order to have really large plants of schizanthus in 7- or 8-inch pots for spring decorations in greenhouse and conservatory you should sow now. Sow seeds thinly in well-drained seed boxes, using the usual compost (see p. 26), and germinate in a frame. Keep the lights on and the frame shaded until the seedlings appear, then remove the shading and begin to give a little ventilation, increasing this until after a week or so the lights are only used to keep off heavy rain. The cooler the conditions under which the plants are grown the better, for schizanthus get drawn very easily.

Sow Winter Spinach and Spinach Beet. Choose a fairly sheltered place and make a sowing of prickly-seeded spinach to stand the winter. Sow the seed thinly in drills 1 inch deep and 1 foot apart.

You can also make a sowing of spinach beet now for use in winter and spring. This useful variety of beetroot is grown solely for its leaves, which are used as a substitute for spinach. Sow the seeds in small groups 8 inches apart, in drills 1 inch deep, and make the drills 15 inches apart. Later, you can single out the clusters of seedlings.

Start to Gather Mushrooms from Outdoor Beds. If you were able to make a mushroom bed in the open early in July (see July, First Week) you should examine it now for the first mushrooms. Gather the 'buttons' (young mushrooms) as they form. The bed should continue in bearing well on into the autumn.

Make New Strawberry Plantations. Strawberry runners that were pegged down early last month (see July, First Week) should now have made good roots and can be severed from their parent plants. A few days later you can lift them carefully and plant them in new beds. Choose a good open position and soil that has been deeply dug and well manured. Plant the strawberries 1 foot apart in rows 2 feet apart. After the first year alternate plants can be removed if overcrowded.

If you want to grow some early strawberries in the greenhouse, pot up a few of the strongest young plants in 6-inch pots, using a compost of three parts of loam, one part of dried manure, and one part of sharp sand, with a sprinkling of wood ashes. Stand the pots in a frame or sheltered place outdoors, but do not cover with any lights as yet.

A STURDY STRAWBERRY PLANT
This is the type of plant that can be obtained by rooting runners in pots.

FOURTH WEEK

Prune Hydrangeas. Most hydrangeas will have finished flowering and will benefit from a little pruning. Cut off each faded flower truss as far back as the first plump-looking growth bud, and remove any thin, weakly looking stems. Of course, if some of the branches are still producing good blooms leave these unpruned.

Lift Spring-sown Onions. Onions sown in January under glass and in March outdoors should now have completed their growth, and there is no point in leaving them in the ground any longer. Lift them carefully with a fork and spread them out on the surface to dry. After a few days you can shake any soil from the bulbs and store them, either on shelves or in shallow boxes in a dry, frost-proof shed or room, or else strung together in ropes after the French fashion.

Sow Onions. This is the time to sow onions, both for use as small salading in the spring and also to provide early bulbs before the spring-sown crop. For the former purpose White Lisbon is the best variety as it is very mild in flavour, but for bulb-making choose one of the Tripoli varieties or Giant Rocca. Select a fairly sheltered place and ground that has been well cultivated but not recently manured. Sow the seeds thinly in drills ½ inch deep and 9 inches apart.

Start to Earth up Maincrop Celery. It is now time to begin to earth up the maincrop celery. The process is exactly as described for early celery (see July, Second Week) except that with these bigger plants more soil will be required. It is quite a good plan to draw the stems together with raffia ties before starting to earth up, so that one can have both hands free for working the soil around the plants.

FLOWERS, VEGETABLES, AND FRUITS IN SEASON DURING AUGUST

Hardy Herbaceous Plants. *Acanthus mollis, Achillea filipendulina, A. Mille-folium* vars., *A. Ptarmica* and vars., *A. sibirica, Aconitum Lycoctonum, A. Napellus* vars., *Adenophora Bulleyana, A. latifolia, A. Potaninii, Althaea rosea* vars. (hollyhocks), alstroemerias (as July), *Anaphalis margaritacea, Anemone japonica* and vars., *Anthemis Cupaniana, A. Sancti-Johannis, A. tinctoria* and vars., *Artemisia lactiflora, Asclepias incarnata, A. tuberosa, Aster acris, A. Amellus* and vars., *A. Frikartii, A. luteus, A. linosyris, A. ptarmicoides, A. Thomsonii, Astilbe Arendsii* hybrids, *Boltonia asteroides, Buphthalmum salici-folium, Campanula alliariaefolia, C. lactiflora, C. latifolia* vars., *C. pyramidalis* and vars., *C. sarmatica, C. Vanhouttei, Catananche caerulea* and vars., *Centaurea montana* and vars., *C. ruthenica, Chelone Lyonii, C. obliqua, Chrysanthemum erubescens, C. macrophyllum, C. maximum* vars. (Shasta daisies), chrysanthemums (early-flowering hybrids), *Cimicifuga dahurica, C. japonica, C. racemosa, Clematis heracleaefolia* and vars., *C. integrifolia, C. recta, Coreopsis grandiflora* and vars., *C. lanceolata* and vars., *Dianthus Allwoodii* vars., *D. Caryophyllus* vars. (border carnations), *D. plumarius* Cyclops, *Dierama pulcherrima, Dracocephalum Ruyschiana, Echinacea purpurea* and vars., *Echinops bannaticus, E. Ritro, E. sphaerocephalus, Erigeron Mesa-grande, E. speciosus* and vars., eryngiums (as July), *Filipendula hexapetala,* gaillardias (hybrids), *Galega officinalis* and vars., *Gaura Lindheimeri, Gentiana asclepiadea, Geum bulgaricum, G. coccineum* vars., *G. Heldreichii, Gypsophila paniculata* and vars., *Helenium autumnale* and vars., *Helianthus multiflorus* and vars. (sunflower), *H. rigidus* and vars. (sunflower), *H. tomentosus, Heliopsis laevis, H. scabra* and vars., *Hemerocallis aurantiaca, H. Forrestii, H. fulva rosea, H. minor, H. multiflora, H. Thunbergii,* hemerocallis hybrids, *Heuchera brizoides, H. sanguineum* and vars., *Hosta fortunei, H. lancifolia* and vars., *H. ovata, H. sieboldiana, H. subcordata, Inula glandulosa, I. Helenium, I. macrocephala, I. Oculus-Christi, I. Royleana, Kniphofia erecta, K. Galpinii, K. macowanii, K. Nelsonii, K. rufa, K. Uvaria* and vars. (red-hot poker), *Lactuca Bourgaei, Lavatera Olbia, Liatris pycnostachya, L. spicata, Ligularia pulcher, L. tanguticus, L. Veitchiana, Linaria dalmatica, Linum narbonense, L. perenne, Lobelia cardinalis, L. fulgens* and vars., *L.*

siphilitica and hybrids, *Lychnis chalcedonica, L. coronaria, Lysimachia ciliata, L. thyrsiflora, Lythrum virgatum* vars., *Malva Alcea* vars., *M. setosa* hybrids, *Meconopsis Wallichii, Monarda didyma* and vars., *Nepeta grandiflora, N. macrantha, N. Mussinii, Oenothera biennis* vars. (evening primrose), *Oe. fruticosa, Oe. glauca, Oe. odorata, Oe. speciosa, Papaver nudicaule* and vars. (Iceland poppies), *Penstemon barbatus, P. gentianoides* hybrids (shelter in winter), *P. isophyllus, Phlox decussata* hybrids, *Phygelius capensis, Physostegia virginiana* and vars., *Phytolacca decandra* (fruits), *Platycodon grandiflorum* and vars., *Polygonum amplexicaule, P. bistorta* vars., *P. campanulatum*, potentilla hybrids, *Poterium canadense, P. obtusum, P. tenuifolium, Romneya Coulteri, R. trichocalyx, Rudbeckia californica, R. laciniata* and vars., *R. maxima, R. nitida* vars., *R. speciosa* (*Newmanii*), rudbeckias (hybrids), *Salvia azurea grandiflora, S. Przewalskii, S. Sclarea* and vars., *S. uliginosa, S. virgata, Saponaria officinalis plena, Scabiosa caucasica* and vars., *Sedum maximum,*

HEMEROCALLIS FULVA (DAY LILY)

The day lilies are among the most colourful of summer-flowering perennials. H. fulva, *2 to 5 feet tall has yellow flowers but there are many fine hybrids in shades of orange and tawny yellow.*

sidalceas (hybrids), *Silphium perfoliatum, S. scaberrimum, Solidago Ballardii, S. caesia, S. serotina, S. Virgaurea* and vars. (golden rod), *Spiraea kamtschatica, S. lobata, S. palmata*, statices (as July), *Stokesia cyanea, Thalictrum dipterocarpum, Tradescantia virginiana, Tropaeolum polyphyllum, Veratrum album, V. nigrum, V. viride*, verbascums (as July), *Verbena bonariensis, V. tenera Mahonetii, V. venosa, Veronica exaltata, V. longifolia* and vars., *V. spicata* and vars., *V. virginica* and vars.

Hardy Bulbs and Tubers. *Allium Beesianum, Amaryllis Belladonna* vars., *Anomatheca cruenta* (shelter), *Antholyza aethiopica, A. crocosmioides, A. paniculata, Crinum longifolium* and vars., *C. Powellii* and vars., *Crocosmia masonorum, Cyclamen europaeum*, gladioli (large-flowered and primulinus vars.), *Lilium auratum, L. Batemanniae, L. Bolanderi, L. cordifolium, L. Henryi,*

L. princeps, L. speciosum, L. superbum, L. tigrinum, L. Wardii, L. Willmottiae, montbretias (hybrids), *Tigridia Pavonia* and vars.

Rock Plants. *Achillea Clavenae, A. tomentosa* and vars., *Androsace lanuginosa* and vars., *Antirrhinum Asarina, A. glutinosum, Arnica sachalinensis, Astilbe simplicifolia, Calamintha alpina, Calystegia japonica, Calandrinia umbellata, Campanula carpatica* and vars., *C. cochleariifolia, C. Portenschlagiana, C. pusilla* and vars., *C. Tommasiniana, C. Waldsteiniana, C. Wockii, C. Zoysii, Ceratostigma plumbaginoides, C. Willmottianum, Chrysanthemum arcticum, Chrysogonum virginianum, Convolvulus althaeoides, C. Cneorum, C. mauritanicus, Corydalis cheilanthifolia, C. lutea, Crucianella stylosa, Erodium chamaedrioides* and vars., *Erythraea Mussonii, Genista tinctoria plena, Gentiana Farreri, G. Freyniana, G. Lagodechiana, G. Purdomii, G. septemfida, Geranium argenteum, G. cinereum, G. sanguineum* and vars.

CAMPANULA MEDIUM
(CANTERBURY BELL)

A popular biennial, the Canterbury bell is excellent for bedding out. It is available in shades of blue, rose, purple and white, and with single or double flowers. 3 feet.

G. subcaulescens, Geum Borisii, G. montanum, Gypsophila cerastioides, G. repens and vars., *Hieracium aurantiacum, H. villosum, Hypericum Coris, H. fragile, H. olympicum, H. repens, H. reptans, Hypsella longiflora, Inula acaulis, I. ensifolia, Linaria aequitriloba, L. alpina, L. hepaticaefolia, L. pallida, Linum alpinum, L. arboreum, L. flavum, L. salsoloides, Lippia repens, Lithospermum prostratum* and vars., *Nierembergia hippomanica, N. rivularis, Oenothera caespitosa, Oe. missouriensis, Oe. pumila, Oe. taraxacifolia, Onosma alboroseum, O. echioides, O. tauricum, Origanum Dictamnus, Othonnopsis cheirifolia, Papaver alpinum, Parochetus communis, Penstemon heterophyllus, Polygonum affine, P. vaccinifolium, Potentilla ambigua, P. nepalensis* and vars., *P. nitida, P. Tonguei, Rhodohypoxis Baurei, Rosa Roulettii, Santolina Chamaecyparissus, Scabiosa graminifolia, S. pterocephala, Sedum Ewersii, S. kamtschaticum* and vars., *S. primuloides, S. Sieboldii, S. Telephium, Silene Schafta, Solidago*

Buckleyi, Spiraea digitata nana, Stachys corsica, Statice minuta, Tunica Saxifraga, Verbena chamaedryfolia, Viola canadensis, V. cornuta and vars., *Zauschneria californica.*

Hardy Aquatics and Bog Plants. *Alisma Plantago, Anagallis tenella, Aponogeton distachyon, Cyperus longus, Eriophorum polystachyon, E. vaginatum, Gentiana Pneumonanthe, Kirengeshoma palmata, Ligularia clivorum, Limnanthemum nymphaeoides, Limnocharis Humboldtii, Lysimachia vulgaris, Lythrum Salicaria* and vars., *Menyanthes trifoliata,* mimulus (as July), *Nartheciumossifragum,* nymphaeas (in var.), *Orontium aquaticum, Parnassia palustris, Phragmites communis, Polygonum sachalinense, Sagittaria sagittifolia* and vars., *Stenanthium robustum, Stratiotes aloides, Typha angustifolia, T. japonica, T. latifolia* (reed mace).

Annuals. Hardy vars. (as June, but sown April and early May), half-hardy vars. (as July), also asters.

Bedding Plants. As July, also dahlias of all types.

COBAEA SCANDENS
(CUPS AND SAUCERS)

A very attractive half-hardy, vigorous climber, perennial in the greenhouse, but killed by frost outdoors. The flowers are much like those of a Canterbury bell but opening creamy white and gradually turning purple.

Hardy Evergreen Shrubs. *Abelia grandiflora* (shelter), *Aplopappus ericoides* (shelter), *Berberis stenophylla semperflorens, Bowkeria Gerardiana* (wall), *Bupleurum fruticosum* (seaside), *Bursaria spinosa* (shelter), *Calluna vulgaris* and vars., *Ceanothus Burkwoodii, Cotoneaster serotina, Daboëcia polifolia, Erica ciliaris* and vars., *E. cinerea* and vars., *E. Mackayi, E. stricta, E. Stuartii, E. Tetralix* and vars., *E. vagans* and vars., *E. Watsonii, E. Williamsii, Escallonia exioniensis, E. floribunda* (shelter), *E. Iveyi, E. macrantha, E. montevidensis, E. Pterocladon, E. rubra,* escallonia (hybrids), *Hebe angustifolia, H. leiophylla, H. obovata, H. salicifolia, H. speciosa* and vars., *Hypericum calycinum, H. galioides, H. Moserianum, Lavandula lantana, L. Spica* (old English lavender), *L. vera* (Dutch lavender), *Myrtus communis, Olearia Gunniana, O. Haastii, O. macrodonta, Osmanthus fragrans, Parasyringa sempervirens, Penstemon cordifolius, Phormium Colensoi, P. tenax, Rhododendron auriculatum, Tamarix*

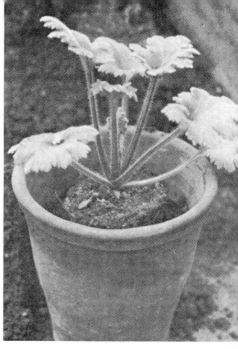

i: A specimen of *Primula sinensis* ready for potting on. *Right:* The plant is placed
he correct depth in the larger pot.

Pulling intermediate carrots.

When planting
narcissus bulbs
they must be well
spaced in the bowls
and firmed.

Bowls of bulbs may
be placed out of
doors and covered
with ashes or
placed in a cool,
dark place indoors.

gallica, Teucrium fruticans, Ulex Gallii, U. nanus, Viburnum coriaceum, Vinca major, V. minor, Yucca filamentosa, Y. gloriosa, Y. recurvifolia.

Hardy Deciduous Shrubs. *Abelia chinensis, A. Schumannii, Abutilon vitifolium, Aesculus parviflora, Amorpha canescens, Aralia chinensis, Buddleia alternifolia, B. variabilis vars., Calycanthus floridus, C. occidentalis, Cassia marylandica, Ceanothus azureus* and hybrids, *Ceratostigma Willmottianum, Clerodendrum Fargesii, C. trichotomum, Clethra alnifolia, Colquhounia coccinea, Colutea arborescens, C. istria, C. orientalis, Cyrilla racemiflora, Cytisus nigricans, C. ratisbonensis* vars., *Desfontainea spinosa* (shelter), *Deutzia corymbosa, Diostea juncea, Fuchsia macrostemma* and vars., *F. Riccartonii, Genista aethnensis, Hedysarum multijugum, Hibiscus syriacus* and vars., *Hydrangea arborescens grandiflora, H. Hortensia* and vars., *H. paniculata grandiflora, Hypericum hircinum, H. Hookerianum, H. patulum* and vars., *Indigofera amblyantha, I. decora, I. Dielsiana, I. Gerardiana, I. hebepetala, I. pendula, I. Potaninii, Itea virginica, Leptodermis oblonga, Leycesteria formosa, Lyonia ligustrina, Magnolia parviflora, Oxydendron arboreum, Perowskia atriplicifolia, Potentilla fruticosa* and vars., *Rosa anemonaeflora, R. Beggeriana, R. Ernestii, R. multibracteata, R. rugosa, Rubus odoratus, R. nutkanus, R. thyrsoideus plenus, R. ulmifolius bellidiflorus, Spartium junceum, Spiraea Aitchisonii, S. assurgens, S. discolor, S. japonica* and vars., *S. Margaritae, S. Menziesii* and vars., *S. sorbifolia, Stewartia pentagyna, S. pseudocamellia, Tamarix pentandra, Tripetaleia bracteata, Zenobia speciosa.*

SAINTPAULIA IONANTHA (AFRICAN VIOLET)

There are many named hybrids of this warm greenhouse perennial, in many shades of blue, violet, pink, and white. It is a popular house plant.

Hardy Evergreen Trees. *Acacia dealbata* (shelter), *Eucryphia nymansensis, E. pinnatifolia, Magnolia grandiflora* and vars., *Xylosma racemosa pubescens.*

Hardy Deciduous Trees. *Aesculus californica, Evodia velutina, Koelreuteria apiculata, K. paniculata, Lagerstroemia indica* (shelter), *Sophora japonica, Stewartia Malachodendron, Tilia petiolaris, T. tomentosa.*

Hardy Climbing Plants. *Berberidopsis corallina* (shelter), *Clematis aethusifolia, C. Durandii* and vars., *C. flammula, C. Hendersonii, C. Jackmanii* and vars., *C. Jouiniana, C. lanuginosa* and vars., *C. montana Wilsonii, C. orientalis, C. patens, C. Pitcheri, C. Rehderiana, C. rubromarginata, C. tangutica, C.*

O

Viticella and vars., *Jasminum officinale* (jessamine), *Lathyrus latifolius* and vars. (everlasting pea), *Lonicera alseuרsmoides, L. Brownii, L. etrusca, L. japonica* and vars., *L. Periclymenum* and vars. (honeysuckle), *L. tragophylla, Periploca graeca, Polygonum baldschuanicum, Rosa bracteata* and hybrids, *R. setigera,* hybrid roses (climbing teas, hybrid teas, and pernetianas, also wichuraiana, multiflora and polyantha ramblers, noisettes, and musk hybrids), *Solanum crispum, S. jasminoides, Tecoma grandiflora Thunbergii, T. radicans, Trachelospermum divaricatum, T. jasminoides, Tropaeolum speciosum, Wisteria frutescens, W. japonica.*

Greenhouse Plants. Achimenes, *Agapanthus umbellatus,* annuals (see June), *Asclepias curassavica,* balsam, begonias (tuberous-rooted), *Bignonia venusta,* boronias, bougainvilleas, *Campanula pyramidalis, C. isophylla,* cannas, carnations (perpetual-flowering), *Cassia corymbosa,* celosias, celsias, *Clianthus Dampieri, C. puniceus, Cobaea scandens, Crassula Bolusii, C. coccinea, Clerodendrum fallax,* crinums, *Cuphea ignea,* daturas, ericas (as July), *Erythrina Cristagalli, Francoa ramosa,* fuchsias, gloxinias, heliotrope, *Hibbertia dentata, Hoya carnosa, Humea elegans, Lagerstroemia indica, Lapageria rosea, Lilium longiflorum, L. speciosum* and vars., *Lasiandra macrantha, Mandevilla suaveolens,* marguerites, *Maurandya Barclaiana, Nerium Oleander, Oxalis Bowiei,* pancratiums, passifloras, *Plumbago capensis, Rehmannia angulata, Rhyncospermum jasminoides, Saintpaulia ionantha,* streptocarpus (sown Jan.), swainsonias, tacsonias, tecomas, *Trachelium caeruleum,* tropaeolums (including double vars.), *Vallota purpurea.*

VALLOTA PURPUREA (SCARBOROUGH LILY)
A strikingly handsome greenhouse bulb, this bears red flowers in August, on stems 2 to 3 feet high.

Vegetables in Store. Onions, shallots.

Vegetables Outdoors. Globe artichokes, broadbeans, french beans, runner beans, globe beetroot, cabbage (sown March), carrots, cauliflowers, celery, ridge cucumbers, endive, kohl-rabi, lettuce, vegetable marrows, mustard and cress, mushrooms, onions, peas, potatoes, radishes, spinach, tomatoes, turnips.

Vegetables under Glass. Cucumbers, mushrooms (cool cellars and outhouses), tomatoes.

Fruits Outdoors. *Apples:* Advance (D), Beauty of Bath (D), Devonshire Quarrenden (D), Early Victoria (C), Ecklinville Seedling (C), George Cave (D), Grenadier (C), Irish Peach (D), Keswick Codlin (C), Lady Sudeley (D), Langley Pippin (D), Leader (D), Lord Grosvenor (C), Maidstone Favourite (D), Scarlet Pimpernel (D), St Everard (D), Tydeman's Early Worcester (D), White Transparent (C). *Blackberries:* Bedford Giant, Himalaya Giant, John Innes, Parsley Leaved. *Cherries:* Emperor Francis Bigarreau (D), Florence (D), Geant d'Hedelfingen (D), Morello (C), Napoleon Bigarreau (D), Tradescant's Heart or Noble (D), Turkey Black Heart (D). *Currants, Red:* Fay's Prolific, Knight's Sweet Red, Laxton's No. 1, Laxton's Perfection, New Red Dutch, Raby Castle, Prince Albert, Rivers' Late Red. *Currants, White:* White Dutch, White Versailles. *Currants, Black:* Baldwin, Daniel's September, Davison's Eight, Seabrook's Black, Tinker, Westwick Choice. *Gooseberries:* Careless, Cousen's Seedling, Keepsake, Lancer, Leveller, Langley Gage, Lancashire Lad, Warrington, Whinham's Industry, Whitesmith. *Loganberry. Lowberry. Melons. Mulberry. Pears:* Clapp's Favourite (D), Early Market (D), Jargonelle (D), *Phenomenal Berry. Plums:* Belgian Purple (CD), Belle de Louvain (C), Blackbird (CD), Blue Rock (D), Blue Tit (D), Bountiful (D), Cambridge Greengage (D), Czar (CD), Denniston's Superb (D), Early Laxton (C), Early Transparent Gage (D), Evesham Wonder (C), Gisborne's Prolific (C), Green Gage (D), Jubilee (D), Laxton's Gage (D), Mirabelle (C), Oullin's Golden Gage (CD), Prosperity (C), Purple Pershore (C), Rivers' Early Damson (C), Supreme (D), Utility (D), Victoria (CD), Yellow Pershore (C). *Raspberries:* Lloyd George. *Veitchberry.*

Fruits under Glass. *Apricots:* Breda, Grosse Pêche, Hemskirk, Kaisha, Luizet, Moorpark, Oullin's Early Peach, Royal, Shipley or Blenheim. *Figs. Grapes:* Black Hamburgh, Buckland's Sweetwater, Foster's Seedling, Madresfield Court, Royal Muscadine. Melons. *Nectarines:* Dryden, Elruge, Hardwick, Humboldt, Lord Napier, Violette Hâtive. *Peaches:* Advance, Crimson Galande, Early Grosse Mignonne, Goshawk, Hale's Early, Kestrel, Peregrine, Rivers' Early York.

September

GENERAL WORK

Plant Narcissi, Lilies, Bulbous Irises, etc. Narcissi (including the trumpet daffodils), crocuses, Spanish, English, and Dutch irises, snowdrops, muscari, scillas, and also all lilies—with the exception of *Lilium candidum* (see July, Fourth Week)—can be planted with fair success at any time during the autumn, but the best results are obtained by early planting. If you can complete this work before September is out, so much the

PLANTING BULBS IN GRASSLAND

A hole is taken out with the special bulb planter, the bulb inserted, and the hole filled in with the ejected turf from the next hole to be taken out.

better. Tulips and hyacinths, however, may with advantage wait a little longer (see October, Fourth Week). All bulbs should be planted on fairly rich, well-worked soil, but preferably not ground that has been recently dressed with animal manure. Artificials of the right type are quite a different matter. A dusting of bone-meal, at 4 ounces per square yard, makes an excellent finish to the preparation of any bulb bed. The actual depth of planting should vary a little according to the nature of the soil, being rather deeper on light than on heavy land, but a fair average is as follows: narcissi, 5 inches deep, 8 inches apart; hyacinths, 6 inches deep, 8 inches apart; chionodoxa, 2½ inches deep, 3 inches apart; Crown Imperial, 6 inches deep, 1 foot apart; crocuses, 2 inches deep,

CUTTINGS OF EVERGREENS

A typical growth from an evergreen shrub with side shoots, each of which would make an ideal cutting. A prepared cutting is shown on the right (shaded).

3 inches apart; dog's-tooth violets, 2 inches deep, 6 inches apart; Spanish, English, and Dutch irises, 4 inches deep, 6 inches apart; snowdrops, 3 inches deep, 3 inches apart; muscari, 3 inches deep, 4 inches apart; *Scilla sibirica*, 2½ inches deep, 2 inches apart; *Scilla campanulata*, 4 inches deep, 4 inches apart; lilies (stem rooting), 8 inches deep, 12 inches apart; lilies (not stem rooting), 6 inches deep, 12 inches apart.

Depths refer to the hole prepared and not to the soil actually covering the top of the bulb. On the important point of whether a lily is or is not stem rooting, the catalogue of any specialist will give you full information and is usually obtainable free for the asking. The list is too long to be printed here (see also note on pot lilies, p. 215).

Do all the planting with a trowel or spade rather than a dibber. The last-named tends to make a pointed hole in which the bulb hangs suspended, with a hole beneath it.

Sow Grass Seed. Grass seed will germinate well enough at any time during September, though, other things being suitable, the sooner it can be sown the better, for then it will be well established before the winter. Details are exactly the same as for spring sowing (see April, First Week).

Take Cuttings of Evergreen Shrubs, etc. Many hardy evergreen shrubs can be propagated quite readily from cuttings taken during September and rooted in a frame or even a sheltered border. The process is similar to that which I have described for summer cuttings (see July, General Work), except that, on the whole, larger shoots are selected. They may be from 6 to 9 inches in length and should be pulled off with a 'heel' or cut closely beneath a joint. Insert them firmly 2 or 3 inches deep in very sandy soil. If in a frame keep the light on, but only shade from very strong direct sunshine. Water sufficiently to keep the soil moist but not sodden. Privet, *Lonicera nitida*, laurel, aucuba, rosemary, and lavender will all root readily in this way, and so will some herbs, such as thyme and sage.

Take Cuttings of Bedding Plants, etc. Throughout September you can take cuttings of a variety of plants, notably bedding calceolarias and penstemons, verbenas, mesembryanthemums, violas and pansies (cut

VIOLA CUTTINGS

The cutting on the left is unsuitable as it has a hollow stem, whereas the one on the right is ideal and should be cut as indicated by the black lines.

back last month), zonal geraniums (including the bedding varieties), antirrhinums, and violets. With all except violets, violas and pansies the method is to prepare cuttings 3 or 4 inches in length from firm, non-flowering shoots. Violet cuttings are prepared from the ends of the runners; pieces about 3 inches in length are ideal. Viola and pansy cuttings are made from young, non-flowering shoots coming from the base of the plant or directly from the roots. Frequently these can be pulled out with a few young, white rootlets attached. Zonal pelargonium cuttings should be rooted in pots, as I have already described (see August, General Work), and must be accommodated in a frost-proof greenhouse from late September onwards, but the others are better inserted directly into a bed of sandy soil prepared in a frame. Dibble them in a few inches apart, water freely, and keep the lights on and shaded until the cuttings are rooted. Then ventilate freely throughout the winter, only keeping the frames closed when frost threatens and removing the lights altogether when the weather is mild.

Prevent Mildew. The foe most to be feared during this month is mildew. It may appear on roses, culinary peas, delphiniums, chrysanthemums, gooseberries, plums, and a variety of other plants and fruits. In all cases it covers leaves and stems with a whitish powdery out-growth. At the first sign of this disease spray plants with weak lime-sulphur (summer strength), Bordeaux mixture, colloidal sulphur, or dinocap, one of the new fungicides.

General Greenhouse Management. Nights now begin to get much colder and one must be watchful with ventilation. The aim should still be an average day temperature of close on 60°, with a night minimum not much below 50°. Side ventilators are not likely to be needed, and even the top ventilators should be closed early in the afternoon if the weather is cold. Shading can be washed off the glass about the middle of the month for all except the most shade-loving plants—some ferns, for example. Syringeing and damping down should also be discontinued gradually. There will soon be too much moisture in the air for most greenhouse plants.

Continue the ripening of early hippeastrums, achimenes, begonias, and gloxinias (see August, General Work). Some of the later batches will also need less water if they have finished flowering.

Pot Lilies for the Greenhouse. I have separated lilies from the other bulbs for the greenhouse because their treatment is rather different and also because it is not so essential to pot early. If you can buy all the bulbs you need early in September, by all means get them potted, because lilies gain nothing by being out of the ground. But a good many bulbs come from abroad—some from the Far East— and these do not usually arrive until later, so you may have to wait awhile if you need any of these (see January, General Work).

Lilies are best grown singly, in pots 6 or 7 inches in diameter according to the size of the bulbs. Set the stem-rooting kinds (see p. 213) well down in the pots and only just cover them with soil now. Then, later on, as the stem grows, you can add top dressings of soil until the pot is almost full. Non-stem-rooting bulbs are potted nearer the surface and are not top dressed. Use the compost described on page 62, but be careful to use lime-free loam. The pots are not plunged under ashes like narcissi, etc., but are stood in an unheated frame or greenhouse to form roots. Do not use any artificial heat until top growth is several inches in length.

Place Bulbs in Ornamental Bowls. Hyacinths and narcissi that are to be grown in undrained ornamental bowls should be obtained as soon as possible. Special bulb fibre containing oyster shell and charcoal must be used for these. Put a few good lumps of charcoal in the bottom of the bowl, then spread a little fibre over it, set the bulbs firmly in position, allowing a clear inch between each, and just cover with more fibre. Water freely and stand in a cool, dark place (a cupboard will serve admirably) until the shoots are about 1 inch in length, when the bowls must be arranged in as light a place as possible. Keep the fibre moist throughout.

Make Successional Sowings. These can no longer be made outdoors as in former months—or at any rate outdoor sowings are only likely to be successful in the mildest districts—but it is a good plan to make yet another sowing of lettuce and endive in unheated frames and also to sow radishes and mustard and cress in the same way.

Plant Spring Cabbages. Cabbages from the July sowing (see July, Third Week) will be ready for removal early in the month to the plot in which they will mature. You could not do better than follow them on after onions that have just been lifted or place them on the ground that has recently been cleared of potatoes. Rake it clean, give it a dusting of old soot, and plant the cabbages about 1 foot apart in rows 18 inches apart. Later in the month the seedlings from the August sowing (see August, Second Week) should be treated in the same way. Coleworts may also still be planted on any available ground. They will come into use late in the autumn.

Continue to Earth up Celery and Leeks. From time to time during the month continue to draw more soil around celery plants and leeks, as described in the notes for May, First Week, July, Second Week, and August, Fourth Week.

Continue to Blanch Endive. During the month you should continue to blanch a few endives as they reach a fair size (see August, General Work).

Treat Vines according to Growth. The same remarks as those I made in last month's notes still apply with equal force (see August, General Work).

Ripen Growth in the Orchard House. Late peaches and nectarines may still be carrying fruits when the treatment recommended in earlier months must still be carried out, but the main effort during September is likely to be directed towards the thorough ripening of growth. This means plenty of ventilation when possible without lowering the temperature too much (55° should be the day minimum, and it is as well that the thermometer should not fall more than a further 5° at night), the discontinuance of ordinary feeding, and a gradual diminution of water supply. If growth tends to be excessive, give a dressing of sulphate of potash at 1 ounce per square yard.

Ripen off Melons in Frames. Melons in the greenhouse are likely to be finished, or nearly so, by this time, but plants in frames should be ripening their fruits and the atmosphere must be kept dry. Do not syringe the leaves at all and reduce the water supply to the roots, giving only sufficient to keep the leaves from flagging. Stand each fruit on an inverted flower pot to expose it to the sun as much as possible, and cover the frames at night with sacks or mats.

Continue to Pick Apples and Pears. Keep a sharp eye on apples and pears and continue to pick them as soon as they are ripe. With certain varieties of pear, such as Beurré Hardy, Jersey Gratioli, Dr Jules Guyot, and Williams, it is even advisable to pick a little before they are ripe and to complete the ripening process in a dry, fairly warm shed or room.

Complete Planting of Strawberries. There is still time to plant rooted strawberry runners in their fruiting quarters, as I explained last month (see August, Third Week), but the sooner the work is completed the better. If for some reason you cannot get them all planted out in September, leave the rest of the plants undisturbed until March (see March, First Week).

FIRST WEEK

Sow Hardy Annuals. A number of hardy annuals may be sown outdoors now to stand the winter and flower in May and June next year. Sow them thinly where they are to flower and cover lightly with soil. Thin the seedlings out to 3 or 4 inches apart as soon as they can be handled, but leave any further thinning until March or April. Among the best varieties for sowing in this manner are annual alyssum, calendula, candytuft, clarkia, annual coreopsis, cornflower, godetia, larkspur, nigella, Shirley and Cardinal poppies, annual scabious and viscaria. Antirrhinums can also be sown now, but unless your garden is fairly sheltered, I advise you to make this sowing in a frame. Give free ventilation, but use the lights to protect the seedlings against frost.

Sow Annuals for the Greenhouse. As I have already explained (see March, First Week), many annuals make first-rate pot plants for the cool greenhouse. If sown now they will start to flower in early spring and continue until May. Sow thinly in well-drained seed boxes or pans and germinate in a frame or unheated greenhouse. Shade until the seedlings appear, but subsequently give them plenty of light and air.

Plant Anemones. Make a first planting of anemones of the St Brigid and Du Caen types. If these are put in in successional batches, it is possible to extend the flowering season. The tubers should be planted 3 inches deep and 6 inches apart. If you wish you can also make a similar planting in a frame, as by this means you can get even earlier blooms—with a bit of luck by January. Place the lights in position, but ventilate moderately when the weather is mild.

Pot and Box Bulbs for Early Flowering. Lose no time in potting or boxing all the hyacinths, early tulips, narcissi (including early trumpet daffodils), ixias, gladioli of the *Colvillei* type, and bulbous-rooted irises, particularly *I. tingitana*, that you require for flowering in the greenhouse during the winter and spring. It is true that this work can be done at almost any time until the end of October, but there is no comparison between the results obtained from early and late potting. Also there is nothing to be gained by spreading the work over a long period. A succession of flowers can be obtained partly by choosing different varieties, some early and some late, and partly by keeping all the bulbs in cool quarters until they are needed and then bringing them into a warm greenhouse a few at a time. It does not much matter what size receptacles you use, but perhaps the best are pots 4 to 6 inches in diameter and boxes about 18 inches by 12 inches and 4 inches deep. Use a compost of loam three parts, moss peat one part, and sharp sand one part, and set the bulbs in this with a clear inch between them. Just cover them with the compost. Then stand all the pots and boxes outdoors in any fairly sheltered place, give them a good soaking, and cover all except ixias, gladioli, and irises with 3 inches of old sifted ashes, moss peat, coconut fibre, or sand. The object is to keep them cool, moist, and dark and so encourage the formation of plenty of roots before top growth starts. The bulbs must remain in this plunge bed for at least 8 weeks before they are brought into the greenhouse.

BULBS IN A PLUNGING BED

Each pot of bulbs has been covered with an empty inverted pot, a plan which, though not essential, certainly makes for cleanliness.

Pot More Freesias. Make a further potting of freesia corms as described in the notes for August, First Week. If these are placed in a frame, and are protected from frost with lights but no attempt is made to force them, they can be introduced to the warm greenhouse a few at a time from November onwards and will supply a succession of flowers in winter and early spring.

Pot on Primulas and Calceolarias. There may be quite a lot of potting on to be done if growth during August has been fairly good. Greenhouse primulas from the April sowing (see April, Fourth Week) should be about ready for their final pots, 5 inches in diameter, while the June-sown primulas (see June, Third Week) are also likely to need potting singly into 3-inch pots. The compost already mentioned so many times (see p. 62) should be used. After potting, the plants can go back into the frame for a few weeks, but will not need much shading now, and they must be ventilated more sparingly.

Greenhouse calceolarias which were given more space in August (see August, Second Week) must also be moved along before they get starved. They can now go into 3½-inch pots, other particulars being the same as for primulas.

Sow Cauliflowers. In a sheltered place make a small sowing of cauliflowers. Scatter the seed thinly, broadcast, and cover with ½ inch of fine soil.

Make a Mushroom Bed under Cover. As I explained in the July notes (see July, First Week), mushrooms can be grown at any time of the year but are easier to manage at certain seasons. Just as July is the ideal time for making outdoor beds, so early September is the best for beds in frames, outhouses, etc.

These beds will start to crop about the middle of October, just as the outdoor mushrooms are coming to an end, and with a little care will continue well into the winter. The method of forming the beds is exactly

SPAWNING A MUSHROOM BED

Small pieces of the spawn are pushed into the bed of prepared manure.

the same as before, except that in frames the whole area is covered with manure to a depth of 2 feet. Also it is particularly important to cover frame beds with an extra thick layer of straw. The frame lights may also be covered with thick mats or sacking, for mushrooms do best in the dark, and the extra covering will help to keep the bed at an even temperature.

SECOND WEEK

Prune Rambler Roses. Most rambler roses will have finished flowering and may be pruned. If they have made a great deal of new growth, much of it from near ground level, you can cut out all the old canes that have just borne flowers, but if there is not much young wood you will have to keep the best of the old and simply remove that which is obviously worn out or diseased. If you have to do this you must be careful to cut back all faded flower trusses, together with any heps they may be bearing. Weeping standard roses are pruned at the same time and in a similar manner. After pruning, train the long shoots round the umbrella-shaped training frames, which should be securely fastened to the stakes supporting the plants.

Lift Maincrop Carrots. Lift the maincrop carrots sown in April (see April, Second Week). If they are left in the ground any longer the roots are liable to crack. Dig them up carefully with a fork, cut off the tops and store the roots in a heap in any shed, cellar, or other frost-proof place. They will keep better and be less likely to shrivel if they are covered with sand or sifted ashes.

Lift Maincrop Beetroot. The main crop of long beetroot sown in May should also be lifted and stored at about this time (and, in any case, before the roots get old and coarse) as I described for early beet in the notes for August, Second Week.

Fix Grease Bands. Now is the time to fix grease bands around fruit trees. They are particularly serviceable on apples, but it is advisable to have them on all the bigger fruits just for safety. These grease bands are

GREASE BANDS

A double line of defence has been prepared on this tree for any insects that crawl over the lower band will be caught on the bands further up the tree.

actually strips of grease-proof paper tied round the trunk or main branches, and also any stakes at least a couple of feet above ground level and covered with a tacky substance. You can buy both paper strips and tacky compound from your local dealer in horticultural sundries. Keep the bands sticky until next March. They will catch all manner of insects that try to crawl over them, and are particularly serviceable against the winter moth, March moth, and woolly aphis (American blight).

Prune Loganberries. By this time loganberries will have finished fruiting and they should be pruned as soon as possible. Simply cut out to the base of the plant all canes that have just borne fruit and train the young canes in their place.

THIRD WEEK

Start to Plant Evergreen Shrubs. From now until about the second week in October is usually the ideal time for planting hardy evergreen shrubs. Of course, you cannot do this work if the weather happens to be hot or the ground is dry, but neither condition is likely to continue for long at this time of the year. Plant very firmly and stake all big specimens at once. Later on, if winds are very cold and drying, erect temporary shelters of hurdles, evergreen boughs, or sacking strained between stakes to protect the shrubs, at any rate on north and east.

Plant Violets in Frames. Violets that have been growing outdoors since April (see April, Second Week) should now be removed to frames for winter flowering. The frames must stand in a sunny and fairly sheltered position and be filled with good loamy soil to within 8 inches of the glass.

Plant the violet clumps almost touching one another. Water them in freely, but do not close the frames as yet. Later on, if frost threatens, put the lights on; but throughout the winter give the plants free ventilation whenever the weather is mild.

Plant Rooted Carnation Layers. Carnation layers pegged down towards the end of July (see July, Third Week) should be well rooted by this time. Scrape away a little of the soil and see how things are. If there are plenty of fibrous roots around the cut area sever the layers from the parent plants and, a few days later, lift them—each with a good ball of soil—and transfer them to their flowering quarters or, alternatively, pot them in 4- or 5-inch pots, place them in a frame, and plant them out in March (see March, Fourth Week). The soil should be good and loamy, with a liberal addition of crushed mortar rubble and a sprinkling of bone-meal.

Prick off Schizanthus. Schizanthus seedlings from last month's sowing (see August, Third Week) will be in need of pricking off. This should be done at the earliest possible moment, because if there is one thing the schizanthus will not stand it is getting drawn up through overcrowding. Prick off the seedlings 2 inches apart each way into deep, well-drained seed trays filled with the same compost as that used for seed sowing.

A CARNATION LAYER
Roots have formed and the layer has been detached.

Pick all Tomatoes. Outdoor tomatoes are not likely to ripen any more on the plants now, so it is as well to pick all the fruits that are showing some trace of colour and stand them in a sunny window to ripen. Absolutely green fruits can be made into tomato chutney. The summer crop of tomatoes under glass will also be coming to an end and, in view of the fact that every inch of greenhouse space is likely to be required in the next few weeks, it will be as well to clear these also, treating them in the same way as the outdoor fruits.

Lift Potatoes for Storing. The exact date at which maincrop and late potatoes should be fit for storing cannot be decided entirely by the calendar as it depends to some extent upon disease and also the weather. If much disease appears, it is wise to lift the tubers at once, before they get badly affected. Similarly, if August is very dry at first and then wet later tubers may begin to make second growth and must be lifted before they have dissipated themselves in a multiplicity of small potatoes. But, given average weather and freedom from disease, lifting commonly becomes general about this time. There is no necessity to wait until haulm dies down if the tubers are a good size and the skin holds really firmly to them. You can easily satisfy yourself on these two points by lifting a sample root. If you decide to lift the whole crop, put aside any damaged tubers for immediate use and store the rest in a frost-proof shed or cellar. An alternative is to make a clamp in the open. This is done by placing a layer of dry straw on the ground, heaping the potatoes on it in a steep-sided bank, covering with more straw and then a good coating of soil beaten down with the back of a spade. It is a wise precaution to draw a few wisps of straw through the soil at intervals along the ridge to allow warm, damp air to escape.

Thin out Vegetable Seedlings. Spinach beet, winter spinach, lettuce, and endive, from the sowings made last month (see August, Third Week and General Work), will need thinning out. Leave the plants of spinach beet about 15 inches apart and the spinach itself about 4 inches apart. The lettuces should be from 8 to 12 inches apart, according to variety, and the endive 12 inches apart. The seedlings of endive and lettuce can be transplanted carefully, either to a very sheltered border or, better still, to a frame. Water them in freely and they will provide a succession to those plants left undisturbed. An alternative method with endive is to thin out the plants now to about 4 inches apart and then lift the bigger plants at the end of October and transfer to a frame. They stand transplanting much better than lettuce, and by means of this late shifting one can sometimes make use of a frame that is filled with cucumbers or melons at the moment.

Prick out Red Cabbage. If you sowed pickling cabbage last month, prick out the seedlings now, 6 inches apart each way, in any fairly sheltered place. The plants will remain in this nursery bed until March, when they should go into their final quarters.

FOURTH WEEK

Pot Cyclamen Seedlings. Cyclamen seedlings from the sowing made in August (see August, Second Week) should be ready for pricking off or potting. Often the seed germinates very irregularly, so, if some of the seedlings are too backward for potting at the moment, leave them in the seed pans, lifting the more forward ones with a sharpened wooden tally. The ideal time for potting is when the seedlings have two or three leaves each. Pot singly in 2-inch pots, using the compost described on page 62. Keep the tiny corms well up on the surface of the soil. After potting, stand the pots on a shelf or staging in the greenhouse, giving them a good light place but shading them for a while from any very strong direct sunshine. Maintain an average day temperature of 55° and 45° at night. Similar remarks apply if you decide to prick off in boxes instead of potting singly.

House Late-flowering Chrysanthemums. It is wise to bring all chrysanthemums that are to flower in the greenhouse into its protection now

A row of celery that has been well earthed up.

Left: Leeks may be blanched by this simple method of placing drain pipes over individual plants. *Right:* A thick covering of straw on the mushroom bed excludes light and helps to keep the bed at an even temperature.

Above, left: When lifted, as shown above, apples will part easily if ready for picking. *Above:* Placing apples in storage racks in a frost-proof shed.
Left: Lifting gladioli ready for storing during the winter.

before frost damages their tender buds. Pot plants should be carried in and set on a hard bottom of ashes or gravel, or be arranged on staging, while plants that have been grown outdoors for lifting (see May, Fourth Week) must be dug up with as much soil as possible and either be planted in the greenhouse borders or else be dropped into suitable boxes and tubs. Give the plants sufficient room for air to circulate between them and light reach their leaves, otherwise you are certain to have trouble with mildew. Ventilate very freely while the weather is mild, but at any threat of frost close the house early in the afternoon and even use a little artificial heat if necessary.

Shelter Tender Plants. It will also be necessary to give some shelter to all tender greenhouse plants that have been outdoors during the summer months. This includes pelargoniums of various kinds (not forgetting the cuttings that have been rooted in pots), marguerites, perennial mesembryanthemums, fuchsias, double tropaeolums, hydrangeas, heliotropes, Indian azaleas, camellias, genistas, arum lilies, and agapanthus (blue Kaffir lily). Any of these that have been used for summer bedding should also be lifted and potted if you wish to save them for another year.

Scarlet salvias should be treated in the same way, unless you intend to raise new plants annually from seed, and similar remarks apply to any particularly choice forms of bedding lobelia or ageratum which you wish to raise from cuttings in the spring. The blue *Salvia patens*, also dahlias and begonias used for bedding may be left outdoors until frost first blackens their foliage. If you have not room for the other bedding plants as they are, you can cut back growth severely so that they do not take up so much space.

A good frame will provide sufficient protection for all these plants for a while if you cover the lights with sacks on frosty nights, but by the end of October it will be safer to have most of them inside the greenhouse, where you can use a little artificial heat to exclude frost.

Perpetual-flowering carnations that have been stood out for the summer should also be brought into shelter before they are injured by frost. Stand them in a light greenhouse with plenty of ventilation and just enough artificial heat to keep out frost and prevent the atmosphere from getting damp and stagnant.

Transplant Parsley to Frame. Lift some of the parsley seedlings from the July sowing (see July, Fourth Week) and transplant them carefully into a frame filled with good soil with which you have mixed some leaf-mould and a little old manure. Set the plants about 6 inches apart each

P

way and water them in freely. They will provide a crop throughout the winter if you use the lights just for frost protection.

Sow French Beans for Forcing. French beans are easier than most vegetables to force, and, if you have space at your disposal in a greenhouse that can be heated to a temperature of about 60°, you may make a sowing now for a winter crop. The method is exactly the same as for early spring crops (see January, Fourth Week).

FLOWERS, VEGETABLES, AND FRUITS IN SEASON DURING SEPTEMBER

Hardy Herbaceous Plants. *Achillea filipendulina*, *A. Ptarmica* and vars., *Aconitum Fischeri*, *A. Fortunei*, *A. Napellus* Spark's var., *A. Wilsonii*, *Actae spicata* (fruits), *Adenophora Bulleyana*, *Anemone japonica* and vars., *Anthemis Sancti-Johannis*, *A. tinctoria* and vars., *Artemisia lactiflora*, *Aster acris*, *A. Amellus* and vars., *A. cordifolius* and vars., *A. ericoides* and vars., *A. Frikartii* and vars., *A. Linosyris*, *A. luteus*, *A. novae-angliae* and vars. (Michaelmas daisies), *A. novi-belgii* and vars. (Michaelmas daisies), *A. ptarmicoides*, *Boltonia asteroides*, *Buphthalmum salicifolium*, *Catananche caerulea* and vars., *Centaurea montana* and vars., *C. ruthenicus*, *Chrysanthemum erubescens*, *C. uliginosum*, chrysanthemums (early-flowering Japanese vars.), *Cimicifuga japonica*, *C. racemosa*, *C. simplex*, *Coreopsis grandiflora* and vars., *Dierama pulcherrima*, *Dracocephalum Ruyschiana*, *Echinacea purpurea* and vars., *Eupatorium purpureum*, galliardias (hybrids), *Galega officinalis* and vars., *Gentiana asclepiadea*, *Geum coccineum* vars., *Gypsophila paniculata* and vars., *Helenium autumnale* and vars. (sunflower), *H. sparsifolius*, *H. tomentosus*, *Heliopsis scabra* and vars., *Hemerocallis fulva rosea*, hemerocallis hybrids, *Hosta fortunei*, *H. longifolia* and vars., *H. ovata*, *H. subcordata*, *Inula macrocephala*, *I. Royleana*, *Kniphofia erecta*, *K. Galpinii*, *K. Nelsonii*, *K. Uvaria* and vars. (red-hot poker), *Lavatera Olbia*, *Liatris pycnostachya*, *L. spicata*, *Ligularia tanguticus*, *L. veitchiana*, *Linaria dalmatica*, *Linum narbonense*, *L. perenne*, *Lobelia cardinalis*, *L. fulgens* and vars., *L. siphilitica* and hybrids, *Lysimachia ciliata*, *L. thyrsiflora*, *Lythrum virgatum* and vars., *Malva Alcea* vars., *M. setosa* hybrids, *Monarda didyma* and vars., *Nepeta grandiflora*, *N. macrantha*, *N. Mussinii*, *Oenothera biennis* and vars., *Oe. speciosa*, *Papaver nudicaule* and vars. (Iceland poppies), *Penstemon barbatus*, *P. isophyllus*, *Phlox decussata* hybrids, *Phygelius capensis*, physalis in var. for fruits (Cape gooseberry, Chinese lantern), *Physostegia virginiana* and vars., *Podophyllum emodi* (fruits), *Polygonum amplexicaule*, *P. campanulatum*, *P. equisetiforme*, potentilla hybrids, *Poterium canadense*, *P. obtusum*, *Romneya Coulteri*, *R. trichocalyx*, *Rudbeckia californica*, *R. laciniata* and vars., *R. maxima*, *R. speciosa* (*Newmanii*) rudbeckia hybrids, *Salvia Przewalskii*, *S. Sclarea* and vars., *S. uliginosa*, *Saponaria officinalis plena*, *Scabiosa caucasica* and vars., *Sedum spectabile* and vars., *Senecio tanguticus*, *Silphium scaberrimum*, *Solidago Ballardii*, *S. Virgaurea* and vars., statices (as July), *Stokesia cyanea*, *Thalictrum dipterocarpum* Hewitt's Double, *Tradescantia* *virginiana, Tricyrtis hirta, T. macropoda, Verbena bonariensis, V. venosa, Veronica exaltata, V. longifolia* and vars.

Hardy Bulbs and Tubers. *Amaryllis Belladonna* (shelter), *Antholyza aethiopica, A. crocosmioides, A. paniculata, Colchicum agrippinum, C. autumnale* and vars., *C. Bornmuelleri, C. byzantinum, C. speciosum* and vars., *Crinum longifolium* and vars., *C. Powellii* and vars., *Crocus cancellatus, C. pulchellus, C. zonatus, Cyclamen europaeum, C. neapolitanum, Lilium auratum, L. formosanum, L. Henryi, L. ochraceum, L. speciosum* and vars., *L. sulphureum* (shelter), *L. tigrinum, Merendera bulbocodium,* montbretias (hybrids), *Nerine Bowdenii* (shelter), *Oxalis lobata, Schizostylis coccinea* and vars., *Scilla autumnalis, Sternbergia lutea, Tigridia Pavonia.*

CEANOTHUS BURKWOODII

A beautiful, evergreen shrub requiring the protection of a wall, this bears deep blue flowers in late summer.

Rock Plants. *Achillea tomentosa* and vars., *Androsace lanuginosa* and vars., *Antirrhinum Asarina, Aster novi-belgii* (dwarf hybrids), *Astilbe chinensis pumila, Calandrinia umbellata, Campanula Zoysii, Ceratostigma plumbaginoides, C. Willmottianum, Chrysogonum virginianum, Convolvulus mauritanicus, Corydalis cheilanthifolia, Erodium chamaedryoides* and vars., *Erythraea Massonii, Gaultheria procumbens* (fruits), *Gentiana Farreri, G. lagodechiana, G. Macaulayi, G. septemfida, G. sino-ornata, Geranium sanguineum* and vars., *Geum Borisii, Hypsella longiflora, Linaria alpina, L. pallida, Lippia repens, Lithospermum prostratum* and vars., *Nertera depressa* (fruits), *Oenothera caespitosa, Oe. missouriensis, Oe. riparia, Oe. taraxacifolia, Origanum Dictamnus, Penstemon heterophyllus, Polygonum affine, P. vaccinifolium, Potentilla ambigua, P. fragiformis, P. nepalensis* and vars., *P. Tonguei, Pyrola rotundifolia, Scabiosa graminifolia, S. pterocephala, Sedum Ewersii homophyllum, S. Sieboldii, Silene Schafta, Solidago brachystachys, S. Buckleyi, Spiraea digitata nana, Statice minuta, Talinum calycinum, Tunica Saxifraga, Verbena chamaedryfolia, Viola canadensis, V. cornuta* and vars., *Zauschneria californica.*

Hardy Aquatics and Bog Plants. *Gentiana Pneumonanthe, Kirengeshoma palmata, Ligularia clivorum, Lythrum Salicaria* and vars., mimulus (as July), *Phragmites communis, Parnassia palustris, Sagittaria sagittifolia* and vars.,

Tolygonum Cookii, P. sachalinense, Stenanthium robustum, Thypha angustifolia, P. japonica, T. latifolia (reed mace).

Annuals. Hardy vars. (as June, but sown in May), half-hardy vars. (as July).

Bedding Plants. As July.

Hardy Evergreen Shrubs. *Abelia grandiflora* (shelter), *Aplopappus ericoides* (shelter), *Berberis stenophylla semperflorens, Bigelowia graveolens, Buddleia auriculata, Bupleurum fruticosum* (seaside), *Ceanothus Burkwoodii, Daboëcia polifolia, Erica ciliaris* and vars., *E. cinerea* and vars., *E. Mackayi, E. stricta, E. Stuartii, E. Tetralix* and vars., *E. vagans* and vars., *E. Watsonii, Escallonia exoniensis, E. Iveyi, E. floribunda* (shelter), *E. montevidensis, E. rubra,* escallonia hybrids, *Hebe angustifolia, H. salicifolia, H. speciosa* and vars., *Hypericum calycinum, H. galioides, H. Moserianum, Osmanthus Aquifolium, O. Fortunei, Parasyringa sempervirens, Pharmium Colensoi, P. tenax, Rhododendron serotinum, Teucrium fruticans, Ulex Gallii, U. nanus, Vaccinium ovatum, Viburnum coriaceum, Vinca major, V. minor, Yucca gloriosa, Y. recurvifolia.*

CLEMATIS JACKMANII

There are many hardy clematises available in a wide range of colour. They are excellent climbers for walls, pergolas, fences or old tree stumps. C. Jackmanii itself has rich violet purple flowers.

Hardy Deciduous Shrubs. *Abelia chinensis, A. Schumannii, Amorpha canescens, Buddleia paniculata, B. variabilis* and vars., *Calycanthus occidentalis, Caryopteris clandonensis, C. Mastacanthus, Cassia marylandica, Ceanothus azureus* and hybrids, *CeratostigmaWillmottianum,Clerodendrum Fargesii, C. trichotomum, Clethra alnifolia, Colletia armata, C. cruciata, Colquhounia coccinea, Colutea arborescens, C. orientalis, Cyrilla racemiflora, Desfontainea spinosa* (shelter), *Desmodium spicatum, Fuchsia macrostemma* and vars., *F. Riccartonii, Hedysarum multijugum, Hibiscus syriacus* and vars., *Hydrangea arborescens grandiflora, H. Hortensia* and vars., *H. paniculata grandiflora, Hypericum hircinum, H. Hookerianum, H. patulum* and vars., *Indigofera amblyantha, I. Dielsiana, I. Gerardiana, I. hebepetala, I. pendula, Itea virginica, Leptodermis oblonga, Leycesteria formosa, Oxydendrum arboreum, Perowskia atriplicifolia, Polygonum vaccinifolium, Potentilla fruticosa* and vars., *Rubus* *thyrsoideus plenus, R. ulmifolius bellidiflorus, Spartium junceum, Spiraea Menziesii* and vars., *Tamarix pentandra, Tripetaleia bracteata, Vitex Agnuscastus* (shelter).

Hardy Evergreen Trees. *Arbutus Unedo* (strawberry tree), *Magnolia grandiflora* and vars.

Hardy Deciduous Trees. *Alnus maritima, A. nepalensis, A. nitida, Aralia chinensis, Laburnum alpinum autumnale, L. caramanicum, L. vulgare semperflorens, Lagerstroemia indica, Sophora japonica.*

Hardy Climbing Plants. *Berberidopsis corallina* (shelter), *Clematis aethusifolia, C. calycina, C. coccinea, C. connata, C. Durandii* and vars., *C. flammula, C. Hendersonii, C. Jackmannii* and vars., *C. Jouiniana, C. lanuginosa* and vars., *C. orientalis, C. paniculata, C. Pitcheri, C. Rehderiana, C. tangutica, C. Viticella* and vars., *Jasminum officinale* (jessamine), *Lonicera alseuosmoides, L. Brownii, L. etrusca, L. Heckrottii, L. japonica* and vars., *L. Periclymenum serotina* (late Dutch honeysuckle), *L. tragophylla, Pilostegia viburnoides, Polygonum baldschuanicum, Rosa bracteata* and hybrids, hybrid roses (climbing teas, hybrid teas and pernetianas, and hybrid musks), *Solanum crispum autumnalis, S. jasminoides, Tecoma grandiflora Thunbergii, T. radicans, Tropaeolum speciosum.*

ABELIA GRANDIFLORA

This is a slightly tender semi-evergreen shrub, reaching 6 feet, which produces pink flowers from July to October. It requires the protection of a warm wall.

Fruiting Trees, Shrubs, and Climbers. *Berberis acuminata, B. Aquifolium, B. aristata, B. brevipaniculata, B. concinna, B. Darwinii, B. dictyophylla, B. Gagnepainii, B. Hookeri, B. Lycium, B. polyantha, B. Prattii, B. pruinosa, B. rubrostilla, B. Sieboldii, B. sinensis, B. Thunbergii, B. vulgaris, B. Wilsonae, B. yunnanensis, Coriaria japonica, C. terminalis, Cotoneaster adpressa, C. amoena, C. bullata, C. buxifolia, C. congesta, C. Dielsiana, C. divaricata, C. Franchetii, C. frigida,*

C. Henryana, C. horizontalis, C. humifusa, C. lucida, C. microphylla, C. rotundifolia, C. salicifolia and vars., *C. Simonsii, C. thymaefolia, Crataegus altaica, C. aprica, C. brachyacantha, C. Carrierei, C. coccinea, C. cordata, C. Crus-galli, C. durobrivensis, C. heterophylla, C. Korolkowii, C. macrantha, C. mollis, C. monogyna* (hawthorn), *C. orientalis, C. oxyacantha* (hawthorn), *C. prunifolia, C. punctata, Euonymus alatus, E. europaeus* (spindleberry), *E. latifolius, Hippophaë rhamnoides* (unisexual), *Lycium chinense* and vars., *Pernettya mucronata, Pyracantha angustifolia, P. coccinea* and vars., *P. Gibbsii, P. Rogersiana, Pyrus alnifolia, P. Aria* (whitebeam), *P. Aucuparia* (mountain ash), *P. baccata* (Siberian crab), *P. Eleyi, P. Malus* vars. (crab apple), *P. munda, P. Niedzwetzkyana, P. prunifolia, P. Ringo, P. toringoides, P. Vilmorinii, Rhaphithamnus cyanocarpus, Rosa alpina, R. altaica, R. Fargesii, R. macrophylla, R. microphylla, R. Moyesii, R. nutkana, R. omeiensis, R. pomifera, R. rugosa* and hybrids, *R. setipoda, R. Soulieana, R. tomentosa, R. Webbiana, Sambucus glauca, S. nigra* and vars. (elderberry), *S. pubens, Skimmia Fortunei, S. japonica* (unisexual), *Viburnum betulifolium, V. Davidii, V. Henryi, V. Lantana* (wayfaring tree), *V. molle, V. Opulus* (guelder rose), *V. prunifolium, V. rhytidophyllum, Vitis heterophylla, V. vinifera purpurea.*

AMARYLLIS BELLADONNA (BELLADONNA LILY)

A beautiful bulb for the foot of a south wall, in rich deep loam. The fragrant flowers in various shades of rose red and pink are produced in August and September, on 18-inch stems before the new leaves.

Greenhouse Plants. Achimenes, *Agapanthus umbellatus, Asclepias curassavica,* begonias (tuberous-rooted), *Bignonia venusta,* bougainvilleas, bouvardias, *Browallia speciosa major* (sown March), *Campanula isophylla, C. pyramidalis,* cannas, carnations (perpetual-flowering), *Cassia corymbosa,* celsias, *Cobaea scandens,* daturas, *Erica insignis, Francoa ramosa,* fuchsias, gloxinias, heliotropes, *Hibbertia dentata, Humea elegans, Lagerstroemia indica,* lantanas, *Lilium longiflorum, L. speciosum* and vars., *Luculia gratissima,* marguerites, *Maurandya Barclaiana,* nerines, *Oxalis variabilis,* petunias, *Saintpaulia ionantha,* streptocarpus, *Trachelium caeruleum, Vallota purpurea.*

Vegetables in Store. Beetroot, onions, shallots.

Vegetables Outdoors. Globe artichokes, french beans, runner beans, beetroot, broccoli, cabbage (sown April), carrots, cauliflowers, celeriac, celery, ridge cucumbers, endive, kohl-rabi, leeks, lettuce, vegetable marrows, mushrooms, mustard and cress, parsnips, peas, potatoes, radishes, spinach, tomatoes, turnips.

Vegetables under Glass. Cucumbers, mushrooms (cool cellars and outhouses).

Fruit Outdoors. *Apples:* Devonshire Quarrenden (D), Ecklinville Seedling (C), Epicure (D), Exquisite (D), Fortune (D), Gascoyne's Scarlet (D), Golden Spire (C), Grenadier (C), James Grieve (D), Keswick Codlin (C), Lady Sudeley (D), Langley Pippin (D), Lord Grosvenor (C), Lord Suffield (C), Maidstone Favourite (D), Peasgood's Nonsuch (CD), St Edmund's Russet (D), St Everard (CD), Stirling Castle (C), Thomas Rivers (C), Worcester Pearmain (D). *Apricots:* Breda Hemskirk. *Blackberries:* Himalaya Giant, John Innes, Parsley-leaved. *Cherries:* Morello (C) (north wall). *Currants, black:* Baldwin, Daniel's September. *Figs. Grapes:* Brant, Early Black July, Miller's Burgundy, Royal Muscadine, Reine Olga. *Melons. Nectarines:* Early Rivers, John Rivers, Lord Napier. *Peaches:* Hale's Early, Peregrine. *Pears:* Beurré d'Amanlis (D), Clapp's Favourite (D), Colmar d'Eté (D), Directeur Hardy (D), Docteur Jules Guyot (D), Fertility (D), Magnate (D), Marguerite Marillat (D), Marquis (D), Michaelmas (D), Souvenir de Congrès (D), Triomphe de Vinne (D), Williams' Bon Chrêtien (D). *Plums:* Belle de Louvain (C), Bradley's King (Damson) (CD), Bryanston Gage (D), Coe's Golden Drop (D), Comte d'Althan's Gage (D), Cox's Emperor (CD), Cropper (CD), Damascene (CD), Diamond (C), Farleigh's Prolific Damson (Cluster or Crittenden), Giant Prune (C), Goldfinch (D), Green Gage (D), Jefferson's Gage (D), Kirke's Blue (D), Late Transparent Gage (D), Merryweather (Damson), Monarch (CD), Pond's Seedling (C), Reine Claude de Bavay Gage (D), Shropshire Prune Damson (CD), Victoria (CD), White Bullace (CD), White Magnum Bonum (D). *Raspberries:* Hailsham, Lloyd George, October Yellow, October Red, November Abundance.

Fruits under Glass. *Apricots:* Grosse Pêche, Moorpark. *Figs. Grapes:* Black Hamburgh, Black Prince, Foster's Seedling, Madresfield Court, Royal Muscadine. *Melons. Nectarines:* Darwin, Newton, Pineapple, Rivers' Orange, Stanwick Elruge, Spenser, Victoria. *Peaches:* Alexandra Noblesse, Barrington, Bellegarde, Dymond, Gladstone, Goshawk, Grosse Mignonne, Lady Palmerston, Late Devonian, Prince of Wales, Princess of Wales, Royal George, Sea Eagle, Salwey, Stirling Castle, Thomas Rivers, Violette Hâtive, Walburton Admirable.

October

GENERAL WORK

Use Slow-acting Fertilizers. October is a good month during which to use such slow-acting fertilizers as basic slag, bone-meal, and kainit. The first supplies phosphates and lime, the second mainly phosphates, and the third mainly potash. Most fruit trees will benefit from a top-dressing of basic slag and kainit applied now, the former at 6 and the latter at 3 ounces per square yard. The herbaceous border may have bone-meal at 4 ounces per square yard, and this will also do a lot of good to bulb beds and to bulbs that are naturalized in grass. Lime can also be applied now. All parts of the vegetable garden can do with a dose every third or fourth year, unless the ground happens to be naturally impregnated with lime or chalk. Use about ½ pound per square yard of hydrated (air-slaked) lime. On light sandy soils ground chalk is really better, but must be given more freely—about 2 pounds per square yard. In all cases the fertilizers or lime need only be scattered over the ground. Rain will wash them in, and if the ground is to be dug or forked later on this will further incorporate them with the soil.

Gather Fallen Leaves, etc. Be careful to sweep up all fallen leaves from time to time during the month. They are a particular source of danger in the rock garden, for if they lie thickly upon the plants they may kill them. All healthy leaves can be built up into a heap in some out-of-the-way corner and left to rot. Similar remarks also apply to any other soft refuse—old pea and potato haulm for example, and the tops of carrots, beetroots, etc. But if there has been any disease in the plants from which leaves or refuse have come, do not keep them in this way but burn them without delay.

Turf and Repair Lawns. This is an excellent time to lay new lawns from turf or to repair worn patches in old ones. Cut out the turf from the worn places with an edging tool and lift with a sharp spade or special turf-lifting tool, making all sides straight. It is a well-nigh impossible task to fit a patch neatly into a curved hole. When laying a number of turves side by side, stagger them like the bricks in a wall so that all the joints do not come together in both directions. This will give a better

232

'bind' until such time as the turves have rooted into their new quarters (see March, General Work, for further particulars).

If your lawn has been used a lot for games during the summer, it will also benefit from a thorough aeration, either with a spiked roller or a fork thrust in at frequent intervals. Then mowing will not be necessary anything like so frequently from early October onwards. An occasional raking with a spring-toothed grass rake will remove moss, and you should also use a birch broom frequently to distribute worm casts. If these are allowed to lie on the grass, they will kill it in small patches.

AERATING A LAWN
A hollow-tine fork is used for the purpose. The ejected plugs of turf can be seen in front of the fork.

Prepare Rose Beds, Fruit Sites, etc. You should get all new rose beds, also the site for new fruit trees and deciduous trees and shrubs of all kinds, prepared as early in October as possible. The ideal time for planting all these things is in November (see November, General Work), and it is all to the good if the ground can have a few weeks in which to settle between digging and planting. Dig the ground at least 2 feet deep, and, unless it is already very rich, work in plenty of well-rotted animal manure or decayed vegetable refuse in the second spit, but keep it away from the surface for it will do no good to freshly planted roots. Finish off with a surface dusting of basic slag at the rate of 6 ounces per square yard. This is most useful, for it sweetens the soil and also adds phosphates to it. If you can also dig or trench any other vacant ground during October so much the better, for, though this work can be done at any time during the summer or winter when the ground is not very sticky, considerable advantage is gained by early soil cultivation. Leave the surface quite rough so that a large area is exposed to the weather.

Lift Begonias, Dahlias, etc. Begonias, dahlias, cannas, and *Salvia patens* that have been growing out of doors during the summer months must be removed to a frost-proof store just as soon as their foliage is blackened by frost. Precisely when this will happen no one can say. Very often it is early in October, but there have been seasons when these plants have continued unharmed until November. So keep a sharp look-out and be ready to dig the tubers up as soon as frost puts a stop to their display. Cut off the dead growth just above the tubers and store the latter in trays and boxes according to their size. It is a good plan to pack them

A BOX OF SALVIA PATENS ROOTS

These plants were lifted before their growth had been killed by frost, so they have been placed in a box to ripen off.

round with dry moss peat or coconut fibre, as this is a protection and keeps them from drying out too much. Do not water at all, but place the boxes in any dry, fairly cool, but frost-proof place. A good outhouse will do well—or a cupboard, so long as it is not alongside a fireplace.

Plant Spring Bedding. As soon as you are able to clear beds of their temporary summer occupants, such as geraniums, marguerites, scarlet salvias, begonias, dahlias, etc. (see September, Fourth Week, and also notes on begonias, dahlias, etc., above), and have cleared out all annuals that have finished flowering, lose no time in planting the spring occupants of the beds. These may include wallflowers, *Cheiranthus Allionii*, forget-me-nots, double daisies, polyanthuses, and coloured primroses, together with various bulbs, particularly tulips and hyacinths. May-flowering tulips can be planted together with forget-me-nots or wallflowers, but the early-flowering tulips and hyacinths are not sufficiently tall to stand above these and so, if you wish to have a groundwork beneath them, use double daisies, arabis, or aubrietas. Wall-flowers and cheiranthuses should be planted from 9 to 12 inches apart, according to the size of the plants; forget-me-nots, double daisies, polyanthuses, etc., 6 to 8 inches apart. I have given distances for bulbs by themselves on pages 213, 214, and 242, but if they are planted with a groundwork of other plants they may be spaced out more: 12 to 15 inches apart will be a good average. The only preparation that the ground will need is a dressing of hop manure at the rate of a double handful per square yard, well forked in, and a top-dressing of bone-meal at 4 ounces per square yard.

Plant Herbaceous Perennials. On light, well-drained soils, October is quite a good month for planting most herbaceous perennials, but it is better to do the work in spring (see March, General Work) on all heavy or wet soils. Details of planting are exactly the same in either case. Perennials and biennials raised from seed in June (see June, First Week) may also be planted now.

Insert Hard-wooded Cuttings. Many shrubby plants, both ornamental and useful, including gooseberries, currants, and rambler roses, can be

HARD-WOODED CUTTINGS

The long black line indicates soil level when the cuttings are correctly inserted, while the short lines show where the cuttings should be trimmed. Buds are left below ground level (left) if sucker shoots are not a disadvantage (as in blackcurrants), but usually it is better to remove these lower buds (right).

increased at this time of the year by means of what the gardener calls 'hard-wooded cuttings.' These differ from summer cuttings (see July, General Work) in being prepared from much riper and firmer wood.

Select shoots of the current year's growth from 6 inches to 1 foot in length according to the nature of the plant. They can either be cut immediately below a joint, exactly like the summer cuttings, or else pulled off the parent plant with a thin strip of older wood (gardeners call these heel cuttings, but most amateurs refer to them as slips). If you adopt the latter method, and it is a good one, trim off the thin piece of bark close to the knob of wood at the base of the cutting (actually what the gardener means by 'heel'). In the case of gooseberries nick out all the lower growth buds to prevent sucker shoots from being formed below the soil. Insert the cuttings to a depth of 3 or 4 inches in sandy soil, in a sheltered place outdoors. These hard-wooded cuttings root slowly and will not be ready for removal to their permanent quarters until the following autumn.

If desired all these cuttings can be treated with a root-forming hormone as described on page 56.

General Greenhouse Management. Nights are now likely to be sufficiently cold to necessitate the use of artificial heat for the majority of favourite greenhouse plants. The ideal temperatures to be aimed at are about 55° by day, rising to 65° or 70° with direct sun heat and never falling below 45° even on the chilliest nights. Damping down and syringeing are not likely to be needed, except for hothouse plants in temperatures over 65°. Supply water to plants in growth in sufficient quantity to keep the soil moist right through, but avoid splashing unnecessarily and be careful to keep water off the leaves and crowns of primulas. Air should be admitted through top ventilators rather than those at the side, and it is unlikely that any ventilation will be needed at night for most of the plants. Chrysanthemums, however, must be kept as hardy as possible or they may contract mildew. If this disease does appear, dust the leaves with flowers of sulphur, space the plants out as much as possible to let in light and air, and use a little artificial heat to dry the atmosphere.

Rest Begonias, Gloxinias, etc. Tuberous-rooted begonias, gloxinias, achimenes, and hippeastrums will be more than ever going to rest and can be finally dried off during this month, after which the begonias may be shaken out of their soil and stored in dry coconut fibre or peat moss. Gloxinias are sometimes treated in the same way, but are really better in the soil in which they have been growing. Tap the dry balls of compost out of the pots, heap them together, and cover them with sacks. Of course, both these and the begonias must be in a dry, frostproof place, but a high temperature is not desirable. Something around 50° is ideal.

Hippeastrums are allowed to get dry in their pots, after which they can stand in any out-of-the-way place—piled up on their sides if that is more convenient. Similar remarks apply to cannas which are grown in pots.

Vallotas are never dried off to quite this extent, but their water supply is greatly reduced during the winter. It is quite sufficient to keep the soil just slightly moist. Reduce the temperature to about 45° if possible. Similar remarks apply to clivias. This is a good time to purchase and pot new bulbs of both these plants. Use the ordinary potting compost and the smallest pots that will hold the bulbs comfortably.

Pot Hardy Plants for the Greenhouse. Several hardy perennial plants commonly grown out of doors also make good pot plants for the greenhouse. They include herbaceous astilbes in a great number of varieties, Solomon's Seal and *Dicentra spectabilis*. Pot these now in the smallest pots that will accommodate the roots and then stand them in a frame or plunge them in ashes or sand in a sheltered place outdoors until you need them. They can be brought into the greenhouse in successive batches from January onwards, and if kept in a temperature of about 60° will grow rapidly and soon come into flower.

Disbud Perpetual-flowering Carnations. Young plants of perpetual-flowering carnations rooted as cuttings in the winter should now be forming flower buds, and to get the best results these must be thinned out. Leave only the central terminal bud on each flower stem and remove all others at as early a stage of development as possible. See that the long, slender stems are properly staked. There is nothing better for this purpose than the circular galvanized wire supports made specially for the purpose.

Protect Cauliflowers. The white hearts (curds) of cauliflowers are liable to be damaged by frost, so look over the bed occasionally and bend some of the outer leaves over any hearts that are forming. This will give them all the protection they need.

Continue to Blanch Endive. Similar instructions to those given in my August and September General notes still apply.

Ripen Growth in Orchard House and Vinery. Your aim should still be to ripen any soft green growth that remains on peaches, nectarines, and apricots in the orchard house. Keep the air as dry as possible by free ventilation and, if possible, the occasional use of artificial heat if the air outside is very damp and stagnant; do not syringe at all unless red spider is still about, and maintain a temperature of 45° to 50°.

Similar remarks apply to vines. With late vines that are still carrying bunches it is a good plan to remove some of the foliage so that berries are exposed to the light and relieved from the danger of drips of water from the leaves.

FIRST WEEK

Protect Outdoor Chrysanthemums. If any of the early-flowering border chrysanthemums are still flowering well, it will be advisable to rig up some kind of temporary shelter over them. Quite an effective method is to drive a few stout stakes, about 5 feet in length, into the bed at con-

A TEMPORARY SHELTER FOR OUTDOOR CHRYSANTHEMUMS
Strips of canvas are stretched over a light wooden framework when frost threatens.

venient points, join them across the top with a few horizontal bars nailed or tied in position, and then throw some sacking over them on frosty nights, making it secure at the corners with string. It does not take much to keep off the light frosts that are quite capable of ruining all the chrysanthemum flowers and buds.

Pot on Cinerarias and Stocks. Cinerarias sown during the third week in June are likely to be in need of a shift into roomier quarters. Give them 5-inch pots and the same compost as before, but rather coarser in texture. You can still keep them in a frame for a few weeks if you are very careful to close it up early in the afternoon and cover with sacks on cold nights, but they will soon have to go into the greenhouse.

Precisely similar remarks apply to stocks intended for winter flowering (see August, First Week).

Pot a Last Batch of Freesias. This is the time to make a last potting of freesias to flower in the spring. Details are as before (see August, First Week), except that now you will have to use the lights considerably more, especially at night, for there will be increasing danger of frost from now on.

Bring Early Arums, Freesias, and Lachenalias into the Greenhouse. If you want to have some arums to cut for Christmas, you must bring a batch of plants into the greenhouse now. Arrange them in a light place not too far removed from the glass and maintain a night temperature of 55°, rising about 10° by day. Water freely.

You may also bring in the first batch of freesias (see August, First Week). Arrange them on the staging and maintain a temperature 5° or so lower than for the arums. Lachenalias in pots and boxes (see August, First Week) may also be brought into the greenhouse now. There is no need to hurry them at all unless you want early flowers. Any temperature above freezing point will serve for them. Both plants like plenty of light and air.

Plant Spring Cabbage. Plant as many as possible of the spring cabbages from the August sowing (see August, Second Week). Any seedlings that remain in the seed beds after the middle of the month are best left undisturbed until February (see February, Second Week).

Complete Earthing up of Late Celery and Leeks. Complete all earthing up of celery as soon as possible. I have already given full particulars in the notes for July, Second Week, and August, Fourth Week. Sometimes rust appears on the leaves at this time of the year. Prompt removal of affected plants, followed by immediate spraying with Bordeaux mixture, will check it.

Leeks should also be earthed up for the last time. The longer the length of fully blanched stem obtained, the better.

SECOND WEEK

Sow Sweet Peas. The best exhibition sweet peas are obtained from sowings made at this time of the year. Some growers sow outdoors where the plants are to bloom, but a far better method in most districts is to sow in pots—about five seeds in a 3-inch pot—and to germinate them in an unheated frame. Once the seedlings are up they can be ventilated very freely—indeed, the lights will only be needed in very frosty or windy weather. The great advantage of this method is that the seedlings are much more under control and can be protected from excessive cold or wet if necessary.

Prick off Cauliflowers. Cauliflowers sown last month (see September, First Week) must now be transferred to a frame. Prepare a bed of finely broken soil in this and dibble the seedlings straight into it 3 inches apart each way. Ventilate freely and only use the lights when there is danger of frost.

Gather all Remaining Apples and Pears. At this time it is wise to complete the gathering of all apples and pears. It is not advisable to let them hang once the weather gets really wintry. Bring all into store. Apples keep very well if carefully packed in boxes deep enough to hold three or four layers. These should be stood in a cool but frostproof place preferably with a slightly moist atmosphere. A shed with an earthen floor is ideal, because there is usually a little moisture arising from the floor. Pears, however, keep more satisfactorily in a rather dry atmosphere; indeed, with them it is really a slow ripening process rather than keeping. Lay them out thinly in a room or cellar with an average temperature of about 50°. Never pile them one on top of the other. Watch carefully for the ripening period as pears spoil quickly.

THIRD WEEK

Lift Gladioli and Montbretias. All gladiolus corms will be better out of the ground now. Dig them up carefully with a fork, shake the soil from the

A GLADIOLUS CORM AFTER
CLEANING
The old corm has been broken away, leaving a clean scar.

roots, tie them up in small bundles by their stems, and hang them up to dry in any frostproof place. They will do well enough in a shed or garage so long as you can keep frost out. Later on, when the foliage has withered *ft:* Resting gloxinias under the greenhouse staging after flowering. *Right:* Planting rbaceous perennials.

ft: Planting tulips in a trench taken out with a spade. *Right:* Laying turf in osition. Note the staggered placing of the turves.

Left: Hardwood cuttings: trimming the leaves and thorns when preparing pyracantha cuttings. *Right:* Preparing cuttings of privet by removing the lower leaves. Those shown on the left are ready for insertion.

Dahlia tubers being stored under staging.

up, you should cut it off just above the corms and place the latter in shallow boxes, in which they can be stored under the same conditions as before. Remove any small corms and keep these for growing on a reserve bed. They may not flower next year, but they can be fattened up for the following season. Tiny cormels (spawn) can also be kept and grown on, but this is more of a specialist's job, and is only worth the candle with new and expensive kinds. Pull off and throw away the old, shrivelled corms that adhere to the bottoms of the new ones.

Choice montbretias are also better out of the ground for the winter, but there is no need to move the old common kinds, for these are hardy

A GLADIOLUS PLANT AS LIFTED

The cormlets will grow on into corms of flowering size and should be detached and replanted in the spring in a nursery bed.

enough to look after themselves. Some people store the choice varieties exactly like gladioli, but I prefer to replant them, close together, in a frame and keep them nearly but not quite dry until early March, when they can be started into growth once more. The lights can be kept on most of the time, but it is a good plan to remove them occasionally for a few hours on mild days, just to give the frame an airing.

Stop Feeding Chrysanthemums. It is rarely wise to continue the feeding of exhibition chrysanthemums after this date. Experience proves that, if feeding is carried on too long, buds tend to decay in the centre. From now on supply with plain water only.

Q

Lift and Store Turnips. Lift a good supply of turnips of reasonable size and store them in a frostproof place for the winter. They will keep quite well in a heap in any dry shed or outhouse, but are all the better for a light covering of dry sand or ashes. Cut off the tops first. If you leave some of the roots in the ground, they will supply a useful crop of turnip tops in late winter and spring.

Cut back Asparagus and Globe Artichokes. The growth of asparagus will have turned yellow and the sooner it is removed the better. Do this with a pair of garden shears and cut off all the tops close to the soil. All rubbish should then be raked together and burned.

The yellowing leaves and stems of globe artichokes should also be cut down. Then fork between the plants lightly and cover the crowns with some sharp dry ashes or a thin layer of leaves as a protection against frost.

FOURTH WEEK

Plant Tulips and Hyacinths. Unlike many other hardy bulbs, tulips and hyacinths do benefit from a thorough drying off and ripening out of the ground, and there is nothing to be gained by planting before late October. This is also convenient, because they can then be planted in the beds just cleared of summer bedding plants and annuals. Give the soil a dusting of bone-meal at the rate of 4 ounces per square yard, fork this in, and then plant the bulbs: the hyacinths 6 inches deep and 8 inches apart, early tulips 3 inches deep and 8 inches apart, May-flowering tulips 4 inches deep and 8 inches apart.

Pot on Greenhouse Plants. Right at the end of October it is a good plan to finish off any greenhouse potting there may be to do before getting really busy with outdoor planting. It is probable that June-sown primulas and calceolarias will be ready for a move into 4- or 5-inch pots, while the early cinerarias, sown at the beginning of May, will require their last shift into the 7- or 8-inch pots in which they will flower. The general potting compost will do admirably, but may be rather coarser in texture for the cinerarias than for the other plants. It is no longer really safe to have any of these plants in frames, and you should remove them to a light airy greenhouse in which you can maintain an average temperature of 55°.

Roses and deciduous pot shrubs such as lilacs, deutzias, forsythias, and cherries, that are to be flowered early in the greenhouse, may also be

repotted now if they need it; but do this work with as little root disturbance as possible. Simply transfer the unbroken pot-ball to a larger
receptacle and work some fresh compost around it. After this treatment
return the plants to a frame or to a plunge bed in a sheltered position
outdoors.

Pot Annuals for the Greenhouse. Annuals sown in September for flowering in the greenhouse in spring should now be ready for potting singly in
3-inch pots. Use the usual compost (see p. 62), and after potting arrange
the plants in a frame or cool greenhouse. Water moderately and ventilate
freely whenever the weather is mild, but be careful to exclude all frost.
Pinch out the points of clarkias to make the plants branch.

Precisely similar remarks apply to schizanthus seedlings pricked off in
September (see September, Third Week). Pinch out the growing tip of
each plant, as advised for clarkias.

With certain annuals grown for greenhouse display, a better effect
is obtained by placing three or four plants in a pot than by potting
singly. Examples are leptosyne, limnanthes, mignonette, nemophila,
phlox, and saponaria.

Lift and Box Mint. A supply of young mint shoots is usually very welcome at Christmas and after, and can be obtained very easily by lifting
a few roots now, laying them thinly on any fairly light compost spread
in deep seed trays, covering them with a further inch of the same com-

BOXING MINT FOR
FORCING
*Short lengths of root
are laid in soil in a
deep seed box and
covered with a little
more fine soil.*

post and bringing them into a warm greenhouse. Any temperature over
50° will secure growth—the higher it is the quicker the roots will grow,
that is all. Keep just moist at first, but when shoots begin to appear,
water more freely.

Make Lily of the Valley Beds. This is a good time at which to make new lily of the valley beds. Choose a cool, semi-shady place and good rich soil with plenty of humus. Plant the crowns separately, 3 inches apart in rows 6 inches apart. The simplest method is to nick out shallow trenches with a spade, lay the roots in these, and just cover the crowns.

FLOWERS, VEGETABLES, AND FRUITS IN SEASON DURING OCTOBER

Hardy Herbaceous Perennials. *Aconitum autumnale, A. Fischeri, A. Wilsonii, Anemone japonica* and vars., *Aster cordifolius* and vars., *A. ericoides* and vars., *A. grandiflorus, A. novae-angliae* vars., *A. novi-belgii* vars. (Michaelmas daisy), *A. ptarmicoides, Boltonia asteroides,* gaillardias, geums, *Helianthus multiflorus* vars., *H. orgyalis, H. rigidus* vars., *H. sparsifolius, Kniphofia maxima globosa, K. multiflora, K. R.* Wilson Kerr, *Liriope spicata, Lobelia fulgens* vars., *Monardella macrantha, Physalis Alkekengi* (fruits), *P. Bunyardii* (fruits), *P. Franchetii* (fruits), *Podophyllum emodi* (fruits), *Scabiosa caucasica* and vars., *Sedum spectabile* and vars., *Solidago Virgaurea* vars., *Stokesia cyanea, Verbena venosa.*

Hardy Bulbs and Tubers. *Colchicum autumnale, C. byzantinum, C. Decaisnei, C. giganteum, C. speciosum* vars., *Crocus asturicus, C. cancellatus, C. caspius, C. Clusii, C. longiflorus, C. ochroleucus, C. pulchellus, C. Salzmannii, C. sativus, C. speciosus, C. zonatus, Cyclamen africanum, C. cilicicum, C. europaeum, C.*

SCHIZOSTYLIS COCCINEA
(KAFFIR LILY)

The Kaffir lily produces its crimson flowers in October and November on stems 1 to 3 feet tall. It is a hardy bulb, often grown in a warm border, but more usually grown in pots in the cool greenhouse.

neapolitanum, Galanthus nivalis Elsae, Leucojum autumnale, Merendera bulbo-codium, M. persica, Narcissus serotinus, Nerine Bowdenii, Schizostylis coc-cinea and vars., *Sternbergia lutea.*

Hardy Rock Plants. *Achillea tomentosa, Androsace lanuginosa Leichtlinii, Ceratostigma plumbaginoides, C. Willmottianum, Gaultheria procumbens* (fruits), *Gentiana Farreri, G. Kurroo, G. Macaulayi, G. sino-ornata, Geum Borisii, Iris lacustris, Lithospermum prostratum* vars., *Nertera depressa* (fruits), *Oxalis lobata, Polygonum vaccinifolium, Potentilla mandschurica, P. nepalensis minor, Sisyrinchium angustifolium convolutum, Tunica Saxifraga, Verbena chamaedryfolia, Viola declinata, V. florariensis, V. gracilis, Zauschneria cali-fornica.*

Hardy Evergreen Shrubs. *Abelia grandiflora, Berberis stenophylla, B. steno-phylla semperflorens, Bigelowia graveolens, Buddleia auriculata, Calluna vulgaris* and vars., *Ceanothus Burkwoodii, Daboecia polifolia, Elaeagnus macrophylla, E. pungens, Erica carnea* Queen Mary, *E. ciliaris* and vars., *E. stricta, E. Tetralix* and vars., *E. vagans* and vars., *E. Watsonii, Escallonia macrantha, E. pterocladon, E. rubra, E. viscosa,* escallonia hybrids, *Hebe angustifolia, H. speciosa* Autumn Glory, *Hypericum Moserianum, H. galioides, H. hircinum, Mahonia fortunei* (shelter), *M. napaulensis* (shelter), *Olearia Fosteri* (shelter), *Ulex nanus, U. europaeus plenus.*

Hardy Deciduous Shrubs. *Abelia Schumannii, Buddleia variabilis* and vars., *Calycanthus occidentalis, Caryopteris Mastacanthus, Ceratostigma plumbagi-noides, C. Willmottianum, Clethra paniculata, Cytisus leucanthus, C. nigricans, Daphne Mezereum autumnalis, Desmodium spicatum, Disanthus cercidifolius, Fremontia californica* (shelter), *Hamamelis virginica, Hypericum Hookerianum, Hydrangea paniculata grandiflora, Indigofera amblyantha, Lavatera Olbia, Osmanthus Aquifolium, Perowskia atriplicifolia, Salix Bockii, Spiraea Mar-garitae, Teucrium fruticans, Vitex Agnus-castus.*

Hardy Evergreen Trees. *Arbutus hybrida, A. Unedo.*

Hardy Deciduous Trees. *Alnus maritima, A. nitida.*

Hardy Climbing Plants. *Clematis apiifolia, C. calycina, C. chinensis, C. connata, C. flammula, C. Jackmanii* hybrids, *C. Jouiniana, C. lanuginosa* hybrids, *C. lasiandra, C. paniculata, C. Rehderiana, C. rubro-marginata, C. Vitalba, Jasminum officinale, Lonicera alseuosmoides, L. Heckrottii, Pileostegia vibur-noides,* roses (climbing hybrid tea and tea, also hybrid musk).

Fruiting Trees, Shrubs, and Climbers. Mainly as September, though birds may strip some varieties. Additional kinds in fruit are as follows: *Aucuba japonica* (unisexual), *Billardiera longiflora, Callicarpa japonica, Celastrus articulatus, C. scandens* (unisexual), *Ilex Aquifolium* and vars. (holly) (unisexual), *I. serrata, Symphoricarpos racemosus* (snowberry), *S. orbiculatus, Taxus baccata.*

Greenhouse Plants. Abutilons, *Bignonia venusta,* bouvardias, *Browallia speciosa major,* carnations (perpetual-flowering), *Cassia corymbosa,* celsias, chrysan-themums, *Cobaea scandens, Erica gracilis, E. verticillata, Eupatorium odoratum, Humea elegans, Luculia gratissima,* marguerites, *Maurandya Barclaiana,* nerines, *Oxalis variabilis, O. versicolor,* pelargoniums (zonal), *Salvia splendens, Saintpaulia ionantha,* streptocarpus, *Trachelium caeruleum.*

Vegetables in Store. Beetroot, carrots, onions, potatoes, shallots.

Vegetables Outdoors. Globe artichokes, broccoli, cabbage (sown April), carrots, cauliflowers, celeriac, celery, coleworts (sown June), endive, kohl-rabi, leeks, lettuce, mushrooms, parsnips, peas, spinach, turnips.

Vegetables under Glass. French beans, cucumbers, mushrooms, mustard and cress, radishes, tomatoes.

MAURANDYA BARCLAIANA

A beautiful half-hardy perennial climber with violet purple flowers in the autumn. Usually grown in the cool greenhouse, it can be grown in pots outdoors and brought indoors before the frosts.

Fruits Outdoors. *Apples:* Allington Pippin (D), Charles Ross (D), Cornish Aromatic (D), Coronation (D), Cox's Orange Pippin (D), Cox's Pomona (CD), Ecklinville Seedling (C), Egremont Russet (D), Ellison's Orange (D), Emperor Alexander (CD), Exquisite (D), Gascoyne's Scarlet (D), Golden Noble (C), Golden Spire (C), Gravenstein (CD), Herring's Pippin (CD), King of the Pippins (D), Laxton's Superb (D), Lord Lambourne (D), McIntosh Red (CD), Mother (American) (D), Peasgood's Nonsuch (CD), Pioneer (D), Rev. W. Wilks (C), Rival (CD), Rosebery (D), Royal Jubilee (C), Schoolmaster (C), St Edmund's Russet (D), Stirling Castle (C), Sunset (D), The Queen (C), Thomas Rivers (C), Wealthy (D). *Figs* (shelter). *Grapes:* Brant, Miller's Burgundy, Royal Muscadine. *Medlars. Peaches:* Dymond, Goshawk, Hale's Early, Peregrine. *Pears:* Beurré Bedford (D), Beurré Diel (D), Beurré Hardy (D), Beurré Superfin (D), Comte de Lamy (D), Conference (D), Durondeau (D), Emile d'Heyst (D), Jersey Gratioli (D), Fondante d'Automne (D), Louise Bonne (D), Maréchal de la Cour (D), Marie Louise (D), Pitmaston Duchess (D), Progress (D), Record (D), Roosevelt (D), Satisfaction (D), Seckel (D), Thompson's (D). *Plums:* Golden Transparent Gage (D), Late Orange (CD), Langley Bullace (C), Merryweather Damson (C), Monarch (CD), President (C), Reine Claude de Bavay Gage (D), Shepherd's Bullace (C), Shropshire Prune Damson (CD), White Bullace (CD). *Quinces. Raspberries* (as September).

Hardy Nuts. Cobnuts, filberts, walnuts.

Fruits under Glass. *Figs. Grapes:* Alicante, Black Hamburgh, Gros Maroc, Lady Hastings, Muscat Hamburgh. *Peaches:* Gladstone, Golden Eagle, Lady Palmerston, Princess of Wales, Salwey, Sea Eagle, Walburton Admirable.

November

GENERAL WORK

Tidy up Herbaceous Borders. By this time most herbaceous perennials will have finished flowering, and the borders may be tidied up for the winter. Cut off all dead or dying stems and leaves, but leave evergreen leaves such as those of kniphofias. Give the ground a dusting of bone-meal if you have not already done this (see October, General Work), and prick over the surface of the border with a fork, but be careful not to disturb roots or to dig up bulbs accidentally. It is really wise to mark the positions of the latter clearly when planting.

Dig all Available Ground. As I have already explained (see October, General Work), the earlier in the autumn ground can be turned over roughly the better. By this time a great deal of the vegetable garden should be free for digging or trenching. The latter, by the by, is simply deep digging to a depth of two or even three spades (almost 3 feet). Very

RIDGING SOIL
It is an excellent plan to throw the soil into steep ridges in the autumn so that a large surface is exposed to frost and wind.

deep trenching can only be practised on rather good soil, but there are few gardens that would not benefit from periodic trenching two spades deep, especially if care is taken to keep the first and second spits (a spit is the depth of a spade) in the same relation one to the other as formerly, and not bring the lower and less fertile soil to the top. Do as much of this work as you can now, and make no attempt to break up the surface as

247

yet. The rougher it is left the greater will be the surface exposed to the beneficial action of wind and frost. Animal manure can be worked in at the same time if required, or alternatively you can apply slow-acting fertilizers or lime, if not already given (see October, General Work). It is not usually wise to apply manure and lime at the same time, as the latter liberates and wastes ammonia from the manure, but they can be used at a few weeks' interval, one way or the other, without ill effect.

Prune Roses. The pruning of almost all bush and standard roses can commence as soon as all leaves have fallen and be continued as convenient until March. The only important exceptions to this are Tea roses which are slightly tender and best left unpruned until early April, and weeping standards which are pruned in late summer or early autumn. If the roses are only required for garden display cut back all strong young growths made last year to a length of about 4 or 5 inches, Weaker shoots should be cut back to a couple of inches, while really thin, spindly wood is best removed altogether. If the roses are required for exhibition, they should be pruned rather more severely, strong shoots being cut back 2 or 3 inches, weaker ones removed. Of course, all dead or damaged growth must be removed first of all.

PRUNING BUSH ROSES

This very severe annual cutting back is necessary if really high-class flowers are desired. Note that each cut has been made just above a dormant growth bud. Normally it is inadvisable to prune so severely.

Newly planted roses should all be pruned in the same way as those required for exhibition. Climbing roses, as distinct from ramblers of the wichuraiana and multiflora types (any catalogue will put you right on this), are also pruned now. Usually it is sufficient to shorten strong growths by about one-third and weaker ones from a half to two-thirds, but occasionally, if a plant has not been making satisfactory progress, rather harder pruning should be carried out.

Polyantha pompon roses should be pruned by removing some of the older stems altogether and shortening the remainder by about half. Floribundas vary more in their growth and some may be treated like hybrid teas while others will thrive with a little thinning only and shortening of young growth by about one-third.

Prune Deciduous Hedges. All deciduous hedges, such as quick (hawthorn), blackthorn, myrobalan plum, sweet brier, beech, and tamarisk, may be pruned during November, and this is a good time to do any hard cutting that may be necessary to keep growth within bounds. The base of a hawthorn or sweet brier hedge sometimes gets bare, but can be kept well furnished with growth by bending down a few long branches and pegging them into position. If the hawthorn branches refuse to bend, half-slit them near the base with a billhook.

Gather Rose Heps. If you have made any special rose crosses and wish to try your hand at seed raising, gather the heps now. Lay them thinly in seed boxes, cover with a little silver sand, and place outdoors in an exposed position for the winter. The more the heps get frozen the better, because this will break them up and prepare the seeds for germination (see March, Second Week). The process is known as stratification, and can be applied to any berries or haws.

Plant Fruit and Ornamental Trees, Shrubs, Roses, etc. This is the great month of the year for planting all deciduous trees, shrubs, and climbers, both ornamental and fruiting. The sooner the work can be completed once the leaves have come off the better, but if you have much to do it will almost inevitably be necessary to spread the planting over several weeks, because it is not possible to work either when the ground is frozen or when it is very wet. However, if you cannot finish it all by the first or second week in December, I advise you to postpone the remainder until early February (see February, General Work) rather than to do it when the ground is very cold and wet.

In almost all cases the details of planting are the same. Protect the roots from sun and drying winds until you are quite ready to plant them. Prepare a hole wide enough to accommodate all the roots spread out in a perfectly natural manner and deep enough to permit the uppermost to be covered with a clear 3 or 4 inches of soil. Cut off any broken or bruised root ends, hold the tree or bush in position in the middle of the hole (it is all to the good if you have someone to help you in this), and throw back the soil a little at a time, gently jerking the plant up and down meanwhile, so that the fine particles of soil work down between the roots. When the hole is almost full, tread the soil down really firmly. Then return the rest of the soil, but leave this loose and level on the surface. All standard trees and large bushes should be made secure to strong stakes driven firmly into the soil, while trained fruit trees must also be tied to their supports without delay. There is nothing that will delay rooting so much as constant disturbance by wind.

Deciduous climbing plants such as honeysuckles, clematises, *Polygonum baldschuanicum*, jasmines, and ornamental vines are usually supplied in pots, and this is a great advantage, as it means that one is practically certain to get the roots intact and uninjured. If they are at all

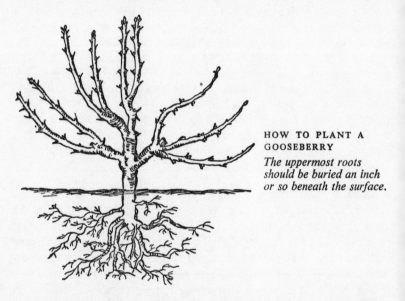

HOW TO PLANT A
GOOSEBERRY
*The uppermost roots
should be buried an inch
or so beneath the surface.*

dry on arrival, soak them in a bucket of tepid water for a few minutes. Then stand them out to drain for an hour or so, and, when you are ready to plant, crack the pot, remove the fragments carefully, loosen the roots in the pot ball a little and work some of the new soil around them. Be sure to make them really firm in their new surroundings and to tie the shoots up to a support at once.

Bush apples, pears, plums, and cherries should be planted 15 feet apart, but standards of these same trees must be allowed from 25 to 30 feet each. Espalier-trained apples and pears and fan-trained plums, cherries, peaches, nectarines, and apricots must be about 12 feet apart.

Cordon apples and pears are planted 2 feet apart, and, if there is more than one row, the rows must be at least 6 feet apart and should run north and south for preference. Bush currants and gooseberries must be at least 4 feet apart each way—it is really wiser to allow blackcurrants 5 feet, as they grow very vigorously. Raspberry canes should be 3 feet apart in rows 6 feet apart, while loganberries, blackberries and other vigorous bramble fruits need nearly twice that amount of space.

For ornamental trees and shrubs, no hard and fast rules for distance can be given, as they differ greatly in growth, but as a general guide I would suggest that most of the smaller shrubs should be planted 3 feet apart and the bigger kinds 5 to 6 feet apart , and that no trees should be closer than 15 feet. Most climbing plants, including roses, should be at least 6 feet apart. Bush roses must be from 18 inches to 2 feet apart each way, while standards should be at least 4 feet apart.

General Greenhouse Management. During foggy November lack of light and a damp coldness in the atmosphere are two of the principal obstacles that one usually has to overcome in the greenhouse. If the glass is at all dirty, wash it thoroughly, both inside and out. Ventilate very cautiously. Open the top ventilators a little for a few hours during the day when the weather is mild and reasonably clear, but keep them shut if it is very cold or foggy. If you have ample artificial heat at your disposal the problem of ventilation is greatly simplified, for the air within the greenhouse can be warmed, dried, and made to rise steadily through the ventilators even when the atmosphere outside is heavy and cold with moisture.

Keep a sharp look-out for decayed leaves or bracts and remove these at once. Dust the plants with flowers of sulphur to prevent the disease from spreading. Avoid splashing water about. Damping down and syringeing will only be required by a few exceptional things, such as tropical foliage plants and winter cucumbers, and as these also require a much higher temperature than the general run of greenhouse plants, they must be grown by themselves. In the mixed greenhouse, where primulas, cinerarias, calceolarias, cyclamens, etc., are growing together with pelargoniums, marguerites, and other stored bedding plants, a day temperature of 55° will serve now, but it should not be allowed to fall below 45° at night.

Attend to Plants in Frames. From now on until the early spring plants in frames will require very careful handling. Some, such as rooted viola, pansy, and violet cuttings, sweet pea seedlings, and also violet clumps, are quite hardy and only in need of protection from hard frost or heavy rains, which might disturb the small cuttings and seedlings or prevent the clumps from flowering. These need very free ventilation. Lights may be removed altogether during the day when the weather is mild, but should be placed on the frames again before the sun sets. Cauliflowers, antirrhinums from late summer cuttings and seeds, bedding calceolarias, and penstemons need just a little more protection, but are almost hardy. They should always be fully exposed on warm, sunny days and ventilated freely whenever there is no frost or very cold wind. Others again, such as pelargoniums, marguerites, and choice fuchsias, are liable to be damaged severely by even a few degrees of frost, and must be well protected with sacks at night. Ventilate the frames on favourable days, but be careful to get the lights back in time to trap sun heat against the night.

In all cases, take advantage of a warm day now and then to have the lights off and examine all plants carefully. Remove and burn any decayed or yellowing leaves. Also stir the surface of the soil with a pointed stick to aerate it.

Water sufficiently to prevent the soil from getting dry, but reduce the amount during frosty weather, especially for the tender plants.

Pot Shrubs for the Greenhouse. November is a good month during which to purchase and pot many deciduous shrubs for early flowering in the greenhouse—hydrangeas, for example; also lilacs, brooms, deutzias, and roses. After potting, stand the hydrangeas in a frame and protect from frost, but plunge the others to the pot-rims in a sunny, sheltered place outdoors. Make no attempt to force these shrubs in a high temperature the first winter, but you can bring them into a cool greenhouse in December or January to get flowers a few weeks ahead of the normal season. You can also purchase Indian azaleas in bud now, either in pots or tapped out of them, and these latter have only to be slipped back into pots to be ready for mild forcing.

Cut back Chrysanthemums. As chrysanthemums in the greenhouse finish flowering, cut them back to within 2 or 3 inches of ground level. This will make more room in the house and will also encourage the roots to throw up sucker shoots which will make the ideal cuttings later on (see December, Third Week).

Successional Sowings. The only successional sowings to be made are mustard and cress and radishes, all in a warm greenhouse or frame over a hotbed. A temperature of from 50° to 60° is necessary to ensure germination and quick growth. If it is 10° higher, so much the better.

Protect Broccoli from Frost. The curds of the early broccolis will be forming now, and though they are much hardier than cauliflowers, it is as well to protect them by bending some of the outer leaves over them. Late cauliflowers will certainly need this protection.

Blanch Endive in Frames. Most, if not all, endive plants will be in frames, and you can blanch them as formerly described (see August, General Work), or, if you want a lot at once, by the even simpler process of covering a whole frame so thickly with sacks that all light is excluded.

Prune Fruit Trees. November is the best month for doing any hard pruning of fruit trees and bushes that may be necessary. However, if you have followed out a system of summer-pruning as I have advised (see June, Second Week, and July, First and Third Weeks), there will not be a great deal to do now. Shorten all the laterals (side shoots) of summer-pruned apples, pears, plums, sweet cherries, apricots, gooseberries, and

A HORIZONTALLY-TRAINED APPLE

If a further pair of arms is required the vertical shoot must be cut back, as indicated by the black line. The young shoots terminating the existing horizontal branches must in any case be shortened by about one-third.

red and white currants to about two, or at most three, dormant growth buds each, unless, with fan-trained trees, there is room to tie in a few at full length. Leading shoots that are going to extend main branches or be the foundation of new branches should be shortened by about one-third of their length, while the central leaders of espalier-trained trees are shortened to about 15 inches if another pair of horizontal arms is required, or cut off altogether if the tree already has sufficient arms. In all these instances I am referring to the shoots actually formed during the past summer. In estimating the length of any stem that is to be pruned there is no need to take into account any of the old wood formed in previous years. In the case of big trees that were not summer-pruned, this hard winter-pruning is not desirable. Instead content yourself with the removal or shortening of thin, weak, or badly placed stems and the removal of all dead or diseased wood. The purpose of this pruning should be to keep the trees reasonably open to light and air.

Peaches, nectarines, and Morello cherries that have been disbudded during the spring and summer (see April, Fourth Week, and July, First Week) are pruned differently. Each old fruiting lateral is cut right out and the new lateral retained at its base for the purpose of replacement is trained in its place. If there is no suitable basal shoot prune to the best young growth available.

Blackcurrants, though not summer-pruned, are now treated in some-what the same way as these peaches, etc.; that is to say, you must cut out as much as possible of the old growth that has just borne fruit to make way for strong young stems. Many of the best may come right from the base of the bush.

Root-prune Fruit Trees. Sometimes failure to fruit is due to too much vigour (see note on ringing, May, First Week). This can be checked by root-pruning during the period at which the trees are dormant. Dig a trench around the tree 4 to 5 feet away from it and then work towards it with a fork, unearthing the roots and carefully preserving all those of a fibrous nature but severing any very stout roots that are plunging down into the subsoil. Do not approach nearer than to within about 18 inches of the tree. Then replace the soil again, spreading out and covering the fine roots. Root-pruning can be practised with safety on stone fruits, such as cherries and plums, for which ringing is unsafe as it may encourage disease.

Ventilate and Prune Trees in Orchard House. All the fruit trees in the orchard house must now be pruned in exactly the same way as those outdoors. No fire heat will be required unless some growth is still un-ripened (see October, General Work), and ventilation can be really free through both top and side ventilators, the house only being closed completely when the thermometer falls much below freezing point.

Ventilate Vines according to Growth. The latest vines may still be carrying bunches of grapes and will need very careful ventilation and heating. The latter will be used to keep the air dry rather than to maintain a high temperature; 50° will be a sufficient average. Ventilation must be given with the same object. In a damp, stagnant, cold atmosphere berries will crack and mould will appear on them. All fallen leaves must be swept up and removed daily. Vines that have finished fruiting are much easier to manage. They can be ventilated freely and will need no fire heat while they remain dormant.

FIRST WEEK

Place Glass over Alpines. Some choice alpines, and especially woolly-leaved plants such as many of the androsaces, suffer badly during the winter from excessive wet, which lodges in their leaves and makes them rot. Plants such as these can be completely protected by covering them now with pieces of glass supported well above the plants on notched sticks or bent pieces of wire. Make no attempt to close in the sides of the shelter. Free circulation of air is essential.

Lift Early-flowering Chrysanthemums. Border chrysanthemums are quite hardy in many gardens, but sometimes they rot off during the winter, so to be on the safe side it is advisable to lift a few plants of each variety now and place them close together in a frame or in boxes, which

BORDER
CHRYSANTHEMUMS
FOR
PROPAGATION
The old roots are lifted and placed close together in a frame with a little soil between them. It is the young shoots which grow up from the roots that make the best cuttings.

can be stood in a cool greenhouse. Simply pack a little light soil between them; that left over from seed trays will do well. Cut off the stems 2 to 3 inches above soil level. No artificial heat will be necessary, and only enough water to keep the soil from drying out. Later on these 'stools', as they are called, will furnish plenty of good cuttings (see February, General Work).

Complete Planting of Tulips and Hyacinths. There is still time to plant tulips and hyacinths (see October, Fourth Week), but the sooner the work is completed the better.

Bring Early Bulbs into Greenhouse. Examine the bulbs that were boxed or potted in September and placed in a plunge bed (see September, First Week). A few of the most forward may now be brought into a moderately heated greenhouse, but do not attempt to force them too fast at first. An average day temperature of 60°, falling to 50° at night, will be ample to begin with, but may rise to 70° once the flower buds are well formed. Another important point is to make quite certain that the bulbs have made plenty of roots before bringing them into the greenhouse at all. You can tap one or two of the pots out carefully without disturbing them, or alternatively you can learn a lot by examining the drainage holes and slits in the bottoms of the pots and boxes. When the soil begins to get full of roots they will start to grow through these drainage openings.

From this time onwards it is advisable to keep an eye on the plunge bed and either to remove forward boxes and pots of bulbs to the greenhouse, or, if you are not ready for them, to place them in an unheated frame, preferably with a north aspect. Here growth can be retarded for weeks without harm to the bulbs.

Start to Force Indian Azaleas, etc. If you want some really early flowers on Indian azaleas, bring the plants into a slightly warmer temperature now—an average of from 65° to 70° will do admirably—and syringe them lightly every morning with slightly tepid water. Various other early-flowering shrubs, such as forsythias, ornamental cherries, *Viburnum Carlesii*, *Jasminum primulinum*, and even lilac can also be brought into the greenhouse now, but do not subject them to temperatures above 60° unless they are really well established in pots.

Sow Broad Beans. There can be no doubt that the very best way to grow early broad beans is to sow seeds in boxes in February and germinate them in a warm greenhouse (see February, First Week). But if you have no glasshouse it is worth making an outdoor sowing now in a sheltered place. Choose a longpod variety and sow the seeds 4 inches apart in drills 2 inches deep and 18 inches apart for dwarf, or 2½ feet apart for tall kinds.

SECOND WEEK

Sow Hardy Culinary Peas. Some people are very successful with culinary peas sown now outdoors where they are to mature. A rather sheltered position and well-drained soil are essentials to success, and you must also use an absolutely hardy variety, such as The Pilot or William the

Planting a rose bush. *Above, left:* Any damaged or long, straggling roots should be trimmed. *Above, right:* Spreading the roots out well.

Below, left: A stick shows the correct depth for planting. *Below, right:* The soil levelled after the rose has been well firmed.

Left: Some alpines need protection against excessive wet. *Right:* Make the cut just above a bud when winter pruning the side growths of a vine back to two buds.

Rhubarb crowns being placed beneath the greenhouse staging for forcing.

First. Other details of sowing are the same as in the spring (see March, Second Week).

Lift Seakale for Forcing. The top growth of seakale should have died down by this time, and the roots will be ready for lifting in preparation for forcing. Dig them up carefully, cut off the side thongs and lay these in bundles in a sheltered position outdoors in readiness for planting out in March (see March, First Week). Then stand the stout central roots, each provided with a crown from which growth will come, against a shady wall or fence and heap ashes or sand around them until only the crowns are visible. They will keep safely like this all the winter, and you can pot up and force a few at a time as you require them. Pot three or four in a 6- or 7-inch pot, using any old potting or seed box compost,

FORCING SEAKALE
(A) *A suitable thong or root prepared for planting and* (B) *a sturdy crown lifted for forcing.* (C) *The top pot is cut away to show crowns being blanched.*

bring them into a warm greenhouse, and cover with another empty pot, blocking up the drainage hole in the bottom of this with a piece of slate or turf. The crowns must be in absolute darkness. Water moderately. In a temperature of about 60° growth will be rapid. When the blanched shoots are about 9 inches in length you can cut them. The forced roots are useless and should be thrown away.

Start to Force Rhubarb. Rhubarb may also be forced from now onwards throughout the winter. Roots started at once in a temperature of about 70° will give good sticks at Christmas. The method followed differs from that for seakale. Strong roots are lifted and allowed to lie on the ground unprotected for a day or so. If it freezes, so much the better. Growth will be all the quicker for this exposure. Then take the roots into a warm greenhouse, stand them quite close together in deep boxes or on the floor under the stages, pack soil between them and keep them absolutely dark by fixing up a screen of sacking, linoleum, or boards. Water

R

moderately and maintain a temperature of from 55° to 75°. A few more roots should be brought in every fortnight or so.

THIRD WEEK

Lift and Store Jerusalem Artichokes, Parsnips, Horseradish, and Salsify.
Jerusalem artichokes will have completed their growth, so cut off all the tops and lift the tubers with a fork. Store the larger tubers in exactly the same way as potatoes (see September, Third Week), and put the smaller tubers on one side in a dry shed or room for planting later on.

Parsnips and horseradish are perfectly hardy, and will not suffer any harm if left in the ground all the winter; indeed, the parsnips are actually improved in flavour by frost, but as it is well-nigh impossible to lift these long roots when the ground is frozen hard, it is as well to dig up a few now and store them in a shed or cellar as a standby. Simply cut off the tops, pile up the roots, and cover them with a little dry sand, ashes, or soil.

At least a portion of the crop of salsify should also be lifted and stored in exactly the same way as the parsnips and horseradish. If you wish, however, you can leave a portion of the bed undisturbed, so that the roots may produce flowering stems in the spring. These shoots, if cut young, can be boiled and eaten like asparagus. They are very palatable.

A STORAGE RACK FOR GRAPES
An ideal method of storing cut bunches of grapes.

FOURTH WEEK

Cut and Store Grapes. There is not much point in trying to keep the bunches of late grapes hanging on the vines any longer, especially if you have a cool, dark, and dry room in which you can store them. Cut each bunch with 9 inches or more of the ripened lateral from which it is hanging, insert the lower end of this into a bottle nearly filled with clean, soft water and containing a few pieces of charcoal, and then stand the bottle in a rack or on a shelf, tilting it sufficiently to prevent the berries from coming into contact with it, or, for that matter, with anything else.

PRUNING A VINE
Each lateral must be cut back to within one or two dormant buds of the main rod or spur.

CLEANING A VINE
Usually most of the old, loose bark can be rubbed off by hand, but a blunt kitchen knife can be used on tough pieces, provided the live bark is not injured.

Prune Early and Maincrop Vines. By this time the leaves should have fallen from early and maincrop vines, and the sooner most of them are pruned the better. Outdoor vines may also be pruned. For both types pruned at this time the method is the same. Cut back every lateral (side) growth to within one, or at most two, dormant growth buds of the main rod or spur. Then rub or pull all loose shreds of bark from the main rods and paint the latter thoroughly with Gishurst compound. Be particularly careful to work this in to all rough, gnarled places round the spur, where insects may be hiding. After pruning and cleaning, cut the ties holding the main rod and lower it on long pieces of cord so that it hangs more or less parallel with the floor. This will discourage sap from rushing up to the top when the vine is restarted and will ensure an even 'break' all over.

FLOWERS, VEGETABLES, AND FRUITS IN SEASON DURING NOVEMBER

Hardy Herbaceous Plants. *Aster grandiflorus, Helianthus orgyalis, H. sparsifolius, Helleborus niger altifolius, Hosta lancifolia tardiflora, Iris unguicularis (stylosa), Liriope spicata, Monardella macrantha,* physalis in variety (fruits), *Podophyllum emodi* (fruits), *Pulmonaria angustifolia azurea, P. saccharata, Viola florariensis.*

Hardy Bulbs and Tubers. *Colchicum byzantinum cilicicum, C. Decaisnei, C. hydrophyllum, Crocus asturicus, C. Boryi* and vars., *C. cancellatus* and vars., *C. caspius, C. Clusii, C. hadriaticus* and vars., *C. hyemalis* and vars., *C. Medius, C. ochroleucus, C. pulchellus, C. Salzmannii, C. speciosus, Cyclamen africanum, C. neapolitanum, Galanthus cilicicus, G. nivalis* vars. (snowdrops), *Merendera bulbocodium, M. persica, Narcissus serotinus, Schizostylis coccinea* and vars., *Sternbergia lutea.*

Rock Plants. *Gentiana Farreri, G. gentilis, G. intermedia, G. Kurroo, G. Macaulayi, G. ornata, G. sino-ornata, Primula Juliana* vars.

Hardy Evergreen Shrubs. *Buddleia auriculata* (shelter), *Erica carnea* vars., *E. ciliaris, E. Maweana, E. darleyensis, E. stricta, Elaeagnus macrophylla, E. pungens, Fatsia japonica, Hebe angustifolia, H. speciosa* Autumn Glory, *Hypericum Moserianum, Mahonia Fortunei, M. napaulensis* (shelter), *Olearia Fosteri* (shelter), *Viburnum Tinus.*

Hardy Deciduous Shrubs. *Chimonanthus fragrans, Colletia armata, Crataegus monogyna praecox, Daphne Mezereum autumnalis, Lonicera Standishii, Viburnum fragrans.*

Hardy Evergreen Trees. *Arbutus hybrida, A. Unedo.*

Hardy Deciduous Trees. *Prunus subhirtella autumnalis.*

Hardy Climbing Plants. *Clematis calycina, C. cirrhosa, Jasminum nudiflorum, Lardizabala biternata* (shelter).

Fruiting Trees, Shrubs, and Climbers. Mainly as October, but most pyrus fruits will have fallen.

Greenhouse Plants. Abutilons, begonias (Gloire de Lorraine and Optima types), *Bignonia venusta, Boronia heterophylla, B. megastigma*, bouvardias, *Browallia speciosa major*, carnations (perpetual-flowering), chrysanthemums, *Crassula lactea*, cyclamen, *Erica gracilis, Eriostemon buxifolia, Libonia floribunda, Oxalis versicolor*, pelargoniums (zonal), *Primula kewensis, Saintpaulia ionantha, Salvia splendens, Sparmannia africana, Trachelium caeruleum*.

PERNETTYA MUCRONATA
The brightly coloured berries of this hardy shrub are a feature of the garden in autumn. The white flowers are produced in spring. It reaches about 5 feet in height.

Flowers in Frames. Violets.

Vegetables in Store. Beetroot, carrots, onions, parsnips, potatoes, shallots, turnips.

Vegetables Outdoors. Jerusalem artichokes, broccoli, brussels sprouts, cabbage (sown April), celeriac, celery, coleworts (sown June), endive, kohl-rabi, leeks, lettuce (shelter), parsnips, savoys, spinach, turnips.

Vegetables under Glass. French beans, cucumbers, endive, lettuce, mushrooms, mustard and cress, radishes, tomatoes.

Fruits in Store. *Apples:* Allington Pippin (D), Beauty of Kent (C), Barnack Orange (D), Bismarck (C), Blenheim Orange (D), Bramley's Seedling (C), Charles Ross (D), Cornish Aromatic (D), Coronation (D), Cox's Orange Pippin (D), Cox's Pomona (CD), Cutler Grieve (D), Egremont Russet (D), Emperor Alexander (CD), Gascoyne's Scarlet (D), Golden Noble (C), Gravenstein (CD), Herring's Pippin (CD), Imperial (D), Joy Bells (D), King of the Pippins (D), Lane's Prince Albert (C), Laxton's Superb (D), Lord Derby (C), Lord Lambourne (D), Margil (D), McIntosh Red (CD), Mother (American) (D), Norfolk Royal (D), Peasgood's Nonsuch (CD), Pioneer

(D), Rev. W. Wilks (C), Ribston Pippin (D), Rival (CD), Roundway Magnum Bonum (D), Royal Jubilee (C), Schoolmaster (C), The Queen (C), Thomas Rivers (C), Triumph (D), Warner's King (C), Wealthy (D), Wellington (C). *Medlars. Pears:* Belissime d'Hiver (C), Beurré Diel (D), Beurré Superfin (D), Charles Ernest (D), Conference (D), Doyenné du Comice (D), Durondeau (D), Emile d'Heyst (D), Forelle (Trout Pear) (D), Maréchal de la Cour (D), Marie Louise (D), Pitmaston Duchess (D), Record (D), Thompson's (D), Victor (D), Wonderful (D). *Plums:* Langley Bullace (C), Shropshire Prune Damson (CD). *Quinces.*

Fruits under Glass. *Grapes:* Alicante, Appley Towers, Canon Hall Muscat, Gros Colmar, Gros Guillaume, Lady Downe's, Lady Hastings, Lady Hutt, Mrs Pearson, Mrs Pince, Muscat of Alexandria, Prince of Wales.

Nuts in Store. Cobnuts, filberts, walnuts.

December

GENERAL WORK

Continue to Dig Vacant Ground. Digging and trenching can be continued throughout the month as opportunity offers, but it is not wise to do this work when there is much snow on the ground, nor when it is frozen, or very wet.

Sterilize Infected Soil. This is a task which can be done at any time of the year, but as it is essential that the soil should have no plants growing in it, and, also, where it has been sterilized by chemical means, that it

STERILIZING SOIL

On the left the soil is being watered with a dilute solution of formaldehyde or cresylic acid and on the right the fumes are being trapped.

should remain unused for a month or so after treatment, December is often the most convenient month for the work. The purpose of sterilization is to rid the soil of all harmful organisms, including insect pests and the spores of fungi, which cause diseases. There is no point in treating soil that is in good order, but if diseases or pests have been rampant, sterilization may be well repaid.

Chemical sterilization is commonly carried out with either formaldehyde or cresylic acid. Formaldehyde of 40% purity (the common commercial strength) is diluted with 49 times its own bulk of water and the soil is then soaked thoroughly with it. Soil can be treated *in situ*, but a more effective method is to spread it out on a hard floor, soak it, and then immediately draw it into a heap and cover with sacks to trap the fumes. You must not use the soil until it has lost all smell of the chemical.

Precisely similar methods are adopted with cresylic acid. This you can purchase in various strengths, but that known as 'pale straw-coloured carbolic acid' is most suitable. Dilute it with 39 times its own bulk of water.

Another method of sterilizing soil is by heat. Steam can be used for supplying this and is the best medium, since it will neither char the soil nor make it sodden. The amount of soil treated at any one time must be sufficiently small to allow the temperature to reach 212°F in about 30 to 40 minutes. This temperature is maintained for 10 minutes, when the soil is removed immediately and allowed to cool down rapidly by being spread out thinly. The soil, unlike that chemically treated, can be used for any purpose as soon as it has cooled, but as the treatment results in a reduction of fertility for a while, it is advisable to counteract this by adding suitable chemicals (see pages 26 and 62).

Small and large proprietary steam sterilizers can be obtained but it is also possible to sterilize soil in a saucepan using boiling water. The soil should be fairly dry to start with, and for a 6-pint saucepan ½ pint of water is sufficient. As soon as it boils, fill the saucepan with soil to within ½ in. of the top and boil for 7 minutes with the lid on. Leave it to stand for 7 minutes more, and then spread it out to cool.

You should note that soil fumigation is a rather different matter from sterilization, as it is directed solely at insect pests—*e.g.*, wireworms, leatherjackets, millepedes, etc., and has no effect upon diseases. Flaked naphthalene is commonly used for the purpose, and is dug into any vacant ground at the rate of 4 ounces per square yard. There are also a number of proprietary soil fumigants, many of them embodying naphthalene in some form or other, which must be used strictly in accordance with manufacturer's instructions.

Start to Propagate Carnations. Perpetual-flowering carnation cuttings may be taken from now until the end of March. They are best prepared from side shoots produced a little way up the flowering stems. Avoid those right at the base and right at the top. Shoots about 3 inches in length are ideal and can be obtained by pulling gently away and down from the plant. The heel or small strip of skin that comes away from the old stem should be trimmed off close to the base of the cutting, which is then ready for insertion. Alternative methods are to cut the shoot just below a joint and not pull it away at the heel, or to pull it upwards so that it slips out of the joint. This last method is known as taking a piping. These cuttings are ready for insertion without further fuss. They should be inserted nearly an inch deep in either pure silver sand or a mixture of good loam and silver sand in about equal parts. They root more quickly and reliably in the pure sand, but need considerably more attention as to watering, which is a nuisance if one has to be away from home most of the day. Carnation cuttings are rooted in a greenhouse maintained at a temperature of about 50°, but it is an advantage to keep them close, either in a propagating box or under a bell-glass, and to warm the soil to about 60°.

Continue to Cut back Chrysanthemums. Throughout the month continue to cut back the later chrysanthemums as soon as they finish flowering (see November, General Work).

Prune Roses. Continue to prune bush and standard roses (see November, General Work).

Stop Sweet Peas. Autumn-sown sweet peas (see September, Second Week) should be pinched at some time during the winter. It does not matter when it is done, so long as it is before the plants have made shoots more than 3 inches in length. Stopping here means that the top of each seedling is pinched out.

Bring More Bulbs into the Greenhouse. Bring in further batches of bulbs to the greenhouse from plunge bed and frame to ensure a succession of flowers later on (see November, First Week).

Continue to Force Seakale and Rhubarb. At intervals of about a fortnight bring in further roots of rhubarb and seakale and force them in the greenhouse (see November, Second Week).

Continue to Protect Broccoli. From time to time during the month you must continue to bend down leaves over the curds of broccoli as they form (see November, General Work).

Successional Sowings. These are exactly the same as last month—mustard and cress and radishes—all in a warm greenhouse or a frame placed on a hotbed.

Continue to Prune Fruit Trees. Throughout the month you can proceed with the pruning of fruit trees and bushes of all kinds (see November,

General Work). It is a mistaken notion that fruit trees must not be pruned when the weather is frosty.

Ventilate Vinery and Orchard House Freely. There is really nothing of importance to add to my November notes on the management of these houses. Free ventilation should be the rule right up to the time at which vines and fruit trees are restarted into growth. If the weather is very cold, close up the houses in sufficient time in the afternoon to keep off the worst frost, but a few degrees of frost will do no harm at all.

FIRST WEEK

Protect Tender Plants, Christmas Roses, and Celery. Very little damage is done by early autumn frosts to such slightly tender plants and shrubs as gunneras, eremuruses, escallonias, evergreen ceanothuses, crinodendrons, etc., but as the winter sets in with greater rigour it is advisable to provide some protection for these if they happen to be growing in rather exposed places. Wall shrubs and climbers about which you are at all nervous can be protected efficiently and without danger by hanging sacking in front of them or fixing wattle hurdles close up to them and then stuffing any intervening space with straw or bracken. The plant must not be entirely shut off from air. Whatever form of protection you use, always leave the top open so that foul air and moisture may escape.

For slightly tender herbaceous plants, the crowns of which may be injured by frost, the best method of protection is to place a piece of fine-mesh galvanized wire-netting over each, humped in the form of a tunnel, heap dry leaves, straw, or bracken on this, and cover with another piece of netting pegged down at the corners.

Christmas roses (hellebores) are not in the least tender, but they will be forming their flower stems now and the blooms will benefit from a little protection to keep off heavy rain and mud splashes. Cover them with spare lights supported on bricks at the four corners, or with cloches of one type or another.

Late celery may be injured by very hard frosts or heavy rain, so it is good policy to cover the ridges at about this time with a little dry straw or bracken, held in position with some wire-netting pegged down to the soil, and also to dig a shallow trench on each side of the ridge to run off surplus surface water.

Prune Clematis Jackmanii. Clematises of the *Jackmanii* and nearly allied *Viticella* classes may be pruned. It is not absolutely essential to do the work at once, so long as it is completed before the end of February, but in the interests of tidiness the sooner it is completed the better. There are two methods of pruning. One is to cut all growth back to within about 1 foot of the ground every year, so keeping the plants fairly small, and the other to allow a framework of main vines to form and then prune each side growth back to one joint.

SECOND WEEK

Make a Mushroom Bed for Succession. This is a very good time to make a mushroom bed in an outhouse, frame, or other covered place, because the bed will start to crop in February and provide a succession to that made in September (see September, First Week). The details are exactly the same as before.

THIRD WEEK

Start to Take Chrysanthemum Cuttings. Some growers start taking cuttings of chrysanthemums considerably earlier than this, but I do not

METHODS OF ROOTING CUTTINGS
Some of the cuttings are being rooted in a propagating frame, while others have been inserted in a shallow bed of sandy soil actually made up on the greenhouse staging. On the extreme left are some rooted cuttings that have been potted singly.

think that the amateur gains anything by being in too much of a hurry. You should start on those varieties that are to be grown for second crown buds, and particularly on November incurves and singles.

The best shoots to select are those that come up through the soil direct from the roots. These should be severed just below soil level when they are a couple of inches or so in length. They are prepared by cutting off the lower leaves with a very sharp knife and trimming off the base cleanly just below a joint; then insert them about ½ inch deep in sandy soil. It does not matter much whether they are in boxes, pots, or directly in a bed made up on the staging in the greenhouse so long as there is ample provision for drainage. The cuttings cannot be rooted out of doors at this time of the year. It is possible to manage them in a well-constructed frame, but it is much easier in a greenhouse with just a little artificial heat to keep out frost. Some growers keep the cuttings close in a frame within the greenhouse, while others prefer to have them open on the staging. Both schemes work well, but using the latter method rather more watering is necessary, and it is advisable to syringe every morning with slightly tepid water.

FOURTH WEEK

Remove Christmas Plants to Glasshouse. The sooner pot plants used in the house for decorations during the Christmas festivities can be returned to the greenhouse the better. They do not like the over-dry atmosphere and everchanging temperature of living-rooms at all, and quickly deteriorate as a result. Palms, aspidistras, and dracaenas will benefit from a thorough sponging down with tepid water into which a few drops of milk have been stirred. After this they should be kept in a rather warm atmosphere for a few days and syringed daily with clear water. Flowering plants such as cyclamens, primulas, cinerarias, and heaths should be given as light a place as possible on the staging in a temperature of from 55° to 60°, and be watered very carefully, all excesses one way or the other being avoided. Remove any withered or mouldy leaves. Berried solanums should also be given plenty of light and a rather higher temperature.

FLOWERS, VEGETABLES, AND FRUITS IN SEASON
DURING DECEMBER

Hardy Herbaceous Plants. *Adonis amurensis, Aster grandiflorus, Helleborus niger* and vars., *Iris unguicularis* (*stylosa*), *Liriope spicata, Monardella macrantha, Petasites fragrans.*

Hardy Bulbs and Tubers. *Colchicum byzantinum cilicicum, C. Decaisnei, C. hydrophyllum, C. libanoticum, Crocus alatavicus, C. Boryi* and vars., *C. caspius, C. hadriaticus, C. hyemalis, C. Imperati, C. medius, C. ochroleucus, C. pulchellus, C. Salzmannii, Cyclamen coum, Galanthus cilicicus, G. nivalis* vars., *Merendera bulbocodium, M. persica, Narcissus serotina, Sternbergia lutea angustifolia.*

Hardy Evergreen Shrubs. *Arctostaphylos tomentosa, Azara integrifolia* (shelter), *Buddleia auriculata* (shelter), *Erica carnea* vars., *E. darleyensis, Fatsia japonica, Lonicera fragrantissima, Mahonia japonica, Olearia Fosteri* (shelter), *Rhododendron* Lee's Scarlet, *Viburnum Tinus* and vars.

Hardy Deciduous Shrubs. *Chimonanthus praecox, Daphne Mezereum autumnalis, Hamamelis mollis, Lonicera Standishii, Rhododendron mucronulatum, Viburnum fragrans.*

STERNBERGIA LUTEA
(WINTER DAFFODIL)
The bright yellow flowers of this hardy bulbous plant are very welcome in late winter. It can also be grown in pots in the cool greenhouse.

Hardy Evergreen Trees. *Arbutus Unedo, Eucalyptus Gunnii.*

Hardy Deciduous Trees. *Crataegus monogyna praecox, Prunus subhirtella autumnalis.*

Hardy Climbing Plants. *Clematis calycina, C. cirrhosa, Jasminum nudiflorum, Lardizabala biternata* (shelter).

Fruiting Trees, Shrubs, and Climbers. *Aucuba japonica, Berberis Hookeri, Celastrus articulatus, C. scandens, Cotoneaster frigida, C. horizontalis, C. microphylla, C. rotundifolia, Crataegus Carrierei, C. cordata, C. Crus-galli, C. spathulata, Hippophae rhamnoides, Ilex Aquifolium* (holly), *Pyracantha angustifolia, P. coccinea, P. Gibbsii, P. Rogersiana, Rosa Fargesii, R. Moyesi, Taxus baccata.* Some of the other varieties mentioned in October may continue, but those listed above are particularly reliable. Much depends upon birds.

Greenhouse Plants. Abutilons, begonias (Gloire de Lorraine and Optima types), *Bignonia venusta,* bouvardias, *Browallia speciosa major,* camellias, carnations (perpetual-flowering), chrysanthemums, cinerarias, *Correa cardinalis*, cyclamen, *Erica gracilis* and vars., *E. hyemalis*, freesias, *Primula kewensis*, *P. obconica*, *P. sinensis* and vars., *Saintpaulia ionantha*.

Flowers in Frames. *Anemone coronaria* vars., violets.

Vegetables in Store. Jerusalem artichokes, beetroot, carrots, onions, parsnips, potatoes, turnips, shallots.

Vegetables Outdoors. Jerusalem artichokes, broccoli, brussels sprouts, celeriac, celery, coleworts (sown July), endive, kales, leeks, lettuce (shelter), parsnips, savoys, spinach, turnips.

Vegetables under Glass. Cucumbers, endive, lettuce, mushrooms, mustard and cress, radishes, rhubarb, seakale.

Fruits in Store. *Apples:* Adams' Pearmain (D), Allington Pippin (D), Annie Elizabeth (C), Barnack Beauty (CD), Barnack Orange (D), Baumann's Red Winter Reinette (CD), Beauty of Kent (C), Belle de Boskoop (CD), Bismarck (C), Blenheim Orange (D), Bramley's Seedling (C), Christmas Pearmain (D),

BROWALLIA SPECIOSA
MAJOR
An annual plant for the warm greenhouse, this has purple to blue flowers in winter. 2 feet.

Claygate Pearmain (D), Coronation (D), Cornish Aromatic (D), Cornish Gilliflower (D), Court Pendu Plat (D), Cox's Orange Pippin (D), Cutler Grieve (D), Gascoyne's Scarlet (D), Golden Noble (C), Gravenstein (CD), Houblon (D), Imperial (D), Joy Bells (D), King of Tompkin's County (D), Lane's Prince Albert (C), Laxton's Pearmain (D), Lord Derby (C), Lord Lambourne (D), Madresfield Court (D), Margil (D), Monarch (C), Newton Wonder (C), Norfolk Royal (D), Orleans Reinette (D), Ribston Pippin (D), Rival (CD), Rosemary Russet (D), Roundway Magnum Bonum (D), Royal Jubilee (C), Royalty (D), Saltcote Pippin (D), Schoolmaster (C), Superb (D), The Queen (C), Thomas Rivers (C), Triumph (D), Wellington (C), William Crump (D), Wyken Pippin (D). *Pears:* Admiral Gervais (D), Bellissime d'Hiver (C), Beurré Six (D), Blickling (D), Catillac (C), Charles Ernest (D), Forelle (D), Glou Morceau (D), Le Lectier (D), Nouvelle Fulvie (D), Santa Claus (D), Vicar of Winkfield (C), Winter Nelis (D).

Fruits under Glass. *Grapes* (as November).

Index

References in parentheses indicate line drawings on the text pages.
The letter 'p' after a number indicates photograph on opposite page.

271

S